SEARCH FOR A PLACE

Black Separatism and Africa, 1860

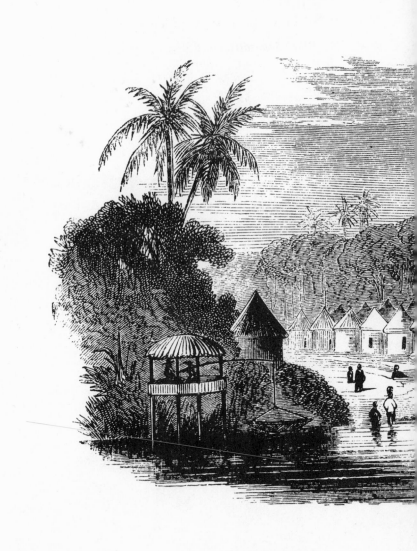

Search For a Place

Black Separatism and Africa, 1860

M. R. DELANY *and* ROBERT CAMPBELL

Introduction by Howard H. Bell

Ann Arbor Paperbacks
The University of Michigan Press

First edition as an Ann Arbor Paperback *1971*
Copyright © by *The University of Michigan 1969*
All rights reserved
ISBN   *0–472–06179–8*
Library of Congress Catalog Card No. *69–15843*
Published in the United States of America by
The University of Michigan Press and simultaneously
in Don Mills, Canada, by Longman Canada Limited
Manufactured in the United States of America

Contents

Introduction, by Howard H. Bell   1

Official Report of The Niger Valley Exploring Party,
by M. R. DELANY   26

A Pilgrimage to My Motherland: An Account
of a Journey Among the Egbas and
Yorubas of Central Africa, in 1859–60,
by ROBERT CAMPBELL   149

Introduction

by

HOWARD H. BELL

Often, present-day black separatists look for ways to restore the balance of justice for centuries of oppression by penalizing the white man. Their counterparts a century ago looked often for a place beyond the borders of the United States where they might develop a powerful black nation, the products of which would compete economically with those of the slave South, and where the Negro's genius for politics and government would be unhampered by meddling whites.

Mindful always of their responsibility to those still in slavery, the Negro separatists of that era reasoned that uplift of the black race, whether in Canada, the Caribbean, Central America, or Africa would have a "reflex influence" on the plight of those still held in bondage and on those only partly removed from its curse in America. A black nation would in time accomplish the goals which an oppressed people could not accomplish for themselves. To support this thesis they pointed to such examples as the Puritans who had been unable to throw off the yoke of oppression in England until some of their number had braved the dangers of a new land and had established a viable government of their own. Of such conviction were Martin R. Delany and Robert Campbell, two black Americans who penetrated into the Egba and Yoruba areas of what is now western Nigeria in the search for a place where, in the Biblical language so meaningful to Americans of the mid-nineteenth century, "Ethiopia might stretch forth her hand."

Campbell begins his narrative at Liverpool, England, June 24, 1859, and ends it at the same city, May 12, 1860. Delany's *Report* is only briefly narrative and is concerned chiefly with conditions that the immigrant would encounter. Delany arrived in Liberia in July 1859; from there he sailed to Lagos, and not until November 5 did he meet Campbell at Abbeokuta, the starting point for their expedition inland as far as Illorin. Thereafter, they remained together except for short intervals.

When the expedition began, Delany was forty-seven years old; Campbell probably twenty years younger. Delany, born in northern Virginia in 1812 to parents who traced their ancestry to African chieftains, grew up with a great pride in all things black—a pride that was to be the sorrow and the joy of an action-packed life. Perennial student, editor, and publisher, Harvard student of medicine, dentist, doctor, orator, explorer, dabbler "in absentia" in Central American politics, army officer, and politician, Delany was ever changing in his career, but it was always associated with the black man and his place in history. In the words of an eminent contemporary, Delany was "the intensest embodiment of black Nationality to be met with outside the valley of the Niger" (*Douglass' Monthly,* August, 1862, p. 695).

Campbell, born in the British West Indies of Negro-Caucasian ancestry (he stated that he was three-fourths white), received a good education, traveled in Central America, and became a teacher of science in the Institute for Colored Youth in Philadelphia. Unlike Delany, he developed no reputation as a militant or separatist, but did develop an interest in Africa as the secrets of that continent began to be revealed through the works of missionaries in the 1850's.

The interest of American blacks in Africa was not new when Delany and Campbell, representing the "General Board of Commissioners" of the colored people, explored the Niger area. As early as 1770 young Negroes had been in training to go to Africa in something of a

2

missionary capacity. The Revolutionary War and its aftermath saw thousands of American blacks being dispersed to various British possessions, with some making their way to Africa. Periodically thereafter certain Negro Americans thought of Africa as a land of opportunity, as a world to which they owed a debt of loyalty for having been the land of their forebears, as a land for missionary effort, or as an area of economic opportunity for which blacks were qualified physically, mentally, and emotionally in greater degree than whites. A number of Negroes from Boston expressed an interest in emigration to Africa in 1787, and before the end of the century a Rhode Island group had asked permission to enter the British colony of Sierra Leone. But the first American Negro to make an individual attempt to tie Africa and North America together commercially by cords of black was Paul Cuffee, a Quaker of Negro-Indian ancestry, a self-made fisherman, whaler, merchant. Cuffee sought with some degree of success to persuade American blacks to take an interest in his joint scheme for emigration and commercial exploitation, but it was brought to a halt by the War of 1812. After the war he did transport a group of emigrants, but died soon afterward.

When in 1816 the American Colonization Society presented its plan for expatriation of free Negroes to the land that was to become Liberia, the great mass of Negro Americans quickly labeled the enterprise as destructive of the black heritage in America and would have nothing to do with it. Of Cuffee's top echelon of former supporters (James Forten, the clergymen Peter Williams, and Daniel Coker) only Coker supported the new effort. Resentment against the plan for expatriation, for whatever reason, and knowledge of the high mortality rate in Liberia were strong influences against any emigration or colonization project for many years. A further deterrent was the widely held abolitionist doctrine that the free Negro should stand by to see the deliverance of the slave from bondage in America. Finally, the expulsive forces were just not strong enough in America to drive many blacks overseas.

The attention of free blacks was eventually turned to lands beyond the borders (except for runaway slaves who found refuge chiefly in Canada) by economic opportunities and Negro nationalism—a kind of militant black unity—which developed concurrently in the decade of the 1850's. Meantime, the foundations for these developments were being laid by evolvement of Negro leadership, capital, and education at home. Before 1830 black leadership had been confined largely to Negro churches, lodges, and self-help associations and had not been noticeable on the national level. Determined to play a larger role in American society, Negroes in 1827 started a new periodical, *Freedom's Journal*, and by 1830 they had begun a series of national conventions, which were to have a telling effect on America—both black and white.

Thereafter, the voice of the Negro gained rapidly in authority as the younger and usually the better educated gained positions of leadership. By 1840 the able young men who boasted a college education were not as prejudiced against emigration as their parents had been. They were willing to consider all avenues of progress, even if it meant leaving their immediate surroundings, and even adventuring on foreign soil. Canada, Haiti, Central America, Liberia had each its appeal to the more venturesome. On the whole, however, the invisible cords of a self-imposed loyalty to those still in bondage, an indefinable reluctance to gamble life and goods in a new land, and a firm belief in their rights as native-born Americans to all of the privileges of free birth and citizenship kept blacks from emigrating for many years.

So long as the Negro community considered emigration as part and parcel of a diabolical scheme of the American Colonization Society to rid the country of free Negroes, there could be no strong support for overseas projects. Occasionally, a minister like Daniel Coker or an editor like John Russwurm would brave the wrath of Negro public opinion to make his home in Africa, but their number was never large nor particularly influential. During these decades it was more acceptable to go to Canada, Haiti, or the British West Indies, where, so the reasoning went, the Negro American could influence the government of his adopted home in the cause of eliminating American slavery, where, so far as the Caribbean area was concerned, he could compete with the South in the production of cotton for the world market, and where, hopefully, he would have a place in the highest ranks of government. So it was that several thousand black Americans made their way to the Caribbean regions during the 1820's and 1830's and some, like Hezekiah Grice and F. E. Dubois, rose to prominence in their adopted lands. Also, substantial communities of free blacks developed in Canada.

Meanwhile, voices began to be raised in defense of the right to choose individually where one would cast his lot. Writing in *The Colored American* for May 3, 1838, "Augustine" contended that animosity of the black community to emigration was simply a reaction to the effort of the American Colonization Society to exile the free Negroes and that this was not a legitimate reason for the opposition. A few months later (September 28) he was examining the belief expressed by some blacks that they should face death rather than allow themselves to be removed from America for any cause whatsoever. "After much reflection upon this highly important point, I am free to acknowledge that I am not one of that number." Noting that too many blacks were "just beginning to live happily in the West Indies, and in Canada, for me to think of dying just now," he suggested that he would "rather be a *living freeman,* even in one of these places, than a 'dead nigger' in the United States."

Another voice in favor of breaking the tie that

5

bound the free Negro to the area close to the slave came from Cleveland, where the Young Men's Union Society labored over a plan to found a colony either within the United States or on its borders. In a series of reports in *The Colored American* for March 2 and 9 and May 18, 1839, the youthful group defended their plan, which called for minimal separation from home territory and for emphasis upon strengthening the black community so that it could withstand pressures exerted toward expatriation to Africa. James M. Whitfield, reporter and defender of the project, would be heard from again. In fact, he became during the 1850's one of the most ardent advocates of Negro emigration, which, to him and his compatriots, was an integral part of Negro nationalism. This movement encompassed a strong pride in the African heritage and a kind of militant unity distrustful of white leadership in projects pertaining to the black community, sought to bypass social and political controls within the nation by setting up black-dominated controls, and planned to establish or support a black nation somewhere beyond the bounds of the United States. Negatively, Negro nationalism may be seen in the unified opposition to the American Colonization Society's effort in Liberia; more positively its embryonic structure may be found in the Negro's defiance in 1840 of the whites who had for a decade made themselves conspicuous in Negro conventions or in the growing feeling expressed openly by the editor of the *Ram's Horn* in 1847 when he suggested that a proposition could be considered legitimately by the Negro community because it was being put forward by a Negro. The black unity—so ready to reject a project proposed by whites and so willing to accept, at least for investigation, a proposition by Negroes—was to become pronounced during the 1850's.

No one year can be singled out as the beginning of a new era in Negro interest in areas beyond the borders of the United States, but the birth of the government of

Liberia in 1847 was significant. No longer to be considered only as a white man's attempt to siphon off the free black, Liberia now emerged as a black nation and therefore a place to which the Negro American could look with hope—even with pride. Henry Highland Garnet launched one of the most spectacular challenges to the philosophy of staying at home while black governments were being born, and black men could be building for a brighter future. In articles in *The North Star* for January 26 and March 2, 1849, he made it clear that he still opposed the American Colonization Society in its philosophy that the Negro could never rise to equality in America, but he was now ready to accept the long-suspect society's ministrations "to the land of my fathers," and like "Augustine" a decade earlier he would rather be free in lands beyond the borders than a slave in the United States. He now looked to Liberia to become of great commercial and political benefit to Africa, and he expected the new government to check the slave trade "by the diffusion of light and knowledge, and by turning the attention of the black traders to some other and honorable business, and by sweeping off the white ones as with the hands of an avenging God."

Garnet's new stand on emigration was followed by a feverish decade of proposals and counterproposals relating to emigration, always with the view that emigration and Negro nationalism went hand in hand. Information on politics and on the agricultural or horticultural potential of Liberia and news of educational advances in the new nation, which hitherto had always been rebuffed by the abolitionist press, now received a respectful hearing by at least some Negro editors; other blacks, especially the younger generation, put their new interest to practical account by trying their luck on foreign soil.

Martin R. Delany with his great pride in the black race was not slow to accept the new interest, and once having done so he became the embodiment of Negro separatism to the great discomfiture of those dedicated to leading the Negro into full equality in the United States. In 1852 he published a booklet entitled *The Condition, Elevation, Emigration, and Destiny of the Colored People of the United States.* Here he claimed credit for having planned at an earlier date an East African commercial-colonization project based on a transcontinental railway reaching from the Red Sea to the west coast. Now willing to suspend the original venture, so long as the black man got credit for the plan, he turned his attention to the more urgent need for developing a powerful and respected Negro nation in the tropics of the Western Hemisphere. But whether his interests lay in the American tropics early in the decade or in Africa in the latter part, he saw the need to develop a strong support from black America. He must change the philosophy which had bound the black man to the area where he could be a symbol of hope to the enslaved and a threat to the enslaver. He must persuade blacks to change an attitude which made them reluctant to lead in any venture, but willing to follow if the white man led the way. He must persuade Negro Americans that once the colored people got together in the American tropics they would be beyond the grasp of the United States. And above all he must persuade them that it was the will of God. He warned against resisting lest "[God's] protecting arm and fostering care . . . be withdrawn from us."

As to those who remained in bondage in America, Delany recognized that blacks must ever be mindful of their condition, but the "reflex influence" would be at work to mitigate their plight. In his words "the redemption of the bondmen depends entirely upon the elevation of the freeman; therefore, to elevate the free colored people of America, anywhere upon this continent, forbodes the speedy redemption of the slaves."

Within a few months Delany was emphasizing the

necessity for having access to all means of progress. In a communication to *Frederick Douglass' Paper* of July 23, 1852, he insisted that the black man must take the lead in developing projects for black people. "We must have a position," he wrote, "independently of anything pertaining to white men or nations." It was time to quit "whimpering, whining, and snivelling at the feet of white men." Still later (April 1, 1853), after Douglass had been in consultation with Harriet Beecher Stowe concerning an educational project, Delany insisted that Douglass had not acted properly. Blacks, not whites, must make plans for blacks. In regard to Mrs. Stowe, Delany insisted "she *knows nothing about us* . . . neither does any other white person—and, consequently can contrive no successful scheme for our elevation." He wanted it clearly understood that "no enterprise, institution, or anything else, should be commenced *for us,* or our general benefit, without first consulting us."

Delany's booklet appeared in 1852. In 1853 the great national Negro convention met at Rochester and set up the Negro National Council, probably in an effort to capitalize on the growing militancy in the Negro community, which was fueling the separatist trend. It was anticipated that this National Council would supervise a national educational institution, a national consumer's union, a national system of arbitration of disputes, a national information agency—all to be formed in the hope of keeping problems of blacks as much as possible in the hands of blacks and out of the hands of whites.

In a countermove the emigrationists were to meet at Cleveland in 1854. Meanwhile, a running literary battle developed between James M. Whitfield, for the separatists, and Frederick Douglass and William J. Watkins, for those favorable to remaining in the United States. These articles were drawn together by M. T. Newsome in a pamphlet entitled *Arguments, Pro and Con, on the Call for a National Emigration Convention* [1854], with an introduction by emigrationist J. Theodore Holly. They ably develop the opposing viewpoints and are especially valuable in seeking to understand the separatist philosophy.

Holly referred to the recently created National Council as "an informal national organization of a denationalized people, whereby an organic, though premature and sickly birth was given to the idea of [Negro] national independence." Whitfield, writing on the same subject, suggested that the effort at Rochester had been "to create a union of sentiment and action among the colored people, and give it efficiency, by forming a kind of national organization here, under the overshadowing influence of their oppressors." Like Delany and most other separatists, Whitfield contended that respect and equality for colored men in America or elsewhere would come only after blacks could show "men of their own race occupying a primary position instead of a secondary and inferior one."

These men knew their history and they knew their times. "Manifest Destiny" had been much in the public mind as the United States relieved neighboring countries of territorial possessions on its trek west and south. But black men were seldom welcome as participants in the American manifest destiny in an age when slavery still existed in nearly half of the states. Whitfield looked beyond the narrow confines of the continent and proclaimed: "I believe it to be the destiny of the negro, to develop a higher order of civilization and Christianity than the world has yet seen." Like Delany he saw manifest destiny for the Negro in the American tropics, beyond the reach of the United States. Then, challenging the discomfited proponents of the National Council, he portrayed emigration as merely the continuation of a logical forward movement begun by them at the great Rochester National Convention. "The child who has ventured to stand alone, must, of necessity, either step on or fall down again and crawl in the dust." Though forward movement might be feeble, it was, in Whitfield's estimation, preferable to "crawling again in the dust to the feet of our oppressors."

Whitfield had shared with Delany an early interest in emigration. Like Delany he suffered for his people when he saw them slow to move into unoccupied or thinly populated lands when they could possess the land for themselves, and then quick to rush in as menials when those lands had fallen to the westward surge of white Americans. "If such a course as this is pursued," inquired the disconsolate Whitfield, "what stronger proof could be desired by our enemies in support of their favorite argument, that the negro is incapable of self-government, and aspires no higher than to be a servant to the whites?"

Repeatedly, the emigrationists were accused of seeking to emigrate en masse, and repeatedly they denied it. Whitfield dealt with the problem more than once in exchanges with opponents in the months between the formation of the National Council at Rochester in 1853 and the emigration convention at Cleveland in 1854. He insisted that emigration en masse was impossible in a society which had passed beyond the pastoral stage, and that mass emigration was not a prerequisite for achieving their goals. He was just as firmly of the opinion that emigration of some of the proscribed group was necessary and that those who did emigrate "should go forth and build up their own institutions, and conduct them in such a manner as to furnish ocular proof of their . . . capacity . . . to fulfill ably all the duties of the highest as well as the lowest positions of society."

The Cleveland National Convention on emigration ruled out opponents of emigration and any who were looking toward Africa. Those interested in emigration to the West Indies, Central America, and South America and those with an interest in Canada were to be given a hearing. They reminded each other that they must always remember the slave, but in so doing they remained firmly of the opinion that by congregating in the American tropics they could be building a new home and a new nation while competing with the American South and thus cutting the slave system down.

In his prepared document on "The Political Destiny of the Colored Race," published as a part of the *Proceedings of the National Emigration Convention,* Delany denied that the blacks were either free men or citizens; he contended that his people could not be free unless they constituted a majority of the ruling class and that emigration was the answer to the plight of the black. Here as elsewhere in his writings, Delany cited the fact that world population was predominantly colored. "The white races," he wrote, "are but one-third of the population of the globe—or one of them to two of us—and it cannot much longer continue that two-thirds will passively submit to the universal domination of this one-third." He recognized readily the great accomplishments of the Caucasian, but unlike earlier blacks in the United States who had "admitted themselves to be inferior, we barely acknowledge the whites as equals." And if equals, or even superiors in some areas of endeavor, the whites were definitely inferior in certain physical qualities: "the whites in the southern part of the United States have *decreased* in numbers, *degenerated* in character, and become mentally and physically imbecile." On the other hand Delany saw the "blacks and colored" as having "steadily *increased* in numbers, *regenerated* in character, and grown mentally and physically vigorous."

Along with the physical ability to live and thrive where the whites could not, Delany saw the darker races as having "the highest traits of civilization." "They are," he said, "civil, peaceable, and religious to a fault." This group would most surely prove their leadership "in the true principles of morals, correctness of thought, religion, and law or civil government."

The ideas of Delany and Whitfield must be related to those of J. Theodore Holly, a former shoemaker, in order to get a clear picture of Negro separatism which so vitally affected the 1850's and which culminated in separate drives toward Africa and Haiti. Holly investigated possibilities of going to Liberia in 1850, but in the following year he attended the North American Convention at Toronto, where the emphasis was on activities in the Western Hemisphere. Holly's principal ideas on Negro nationalism are presented in a series of articles in *The Anglo-African Magazine* from June to November 1859. Although his emphasis is on Haiti, the Negro separatist philosophy is orthodox and applicable to other areas. He saw the Haitian government as the "most irrefragable proof of the equality of the negro race." He would direct American Negroes to Haiti so that they might offer their skills to a less-developed people, but people with whom they could find easy assimilation. He saw American Negro emigration as a necessity "for the political enfranchisement of the colored people of the United States," but also as the only logical source from which Haiti could draw in its effort to improve.

Turning his attention to the significance of a Negro nation, Holly contended, as did most other separatists, that the black man was exploited on a world-wide basis because there was no powerful Negro nation to call a halt to such abuse. The appearance of such a nation would stop the African slave trade and portend the end of slavery itself. From this nation "a reflex influence will irradiate, not only to uproot American slavery, but also to overthrow African slavery and the slave-trade throughout the world."

In a pamphlet publication, *A Vindication of the Capacity of the Negro for Self-Government* (1857) Holly stated his views on the comparative qualities of white and black. "I have made no allowance," he wrote, "for the negroes just emerging from a barbarous condition and out of the brutish ignorance of West Indian slavery." His reason for not making any allowance was his "fear that instead of proving negro equality only, I should prove negro superiority."

Between 1854 and 1858 Holly and Delany worked together through the Board of Commissioners of colored people organized at the Cleveland emigration convention in 1854. Their emphasis was on a black empire in the American tropics. New interest in Africa from various sources, including missionary accounts, was becoming more pronounced as the decade progressed, and Delany's earlier interest in that continent was renewed to the extent that he transferred his efforts from the American tropics to Africa.

The year 1858 is important in the African phase of Negro separatism. The African Civilization Society was launched at Philadelphia, with Henry Highland Garnet, veteran of many a battle within and without the Negro community for the betterment of the race, as president of the new organization. This new organization was the outgrowth of a great deal of planning and support from Philadelphia whites, notably Benjamin Coates, Christian and colonizationist in sympathy, but a member of the American Colonization Society, and therefore suspect to most blacks even in 1858. The society began immediately to plan for an expedition to Africa, and there is some reason to suspect that Delany's decision to go to the Niger River area was dictated by the prior decision of the African Civilization Society to seek to exploit that district. Delany had earlier considered territory farther south. Garnet knew how to arouse the interest of the black community in his new project, and he proceeded to do so by public debates and by provoking Frederick Douglass into editorializing on the disadvantages of going to Africa in language no longer convincing.

Also in 1858, Delany and his colleagues met in convention for the third time to deliberate on what course to follow. Delany surrendered the presidency to William H. Day, but remained in a position of responsibility by being accorded the office of foreign secretary. Delany demanded immediate and specific action on Africa. His colleagues were willing to seek money to build up a press, schools, and churches in Canada and use these facilities to train young people to go as missionary teachers to Africa. At his own insistence Delany was authorized to be a commissioner to explore Africa and to name his own colleagues. He was also given the dubious privilege of raising the funds necessary for the expedition. It was characteristic of Delany that he assumed the arduous task willingly and went to work with his usual optimism. The funds would be available, and it was important that they come from the black community.

Thus, Delany and Garnet became rivals in an effort to explore within the Niger area. Delany had the formidable task of selecting capable members for the expedition, with no organizational backing for either men or money. Garnet had the support of the African Civilization Society, with access to money from interested whites. But if the two men were rivals, they still had much in common. Both had had an honorable career in efforts to improve the position of the blacks in America. Both had opposed emigration. Both had come to believe in emigration as a legitimate way of progress and to believe in a Negro nation. Both now looked to Africa as the land of promise.

Neither man expected miracles in planning for a home in Africa. They did not expect to lead a mass emigration. Both expected to develop small settlements of American blacks in Africa—people carefully chosen who would demonstrate Christianity, morality, and good character. They should have skills in agriculture, the mechanical arts, and commerce; they should come well recommended. It was expected that these enclaves of Americans would influence the people of Africa to accept their way of life. Meantime, the new community would raise cotton or other crops to compete with the American South and thus hasten the day when slavery would be no more. And if there were still slaves being put on board ship from Africa, that curse could also be eliminated by the influence of the new settlers.

Delany's unwillingness to use money from whites quickly got him into financial difficulties which Garnet's easier acceptance of proffered aid allowed him to avoid. In fact, it was Garnet's organization, the African Civilization Society, which put up the money necessary to send one of Delany's chosen colleagues on his way to Africa via England. This was, of course, without Delany's consent. The man in question was Robert Campbell. Campbell's residence at Philadelphia made him a natural target for those interested in the African Civilization Society, for Philadelphia was also the home of Benjamin Coates, to whom Frederick Douglass once referred as the real head of the African Civilization Society. When Delany had trouble raising funds for the expedition, which was to have lasted for three years and to have had five members, Campbell was induced to accept aid from the rival organization and departed for England. In so doing Campbell not only violated a trust, he also offended Delany's black nationalism, even compounding the offense by accepting more money—this time from Englishmen—on his way to Africa.

With Campbell already on his way, Delany had to secure emergency financing and betake himself to Africa in order to maintain some semblance of control. The men were gone about a year. They visited England together on their way home and were accorded a hero's welcome.

Their separate reports, though partly covering the same material, are in most respects highly individualistic. Of the two accounts, Delany's is the more mission-minded; Campbell's the more practical and factual. Both were familiar with Thomas Jefferson Bowen's *Central Africa* (1857) and seem to have used information from it to some extent. Delany was familiar with David Livingstone's *Missionary Travels and Researches in South Africa,* first published in London in 1857, and this work seems to have influenced his thinking on Africa, but bears little relation to the printed report. Campbell appreciated Charlotte Tucker's *Abbeokuta,* which by 1854 had reached a fourth edition. Miss Tucker, unlike Bowen and Livingstone, had not lived in Africa but had drawn her information from missionary sources and from her familiarity with the lives of some of the missionaries.

Bowen, a white Southern Baptist missionary, had the advantage of having spent some seven years in the interior of Africa, mostly in the Egba-Yoruba country. He was a missionary first, a rather good observer second. But he had one overwhelming disadvantage. He was a white man in a black society that had not been cowed by colonialism, nor was it a society particularly receptive to the Christian religion which Bowen was seeking to propagate. His observations were from the outside, sometimes so literally from the outside that he was not allowed to sleep within the walls of the town. Delany and Campbell, though classified as "white men" because they had accepted the Euro-American way of life, had the great advantage of being considered as relatives of the Africans, even though Campbell had to make a point of explaining that he was indeed of African ancestry. Delany was never troubled by any such necessity for explanations. His face was proof positive that Africa was indeed the land of his fathers.

In reporting on their sojourn in Africa, whether in Liberia or in Egba-Yoruba area from Lagos to Ilorin, Delany seldom forgets his mission. He must develop a Negro nation. He must read into the record the achievement of the black man and his plans for the future, for white historians had deprived the Negro of his rightful place in history by simply failing to record the accomplishments of other groups than their own. He suffered for the race when he recounts how his young colleague had taken things into his own hands and had, in his estimation, sullied the banner of Negro nationalism by accepting money from, and thereby an obligation to, the African Civilization Society.

Delany reports courteous treatment at the hands of the Liberians, even though his fame as an opponent of the American Colonization Society's child had preceded him. He found it possible to explain his position to their satisfaction and his role as an emissary from American blacks to inspect the land for future settlement. He gives an account of the climate, soil, plants, animals, and people of Liberia and offers suggestions for improvement of health, welfare, housing, government, and crops. Continuing his journey to meet Campbell who had preceded him to Africa and who had moved on to the Niger area, Delany again gives brief details on the land, the products, way of life, diseases, and treatment. He devotes a section to missionaries, where his anti-Catholic bias is noticeable, and suggests that the correct kind of missionary effort would quickly bring positive results. Such missionaries should be black. He discusses commerce, transportation, crops—including cotton—and sees in this and other tropical or semitropical crops the hope of competing successfully with the economy of the American South. The "reflex influence" could work also in Africa. And of course there is the reproduction of a treaty with the African kings calling for black settlements in the Niger area.

By page count slightly more than one-third of Delany's report is devoted to details of the history of the movement before the African experience itself or to the visit to England on the way home. Only about one-half of his report pertains to the Niger Valley experience.

Delany can be described as forceful and positive in his writings—as indeed he was in life—but he was not well organized or polished in his literary style. The great merit of his report is that it conveys in a most positive manner the dreams and ambitions of a man who hungered for a place for his people and a recognition of their contribution to man and to civilization.

Campbell's account is devoted entirely to the African experience. It is far more readable, better arranged, and more detailed insofar as Yoruban Africa is concerned. The report plunges immediately into the recital of the sojourn in Africa and closes with the treaty between the explorers and the African kings. If there is a Negro nationalist in Campbell it is quietly implicit in the last paragraph of his preface: "I have determined, with my wife and children, to go to Africa to live." His determination is evinced in *The Anti Slavery Reporter* for April 18, 1863, which reports Mr. R. Campbell to be operating a new paper, the *Anglo-African,* at Lagos.

Campbell comments regularly on social and economic conditions, war and peace, religion and politics, geography and climate, and health and housing. Indeed, these topics were covered again and again by both men. Of the two, Campbell was much more likely to record the fact, perhaps in greater detail, but he was much less inclined to rebuild African society on the spot. While Delany offers suggestions on how to improve coffee tree culture or how to improve ventilation, or on why horses did not live in Liberia, Campbell is more likely to give a description of people, of a social gathering, or of a dramatic confrontation between his party and a wandering band of soldiers.

On the way home the two explorers stopped off in England in May 1860 and were assured of the interest of Englishmen in developing the cotton industry in Africa. They were told that the African Aid Society would be at their service in exploiting the resources of the continent. What neither report records is that within a few months the African kings reneged on their treaty, the British government began to pressure the African Aid Society into withholding further succor for the would-be immigrants, and Delany made a kind of peace with the African Civilization Society after he had dictated some modification of the constitution requiring that blacks be in command. By that time the American Civil War had begun, and the interest in Africa had to take second place in the lives, though perhaps not in the hearts, of men like Martin Delany. When he died in 1885, somewhat past the Biblical three score years and ten, he was once again involved in an enterprise concerning blacks beyond the borders of the United States.

Delany's report preserves information on the history of the separatist movement, culminating in the effort to transfer Christian black communities from America to Africa. Delany remained defensively aware of his own place in history and defensively aware of the Negro's struggle for recognition and fulfillment. To the end of his life he saw black men as a noble race and the only source from which the regeneration of Africa might be achieved. Campbell, less defensive, less volatile, recorded more of Africa and less of the history of a movement to vindicate the black man's place in history. Together the two throw valuable light on a facet of history little known to a generation which has developed its own brand of black nationalism.

These two black nationalist movements, separated by the Civil War and more than a century of unkept promises, have more in common than at first meets the eye. Both have elements of pride in race, which has been too often lacking among the oppressed. Both look to the Negro as the means of salvation, not only for Africa but also for America. Both are aggressively aware of black unity which scoffs at claims of white superiority, but is ready to accept black superiority. Both demand the fulfillment of economic and social equality. Both are disdainful of white-led, or even white-participating efforts at betterment of conditions for the Negro. Both demand black leadership for black projects.

Black nationalism of the 1960's is, however, better educated, more aggressive, more sophisticated, more ruthless than the Negro nationalism of the 1850's. Whitfield and Holly and Delany looked for a place where the black man might prove his capacity for government; the black nationalist of today is more likely to suggest that a substantial portion of the United States be assigned to Negroes for past misdeeds of the nation.

Perhaps one of the greatest differences, and one of the happiest, between the nationalists of the 1850's and those of today is the greater confidence which the twentieth century has brought to the black man. One cannot read Delany without being painfully aware of his great sense of hurt and frustration, but there were relatively few who believed him when he spoke of the great soul and the potentially great accomplishments of the blacks. Today there are literally millions of people in the United States and in Africa who do believe what only the few believed about the black man's greatness a century ago.

This new confidence is in part due to the development of Africa during the intervening years. The Negro nationalists of the 1850's had to persuade themselves, and seek to persuade others, that their confidence in the black man would be vindicated. It is somewhat ironic that the "reflex influence" which was cited so often by Negro nationalists of the past century came to fruition only in the 1960's after Africa had suddenly spawned its independent members of the family of nations. It is even more ironic that, except for Liberia, the reflex influence came not from the emigrant American black men, but from the native population which had emerged to independence under the aegis of European powers.

Even though Delany and Campbell failed to lead many emigrants to Africa, the back-to-Africa movement of the period should not be written off as inconsequential. There were in Africa at that time thousands of blacks who had made their way back from the Western Hemisphere and had settled in Liberia, or Sierra Leone, or the Niger River area. They had come not only from the United States but from Latin America and British American areas as well.

This return to Africa was nationalistic, as portrayed in the lives of men like Delany and Campbell. It had a strong economic bent as demonstrated by a Negro emigrationist's reference to the meeting between Diogenes and Alexander the Great, when Diogenes had asked the great one to get out of his light: "We, too, asked this [of the whites] a long time; finding, however, they wouldn't mind us, we came around to the east, so as to get between them and the sun, and get the early sun on our sugar, coffee, and cotton, that by and by we may somewhat obstruct their view" (*African Repository,* Feb., 1860, p. 56). Finally, the return to Africa was never devoid of the religious element. The bondage and redemption of the children of Israel had too many similarities to the later bondage and hopeful redemption of the blacks to escape notice.

It was Alexander Crummell, emigrationist in Liberia, who pointed up these similarities. Recalling the centuries of suffering and servitude of the Israelites he yet saw that bondage as a time of preparation, for God was always with them and led them into new knowledge and acquaintance with a high civilization. So it was for the Negro in the Americas, where God had been preparing him for new duties. "The day of preparation for our race is well nigh ended; the day of duty and responsibility on our part, to suffering, benighted, Africa, is at hand" [Alexander Crummel, *Africa and America* (1891), p. 421].

Contents

Political Movements — Section I   27

Succeeding Conventions — Section II   31

History of the Project — Section III   32

Arrival and Reception in Liberia — Section IV   47

Liberia; Climate, Soil, Productions, etc. — Section V   52

Diseases, Cause, Remedy — Section VI   64

The Interior; Yoruba — Section VII   67

Topography, Climate, etc. — Section VIII   70

Diseases of This Part of Africa, Treatment, Hygiene, Aliment — Section IX   87

Missionary Influence — Section X   102

What Africa Now Requires — Section XI   107

To Direct Legitimate Commerce — Section XII   111

Cotton Staple — Section XIII   116

Success in Great Britain — Section XIV   122

Commercial Relations in Scotland — Section XV   137

The Time to Go to Africa — Section XVI   143

Concluding Suggesions — Section XVII   145

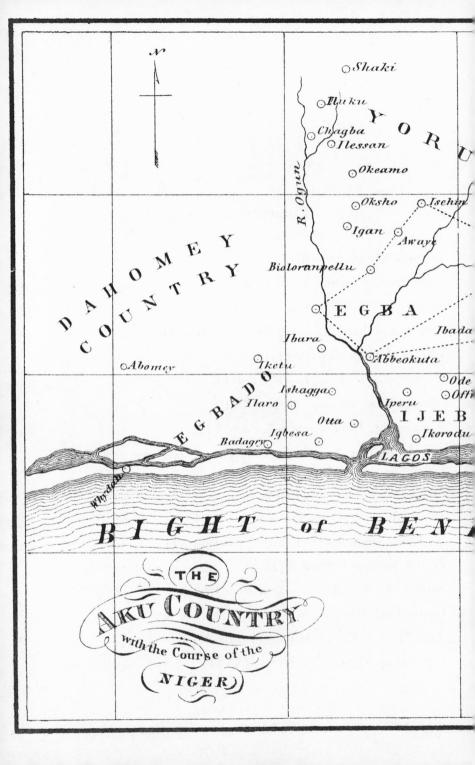

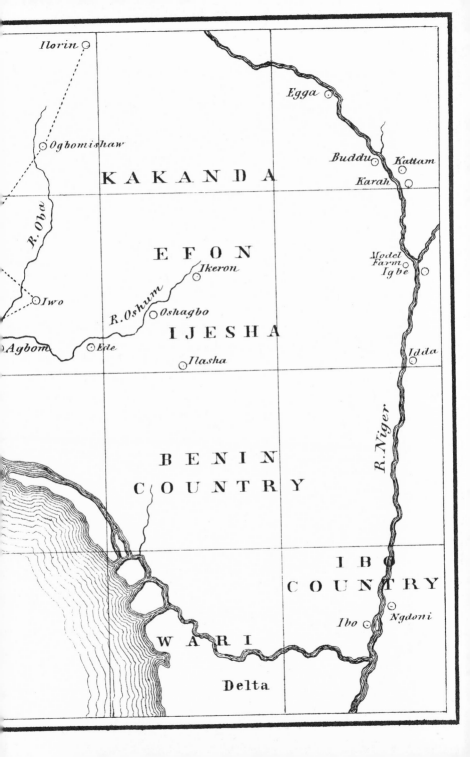

Official Report

OF

THE NIGER VALLEY

EXPLORING PARTY

BY
M. R. DELANY
Chief Commissioner to Africa

REPORT

OF

THE NIGER VALLEY
EXPLORING PARTY

SECTION I

POLITICAL MOVEMENTS

On or about the latter part of July, 1853, the following
document was sent on, and shortly appeared in the columns of "FREDERICK DOUGLASS' PAPER," Rochester, N.Y.,
and the "ALIENED AMERICAN," published and edited by
William Howard Day, Esq., M.A., at Cleveland, Ohio,
U.S., which continued in those papers every issue, until
the meeting of the Convention:

CALL FOR A NATIONAL EMIGRATION CONVENTION OF COLORED MEN

*To be held in Cleveland, Ohio, on the 24th, 25th, and
26th of August, 1854*

MEN AND BRETHREN: The time has fully come when we,
as an oppressed people, should do something effectively, and
use those means adequate to the attainment of the great
and long desired end—do something to meet the actual
demands of the present and prospective necessities of the
rising generation of our people in this country. To do this,
we must occupy a position of entire *equality*, of *unrestricted*
rights, composing in fact, an acknowledged *necessary* part of
the *ruling element* of society in which we live. The policy
necessary to the *preservation* of this *element* must be *in our
favor*, if ever we expect the enjoyment, freedom, sovereignty,
and equality of rights anywhere. For this purpose, and to this
end, then, all colored men in favor of Emigration out of the
United States, and *opposed* to the American Colonization
scheme of leaving the Western Hemisphere, are requested to
meet in CLEVELAND, OHIO, TUESDAY, the 24th day of AUGUST,
1854, in a great NATIONAL CONVENTION, then and there to con-

sider and decide upon the great and important subject of Emigration from the United States.

No person will be admitted to a seat in the Convention, who would introduce the subject of Emigration to the Eastern Hemisphere—either to Asia, Africa, or Europe—as our object and determination are to consider our claims to the West Indies, Central and South America, and the Canadas. This restriction has no reference to *personal* preference, or *individual* enterprise; but to the great question of national claims to come before the Convention.

All persons coming to the Convention must bring credentials properly authenticated, or bring verbal assurance to the Committee on Credentials—appointed for the purpose—of their fidelity to the measures and objects set forth in this call, as the Convention is specifically by and for the friends of Emigration, and none others—and no opposition to them will be entertained.

The question is not whether our condition can be bettered by emigration, but whether it can be made worse. If not, then, there is no part of the wide spread universe, where our social and political condition are not better than here in our native country, and nowhere in the world as here, proscribed on account of color.

We are friends to, and ever will stand shoulder to shoulder by our brethren, and all our friends in all good measures adopted by them for the bettering of our condition in this country, and surrender no rights but with our last breath; but as the subject of Emigration is of vital importance, and has ever been shunned by all delegated assemblages of our people as heretofore met, we cannot longer delay, and will not be farther baffled; and deny the right of our most sanguine friend or dearest brother, to prevent an intelligent inquiry into, and the carrying out of these measures, when this can be done, to our entire advantage, as we propose to show in Convention—as the West Indies, Central and South America—the majority of which are peopled by our brethren, or those identified with us in race, and what is more, *destiny,* on this continent—all stand with open arms and yearning hearts, importuning us in the name of suffering humanity to come—to make common cause, and share one common fate on the continent.

The Convention will meet without fail at the time fixed for assembling, as none but those favorable to Emigration are admissible; therefore no other gathering may prevent it. The number of delegates will not be restricted—except in the town where the Convention may be held—and there the number will be decided by the Convention when assembled, that they may not too far exceed the other delegations.

The time and place fixed for holding the Convention are ample; affording sufficient time, and a leisure season generally —and as Cleveland is now the centre of all directions—a good and favorable opportunity to all who desire to attend. Therefore, it may reasonably be the greatest gathering of the colored people ever before assembled in a Convention in the United States.

Colonizationists are advised, that no favors will be shown to them or their expatriating scheme, as we have no sympathy with the enemies of our race.

All colored men, East, West, North, and South, favorable to the measures set forth in this Call will send in their names (post-paid) to M. R. DELANY, or REV. WM. WEBB, Pittsburgh, Pa., that there may be arranged and attached to the Call, *five* names from each State.

We must make an issue, create an event, and establish a position *for ourselves.* It is glorious to think of, but far more glorious to carry out.

REV. WM. WEBB, M. R. DELANY, H. G. WEBB, THOS. A. BROWN, JOHN JONES, R. L. HAWKINS, SAMUEL VENERABLE, JOHN WILLIAMS, A. F. HAWKINS, S. W. SANDERS, JEFFERSON MILLER, *Pittsburgh, Pa.;* REV. A. R. GREEN, P. L. JACKSON, J. H. MAHONEY, G. HARPER, JONATHAN GREEN, H. A. JACKSON, E. R. PARKER, SAMUEL BRUCE, *Alleghany City;* J. J. GOULD BIAS, M.D., REV. M. M. CLARK, A. M. SUMNER, JOHNSON WOODLIN, *Philadelphia;* JAMES M. WHITFIELD, JOHN N. STILL, STANLEY MATTHEWS, *New York.*

This Call was readily responded to by the addition of names from other States, which appeared in subsequent issues.

At the Convention, which according to the Call sat in Cleveland successively on Thursday, 24th, Friday, 25th, and Saturday, 26th of August, 1854, the following States were represented: Rhode Island, New York, Pennsylvania, Ohio, Michigan, Wisconsin, Indiana, Missouri, Kentucky, Tennessee, Louisiana, Virginia, and the Canadas; the great body consisting of nearly sixteen hundred persons. W. H. DAY, Esq., editor of the *Aliened*

American, entered the Convention, and the Chairman invited him forward, offering him the privileges of the Convention, stating that wherever colored people were, William Howard Day was free—whether or not he altogether agreed in sentiment on minor points; and the Convention unanimously concurred in the invitation given.

Mr. Day subsequently proffered to the Convention any books or documents at his command for the use of that body.

The following permanent Institution was established:

ORGANIZATION OF THE NATIONAL BOARD OF COMMISSIONERS

Central Commissioners, Pittsburgh, Pennsylvania— M. R. DELANY, President; WM. WEBB, Vice-President; THOS. A. BROWN, Treasurer; EDW. R. PARKER, Auditor; CHAS. W. NIGHTEN, Secretary; PROFESSOR M. H. FREEMAN, A.M,. Special For. Sec.; SAMUEL VENERABLE, ALFRED H. JOHNS, SAMUEL BRUCE, PARKER SORRELL.

DEPARTMENTS

Committee on Domestic Relations.—SAMUEL BRUCE, Chairman; SAMUEL VENERABLE, CHARLES W. NIGHTEN. *Financial Relations.*—THOMAS A. BROWN, Chairman; PARKER SORRELL, ALFRED H. JOHNS. *Foreign Relations.*— REV. WM. WEBB, Chairman; M. R. DELANY, EDW. R. PARKER. *Special Foreign Secretary.*—PROF. MARTIN H. FREEMAN, A.M. *State Commissioners.*—*Massachusetts—* WM. C. NELL, Boston; C. L. REMOND, Salem. *New York, Buffalo.*—JAMES M. WHITFIELD, J. THEODORE HOLLY. *Ohio, Cincinnati.*—AUGUSTUS R. GREEN, PHILIP TOLIVAR, Jun. *Michigan, Detroit.*—WILLIAM C. MUNROE, WILLIAM LAMBERT. *Kentucky, Louisville.*—CONAWAY BARBOUR, JAMES H. GIPSON. *Missouri, St. Louis.*—REV. RICH'D ANDERSON, REV. JORDAN BROWN. *Virginia, Richmond.*— RICHARD HENDERSON, JOHN E. FERGUSON. *Tennessee,*

Nashville.—ELDER PETER A. H. LOWRY, CHARLES BARRATT. *Louisiana, New Orleans.*—JORDAN B. NOBLE, REV. JOHN GARROW. *California, San Francisco.*—HENRY M. COLLINS, ORANGE LEWIS.

SECTION II

SUCCEEDING CONVENTIONS

The Second Convention, pursuant to a call, was held in Cleveland, in August, 1856, when some modification and amendments were made in the Constitution, and some changes in the officers of the Board; but the president was unanimously re-elected, and continued in office until the close of the Third Convention, which met pursuant to a call in the town of Chatham, Canada West, in August, 1858, when, resigning his position in the Board, the following officers succeeded to the

GENERAL BOARD OF COMMISSIONERS

CENTRAL COMMISSIONERS—CHATHAM, CANADA
WILLIAM HOWARD DAY, President
MATISON F. BAILEY, Vice-President
GEORGE WASH. BRODIE, Secretary
JAMES MADISON BELL, Treasurer
ALFRED WHIPPER, Auditor
MARTIN R. DELANY, Foreign Secretary

NOTE.—The names only of the Central Commissioners are here given, the others being re-elected as chosen in 1856, at Cleveland.

OTHER MEMBERS

ABRAM D. SHADD
J. HENRY HARRIS
ISAAC D. SHADD

At an Executive Council Meeting of the Board, September 1st, 1858, the following resolution, as taken from the Minutes, was adopted: That Dr. Martin R. Delany, of Chatham, Kent County, Canada West, be a Commissioner to explore in Africa, with full power to choose his own colleagues.

SECTION III

HISTORY OF THE PROJECT

In the winter of 1831–2, being then but a youth, I formed the design of going to Africa, the land of my ancestry; when in the succeeding winter of 1832–3, having then fully commenced to study, I entered into a solemn promise with the Rev. Molliston Madison Clark, then a student in Jefferson College, at Cannonsburg, Washington County, Pennsylvania, being but seventeen miles from Pittsburgh, where I resided (his vacations being spent in the latter place), to complete an education, and go on an independent and voluntary mission—to travel in Africa—I as a physician and he as a clergyman, for which he was then preparing.

During these vacations of about seven weeks each, Mr. Clark was of great advantage to me in my studies, he being then a man of probably thirty years of age, or more, and in his senior year (I think) at college.

This design I never abandoned, although in common with my race in America, I espoused the cause, and contended for our political and moral elevation on equality with the whites, believing then, as I do now, that merit alone should be the test of individual claims in the body politic. This cause I never have nor will abandon; believing that no man should hesitate or put off any duty for another time or place, but "act, act in the *living present,* act," *now* or *then.* This has been the rule of my life, and I hope ever shall be.

In 1850, I had fully matured a plan for an adventure, and to a number of select intelligent gentlemen (of African descent, of course) fully committed myself in favor of it. They all agreed that the scheme was good; and although neither of them entered personally into it, all fully sanctioned it, bidding me God-speed in my new adventure, as a powerful handmaid to their efforts in contending for our rights in America.

In 1854, at the great Emigration Convention in Cleveland, my paper, read and adopted as a "Report on the Political Destiny of the Colored Race on the American Continent," set forth fully my views on the advantages of Emigration.

Although the Call itself strictly prohibits the introduction of the question of emigration from the American Continent or Western Hemisphere, the qualification which directly follows—"This restriction has no reference to *personal* preference, or *individual* enterprise"—may readily be understood. It was a mere policy on the part of the authors of those documents, to confine their scheme to America (including the West Indies), whilst they were the leading advocates of the regeneration of Africa, lest they compromised themselves and their people to the avowed enemies of the race.

The Convention (at Cleveland, 1854), in its Secret Sessions made, Africa, with its rich, inexhaustible productions, and great facilities for checking the abominable Slave Trade, its most important point of dependence, though each individual was left to take the direction which in his judgment best suited him. Though our great gun was leveled, and the first shell thrown at the American Continent, driving a slaveholding faction into despair, and a political confusion from which they have been utterly unable to extricate themselves, but become more and more complicated every year, *Africa was held in reserve, until by the help of an All-wise Providence we could effect what has just been accomplished with signal success*—a work which the most sanguine friend of the cause believed would require at least the half of a century.

It is a curious, and not less singular historical fact, that a leading political journal, and the first newspaper which nominated Mr. James Buchanan, many years ago, for the Presidency of the United States; and at a time whilst he was yet at the Court of St. James (1854), as Envoy Extraordinary, this paper was strongly urging his claims as such, thus expresses itself, which gives a fair idea of the political pro-slavery press generally, especially in Pennsylvania, Mr. Buchanan's native State. I intended to give the article entire, as alarm will be seen even at the commencement; but pressure for space will prevent my quoting but a few sentences. It is from the Pittsburgh *Daily Morning Post,* Wednesday, October 18th, 1854:

A GRAND SCHEME FOR THE COLORED RACE

In August last, a National Convention of colored people was held at Cleveland, Ohio. It was composed of delegates from most of the States. It was called the 'National Emigration Convention,' and its objects were to consider the political destinies of the black race; and recommend a plan of Emigration to countries where they can enjoy political liberty, and form nations 'free and independent.'

The Committee then proceeds to mark out a grand scheme by which the Negro race may be regenerated, and formed into free, intelligent, and prosperous nations. The West India Islands, Central America, and all the Northern and middle portions of South America, including the whole of Brazil, are designated as the regions desired; and that can be obtained as the seat of negro civilization and empire. These regions and islands together are represented as containing twenty-four and a half millions of population; but one-seventh of which, some three and a half millions, are whites of pure European extraction; and the remainder, nearly twenty-one millions, are colored people of African and Indian origin. This immense preponderance of the colored races in those regions, it is supposed, will enable them, with the aid of Emigration from the United States, to take possession of all those countries and islands, and become the ruling race in the empires to be formed out of those wide and fruitful realms. The Committee expresses full confidence in the practicability of this great undertaking; and that nothing is wanting to its success at no distant day but unanimity of sentiment and action among the masses of the colored people. The climate of those regions is represented as entirely congenial to the colored race, while to the European races it is enervating and destructive; and this fact, added to the present immense superiority of numbers on the part of the negroes, is relied on as a sure guarantee of the success of the great enterprise; and that their race could forever maintain the possession and control of those regions.

Other great events, it is supposed, will follow in the train of this mighty movement. With the West India Islands, and Central and South America, composing free negro nations, slavery in the United States would, they suppose, soon be at an end. The facility of escape, the near neighborhood of friends and aid, it is urged, would rapidly drain off from the Southern States all the most intelligent, robust, and bold of their slaves.

Dr. M. R. Delany, of Pittsburgh, was the chairman of the committee that made this report to the convention. It was, of course, adopted.

If Dr. D. drafted this report, it certainly does him much credit for learning and ability; and cannot fail to establish for him a reputation for vigor and brilliancy of imagination never yet surpassed. It is a vast conception of impossible birth. The Committee seem to have entirely overlooked the strength of the 'powers on earth' that would oppose the Africanization of more than half the Western Hemisphere.

We have no motive in noticing this gorgeous dream of 'the Committee,' except to show its fallacy—its impracticability, in fact, its absurdity. No sensible man, whatever his color, should be for a moment deceived by such impracticable theories.

On the African coast already exists a thriving and prosperous Republic. It is the native home of the African race; and there he can enjoy the dignity of manhood, the rights of citizenship, and all the advantages of civilization and freedom. Every colored man in this country will be welcomed there as a free citizen; and there he can not only prosper, and secure his own comfort and happiness, but become a teacher and benefactor of his kindred races; and become an agent in carrying civilization and Christianity to a benighted continent. That any one will be turned aside from so noble a mission by the delusive dream of conquest and empire in the Western

Hemisphere is an absurdity too monstrous and mischievous to be believed. Yet 'the Committee's Report' was accepted, and adopted, and endorsed by a 'National Convention;' and is published and sent forth to the world.

In July, 1855, Rev. James Theodore Holly, an accomplished black gentleman, now rector of St. Luke's Church, New Haven, Connecticut, U.S., was commissioned to Faustin Soulouque, Emperor of Hayti, where he was received at court with much attention, interchanging many official notes during a month's residence there, with favorable inducements to laborers to settle.

During the interval from the first convention, 1854 to 1858, as President of the Council, I was actively engaged corresponding in every direction, among which were several States of Central and South America, as well as Jamaica and Cuba; the Rev. J. T. Holly, who, during two years of the time, filled the office of Foreign Secretary, contributing no small share in its accomplishment.

Immediately after the convention of 1856, from which I was absent by sickness, I commenced a general correspondence with individuals, imparting to each the basis of my adventure to Africa to obtain intelligent colleagues. During this time (the Spring of 1857), "Bowen's Central Africa" was published, giving an interesting and intelligent account of that extensive portion of Africa known on the large missionary map of that continent as Yoruba. Still more encouraged to carry out my scheme at this juncture, Livingstone's great work on Africa made its appearance, which seemed to have stimulated the Africo-Americans in many directions, among others, those of Wisconsin, from whom Mr. Jonathan J. Myers, a very respectable grocer, was delegated as their Chairman to counsel me on the subject. In the several councils held between Mr. Myers and myself, it was agreed and understood that I was to embody their cause and interests in my mission to Africa, they accepting of the policy of my scheme.

At this tme, I made vigorous efforts to accomplish my design, and for this purpose, among others, endeavored to obtain goods in Philadelphia to embark for Loando de St. Paul, the Portuguese colony in Loango, South Africa, where the prospect seemed fair for a good trade in beeswax and ivory, though Lagos, West Central Africa, was my choice and destination. Robert Douglass, Esq., artist, an accomplished literary gentleman (landscape, portrait painter, and photographer) of Philadelphia, with whom I was in correspondence, sent me the following note:

MR. M. R. DELANY:—   PHILADELPHIA, June 17, 1858

DEAR SIR—I think very highly of the intended Expedition to the 'Valley of the Niger.' I would be pleased to accompany it professionally, if I were to receive a proper outfit and salary. Dr. Wilson declines; but Mr. Robert Campbell, of the 'Institute for Colored Youth,' a very accomplished Chemist, &c., &c., &c., says he will gladly accompany the Expedition, if a proper support for his family in his absence were assured. Rev. William Douglass, in conversation with me, has expressed very favorable views. Hoping you may be very successful, I remain in expectation of receiving more detailed accounts of the plan, its prospects and progress,

Your friend and well-wisher,
661, N. Thirteenth St., Phil.   ROBERT DOUGLASS

Up to this time, I had never before known or heard of Mr. Campbell, who is a West India gentleman, native bred in Jamaica, but the recommendation of Mr. Douglass, an old acquaintance and gentleman of unsullied integrity, accompanied as it was by the following note from Dr. Wilson, also an accomplished gentleman of equal integrity, a physician, surgeon, and chemist, who, being selected by me as Surgeon and Naturalist of the party, also recommended Mr. Campbell in a detached note which has been mislaid, was sufficient at the time:

DR. DELANY:—   PHILADELPHIA, June 7th, 1858

DEAR SIR—I received your note of May 25th, through the kindness of R. Douglass, Jr., and can truly say, I am highly gratified to learn of so laudable an enterprise and expedition; and would be happy and proud to be numbered with the noble hearts and brilliant minds, identified with it. Yet, whilst I acknowledge (and feel myself flattered by) the honor conferred upon me in being selected for so important and honorable position, I regret to inform you, that it will be wholly out of my power to accept.

Very respectfully,

838, Lombard Street.   JAMES H. WILSON

I have been the more induced to give the letters of Mr. Douglass and Dr. Wilson in favor of Mr. Campbell, because some of my friends were disposed to think that I "went out of the way to make choice of an entire stranger, unknown to us, instead of old and tried acquaintances," as they were pleased to express it. I had but one object in view—the Moral, Social, and Political Elevation of Ourselves, and the Regeneration of Africa, for which I desired, as a *preference,* and indeed the only *adequate* and *essential* means by which it is to be accomplished, men of African descent, properly qualified and of pure and fixed principles. These I endeavored to select by corresponding only with such of my acquaintances.

At the Council which appointed me Commissioner to Africa, having presented the names of Messrs. Douglass and Campbell, asking that they also might be chosen; at a subsequent meeting the following action took place:

Whereas, Dr. Martin R. Delany, Commissioner to Africa, having presented the names of Messrs. Robert Douglass and Robert Campbell of Philadelphia, Pa., U.S., requesting that they be appointed Commissioners, the Board having made him Chief Commissioner with full power to appoint his own Assistants, do hereby sanction the appointment of these gentlemen as Assistant Commissioners.

A paper was then laid before the Council, presenting the name and scheme of the party, which was received and adopted.

Dr. Amos Aray, surgeon, a highly intelligent gentleman, and Mr. James W. Purnell, also an intelligent young gentleman, bred to mercantile pursuits, having subsequently sent in their names and received appointments by the Chief Commssioner, the following document was made out:

AFRICAN COMMISSION

The President and Officers of the General Board of Commissioners, viz: William H. Day, A.M., President; Matison F. Bailey, Vice-President; George W. Brodie, Secretary; James Madison Bell, Treasurer; Alfred Whipper, Auditor; Dr. Martin R. Delany, Special Foreign Secretary; Abram D. Shadd, James Henry Harris, and Isaac D. Shadd, the Executive Council in behalf of the organization for the promotion of the political and other interests of the Colored Inhabitants of North America, particularly the United States and Canada.

To all, unto whom these letters may come, greeting: The said General Board of Commissioners, in Executive Council assembled, have this day chosen, and by these presents do hereby appoint and authorize Dr. Martin Robison Delany, of Chatham, County of Kent, Province of Canada, Chief Commissioner; and Robert Douglass, Esq., Artist, and Prof. Robert Campbell, Naturalist, both of Philadelphia, Pennsylvania, one of the United States of America, to be Assistant Commissioners; Amos Aray, Surgeon; and James W. Purnell, Secretary and Commercial Reporter, both of Kent County, Canada West, of a Scientific Corps, to be known by the name of

THE NIGER VALLEY EXPLORING PARTY

The object of this Expedition is to make a Topographical, Geological and Geographical Examination of the Valley of the River Niger, in Africa, and an inquiry into the state and condition of the people of that Valley, and other parts of Africa, together with such other scientific inquiries as may by them be deemed expedient, for the purposes of science and for general information; and without any reference to, and with the Board being entirely opposed to any Emigration there as such. Provided, however, that nothing in this Instrument be so construed as to interfere with the right of the Commissioners to negotiate in their own behalf, or that of any other parties, or organization for territory.

The Chief-Commissioner is hereby authorized to add one or more competent Commissioners to their number; it being agreed and understood that this organization is, and is to be exempted from the pecuniary responsibility of sending out this Expedition.

Dated at the Office of the Executive Council, Chatham, county of Kent, Province of Canada, this Thirtieth day of August, in the year of our Lord, One Thousand Eight Hundred and Fifty-eight.

By the President,
WILLIAM HOWARD DAY
ISAAC D. SHADD, Vice-President*
GEORGE W. BRODIE, Secretary

So soon as these names with their destined mission were officially published, there arose at once from mistaken persons (*white*) in Philadelphia, a torrent of opposition, who presuming to know more about us (the blacks) and our own business than we did ourselves, went even so far as to speak to one of our party, and tell him that we were *not ready* for any such *important* undertaking, nor could be in *three years yet to come!* Of course, as necessary to sustain this, it was followed up with a dissertation on the *disqualification* of the Chief of the Party, mentally and physically, *external* appearances and all. So effectually was this opposition prosecuted, that colored people in many directions in the United States and the Canadas, were not only affected by it, but a "Party" of three had already been chosen and appointed to supersede us! Even without any knowledge on my part, claims were made in England in behalf of the "Niger Valley Exploring Party," solely through the instrumentality of these Philadelphians.

Such were the effects of this, that our preparatory progress was not only seriously retarded (I having to spend eight months in New York city to counteract the influence, where six weeks only would have been required), but three years originally intended to be spent in exploring had to be reduced to one, and the number of Commissioners from five to two, thereby depriving

* Mr. Shadd was elected Vice-President in the place of Mr. Bailey, who left the Province for New Caledonia.

Mr. Robert Douglass from going, an old friend and most excellent gentleman, whose life, as well as that of his father before him, had been spent in efforts, not only of self-elevation, but the elevation also of his people. Many years ago, the accomplished articles of "Robet Douglass, Jun," to the *United States Gazette,* and other public journals, forced those negro-hating periodicals to respect at least the writer, if not his race. Dr. Aray, also an excellent gentleman who had given up business to join the party, was doomed to disappointment. And of Mr. Jas. W. Purnell—who met me in New York two weeks after my arrival, and through the whole eight months of adversity and doubtful progress, stood by me, performing the duty of Secretary, writing in every direction, copying, and from dictation for hours at a time—I cannot say too much. For a young gentleman inexperienced in such matters, he has no superior; and for integrity, true-heartedness, and trustworthiness, in my estimation, he has few if any rivals. To his great and good uncle, under whom he was brought up, much of his character is to be credited.

As an expression of the feelings of the most intelligent emigrationists with whom I corresponded generally in America, I give below two extracts from letters of Professor Freeman. The Professor is now as he then was, the Principal of Avery College.

ALLEGHANY CITY, April 14, 1858

MY DEAR FRIEND—Your letter of condolence was duly received, for which we tender you our warmest thanks.

I have read Bowen's work, and shall to-day purchase Livingstone's. I am more and more convinced that Africa is the country to which all colored men who wish to attain the full stature of manhood, and bring up their children to be men and not creeping things, should turn their steps; and I feel more and more every day, that I made a great mistake in not going there, when I was untrammelled by family ties, and had the opportunity.

Respectfully yours,
M. H. FREEMAN

Again the Professor says:

I see that Emigration has broken out in the East, and that
_____ can notice one now without scoffing at, which he
could not in 1854. Well, people can grow wondrously wiser in
four years. But it will take several more *Olympiads* to bring
the leaders among us up to the old Cleveland Platform of 1854.

All the fault of that movement was this, that it was at
least one generation ahead of the colored *heads* of our people.
We may, if we please, refuse to emigrate, and crouch like
spaniels, to lick the hand that beats us; but children's children
at the farthest, will have outgrown such pitiful meanness, and
will dare to do all that others have dared and done for the
sake of freedom and independence. Then all this cowardly
cant about the unhealthy climate, the voracious beasts, and
venomous reptiles of Africa, will be at a discount, instead of
passing current as now for wisdom and prudence.

Mr. Campbell, who finally agreed voluntarily to be
one of the "Niger Valley Exploring Party," spent some
time with us in New York and some time in Philadelphia,
but finally, in consequence of the doubtful prospects of
my success, left, it would seem, at the suggestion and with
the advice and recommendation of parties in Philadelphia, disconnected with and unknown to me, from whom
he received letters of introduction for England. In justice to myself and party as organized, as well as the great
cause and people whom I represent, I here simply remark, that this was no arrangement of mine nor our
party, as such at the time; and whatever of success the
visit was attended with, and benefit thereby accrued
mutually to us in Africa, I as frankly decline any authority in the matter and credit to myself, as I should had
the result proved what it might have done otherwise. I
am only willing to claim that which is legitimately mine,
and be responsible for my own doings whether good or
bad; but this act the integrity of the Party was forced to
acknowledge, as the following circular published in England will show:

Exploring Party

EXPEDITION TO AFRICA

TO PROMOTE THE CULTIVATION OF COTTON AND OTHER PRODUCTS OF SLAVE-LABOR, BY EMIGRANTS FROM AMERICA

A party, consisting of Martin R. Delany, M.D., Robert Campbell, J. W. Purnell, Robert Douglass, and Amos Aray, M.D., (the last two subsequently omitted) has been commissioned by a Convention of Colored Persons, held at Chatham, C.W., to proceed to Africa, and select a location for the establishment of an Industrial Colony.

While such an enterprise is of importance in the Evangelization and Civilization of Africa, and in affording an asylum in which the oppressed descendants of that country may find the means of developing their mental and moral faculties unimpeded by unjust restrictions, it is regarded as of still greater importance in facilitating the production of those staples, particularly Cotton, which now are supplied to the world chiefly by Slave Labor. The effect of this would be to lessen the profits of Slavery. to render in time the slave a burden to his owner, and thus furnish an irresistible motive to Emancipation. Africa possesses resources which, properly developed, must doubtless render her eventually a great, if not the greatest, producer of all the products of Slave Labor. And how would all good men rejoice to see the blow which shall effectually prostrate the giant Slavery, struck by the Black Man's arm! It is necessary, however, that civilized influences be diffused in her midst, or, at least, that facilities for rendering available her products, be supplied equal to the demand for them.

It is the purpose of the party to proceed to Lagos, thence through Abbeokuta to Rabba, on the Niger, about 350 miles from the coast; to study the Agricultural and Commercial facilities of the country, and the disposition of the Natives towards strangers as settlers; also to negotiate for the grant or purchase of land, and to ascertain the conditions on which we might be protected in the usages of civilized life.

These objects being accomplished, the party will return and report the result of their labors, when a considerable number of intelligent and enterprising persons from the United States and Canada, many of them intimately acquainted with the production of Cotton, and its preparation for market, will be prepared to emigrate.

Towards defraying the expenses of this undertaking, £500

has been subscribed in America. This amount has been expended in providing for the families of two of the party in their absence; in paying the passage of Martin R. Delany and J. W. Purnell to Africa, direct from America, and providing them a few articles of outfit; in defraying the current expenses of the party since the 1st December ult., while engaged in soliciting subscriptions, and otherwise forwarding the objects of the Expedition; and in providing the Subscriber with the means of coming hither.

It is desired to raise in this country, in time to enable the Subscriber to depart for Africa in June by the steamer from Liverpool, an additional sum of £250, with which to provide other articles of outfit, and goods for trading with the natives for the means of subsistence, as well as to provide for other necessary and contingent expenses.

The Subscriber will take the liberty of calling upon you personally, at an early day, to solicit your aid in this enterprise.

MANCHESTER, May 13th, 1859   ROBERT CAMPBELL

Grant, for charity's sake, that it was done with the best of motives, it was flagrantly and fatally at variance with every principle of intelligent—to say nothing of enlightened—organizations among civilized men, and in perfect harmony with that mischievous interference by which the enemies of our race have ever sought to sow discord among us, to prove a natural contempt for the Negro and repugnance to his leadership, then taunt us with incapacity for self-government. These flambeaus and rockets directed with unerring precision, taking effect in the very centre of our magazine, did not cause, in those for whom it was intended, a falter nor a wince in their course, but steadily and determinedly they pressed their way to the completion of their object under prosecution. In this design the enemy was thwarted.

I drop every reflection and feeling of unpleasantness towards my young brother Campbell, who, being a West Indian, probably did not understand those *white Americans,* and formed his opinion of American *blacks* and their capacity to "lead," from the estimate they set upon them. I owe it to posterity, the destiny of my race, the great adventure into which I am embarked and the position I sustain to it, to make this record with all Christian (or *African,* if you please) forgiveness, against this most glaring and determined act of theirs to blast the negro's prospects in this his first effort in the Christian Era, to work out his own moral and political salvation, by the regeneration of his Fatherland, through the medium of a self-projected scheme; and thereby take the credit to themselves. It was too great an undertaking for negroes to have the credit of, and therefore they *must* go *under* the auspices of some white American Christians. To be black, it would seem, was necessarily to be "ungodly"; and to be white was necessarily to be "godly," or Christian, in the estimation of some.

With a grateful heart, I here as freely record as an equal duty I owe to posterity, my unfeigned thanks to all those gentlemen who took an active part and in any way aided the mission on my behalf, either from the pulpit, by the contribution of books, stationery, charts, instruments, or otherwise, especially those who made each the *one hundred dollar contribution,* and the two in New York, through whose instrumentality and influence these were obtained. Those disinterested and voluntary acts of kindness I never shall forget whilst reason occupies her throne, and would here willingly record their names, had I their consent to do so.

I sailed from New York May 24th, in the fine *barque Mendi*—Captain M'Intyre—vessel and cargo owned by Johnson, Turpin and Dunbar, three enterprising colored gentlemen of Monrovia, Liberia, all formerly of New York, U.S. In the name of the General Board of Commissioners for the promotion of the political and other interest of the colored people of the United States and the Canadas, by self-exertion, I thank them.

I cannot close this section without expressing my

obligations to Captain M'Intyre for his personal kindness to me; and also to his first officer, Captain Vernon Locke, (himself a ship-master, who took the position of first officer for the voyage, and who had been, for the last three or four years, collecting scientific information by astronomical, meteorological, and other observations, for Lieutenant Maury, Director of the Observatory at Washington, D.C., U.S.,) I am greatly indebted for many acts of kindness in facilitating my microscopic and other examinations and inquiries, during the voyage. Concerning the *nautilus and whale,* I learned more through this accomplished seaman than I had ever learned before. The first by examination of the mollusca, which were frequently caught by Captain L. for my accommodation—and of the latter, by oral information received from him (who had been a great whaler) on frequently observing those huge monsters during the voyage.*

---

* On the 16th day of June, lat 35 deg. 35 min., long. 38 deg. 39 min., a very large school (the largest Captain Locke said that he had ever seen or read of), probably *five hundred,* of sperm whales made their appearance in the segment of a circle to windward and leeward of the vessel about noon, continuing in sight, blowing and spouting, filling the air with spray for a long time, to our amusement and delight. The captain said, though an old whaler, he had never known of sperm whales in that latitude before; and from the immense number, and as they were frequently seen as we approached Africa many times on different days afterwards, that he thought a new whaling point had been discovered. Other whales were also seen frequently in these latitudes—lazy, shy "old bulls," which floated with their huge backs and part of their heads out of water, so as to expose their eyes, when they would suddenly disappear and as quickly appear again; but the great quantity of *squid spawn,* the peculiar *mollusca* upon which the sperm whale feeds, made it ominous, according to the opinion of Captain Locke, that a great new sperm whale fishery had been discovered, the spawn being seen during several days' sail before and after observing the great school.

NOTE.—I should not close this part of my report without stating that, during the year 1858, Mr. Myers wrote to the Royal Geographical Society, London; Thomas Clegg, Esq., Manchester; Dr. Livingstone, and perhaps others, all over *my name* as secretary and himself chairman. The letters referred to were written (without my knowledge) by a son of Mr. Myers; and I only mention the fact here because I am unwilling to claim the honor of the authorship of correspondence carried on through a lad of sixteen years of age.

SECTION IV
ARRIVAL AND RECEPTION IN LIBERIA

Saturday, July 10th.—I landed on the beach at Grand Cape Mount, Robertsport, in company with Messrs. the Hon. John D. Johnson, Joseph Turpin, Dr. Dunbar, and Ellis A. Potter, amid the joyous acclamations of the numerous natives who stood along the beautiful shore, and a number of Liberians, among whom was Reverend Samuel Williams, who gave us a hearty reception. Here we passed through the town (over the side of the hill), returning to the vessel after night.

Arrival in Africa

Monday, July 12th.—The roadstead of Monrovia was made about noon, when I, in company with B. E. Castendyk, Esq., a young German gentleman traveling for pleasure, took lodgings at Widow Moore's, the residence of Rev. John Seys, the United States consular agent, and commissioner for recaptured Africans.

Monrovia

On the day after my arrival, the following correspondence took place:

Residence of the United States Consular Agent
Monrovia, Liberia, July 12th, 1859

To His Excellency, the President of the Republic of Liberia: Sir—By a Convention of Colored People of the United States and the Canadas, Martin R. Delany, Robert Douglass, Robert Campbell, Amos Aray, and James W. Purnell, were appointed as Commissioners under the name of the 'Niger Valley Exploring Party,' to make an Exploration through different parts of Africa.

I have arrived, Sir, near your Government, and expect soon to meet other members of the party. Any aid, orally, documentary, or in the person of an Official Commissioner, which you may please to give to facilitate the mission in Liberia will be gratefully and highly appreciated. I ask the favor of an interview with your Excellency, either privately or in Cabinet Council, or with any other gentlemen that the occasion may suggest, at such time as may be designated.

I am happy, Sir, of the opportunity of giving your Excellency assurance of my most distinguished consideration.

M. R. DELANY

His Excellency, President Benson.

Government House, Monrovia, July 13, 1859

Sir—I have the honor to acknowledge the receipt of your note of the 12th instant, conveying to me the information of your appointment (in connection with colleagues expected soon to arrive), by a Convention of the colored people of the United States and the Canadas, 'Commissioners,' under the name of 'The Niger Valley Exploring Party;' and of your arrival near this Government. You have also been pleased to signify, that you will duly appreciate any aid, oral, documentary, or in the form of an official Commissioner this Government may feel disposed to afford you, in facilitation of the enterprise.

In reply, I have to express my deep regret, that the receipt of your very interesting note is on the very eve of my leaving this city on an official visit to the leeward counties, which will, for the present, deprive me of the pleasure I had anticipated of an interview with you on the very interesting and highly important objects of your mission.

The Hon. John N. Lewis, Secretary of State, with whom I will converse on the subject matter of your note before leaving, will be pleased to grant you an audience; and will, with pleasure, meet your wishes, so far as he can consistently.

Please be re-assured of the deep interest I feel in your very laudable enterprise; and that, if it were not for very important despatches received last week from the county of Maryland, which make it absolutely necessary that I should delay no time in reaching there, I would defer my departure a couple of days for the express purpose of consultation with you in person.

I have the honor to be most respectfully,

Your very obedient servant,

To M. R. Delany, Esq., &c.   Stephen A. Benson

———

Monrovia, July 13, 1859

Martin R. Delany, Esq.:

Dear Sir—The undersigned, citizens of the city of Monrovia, having long heard of you and your efforts in the United States to elevate our down-trodden race, though those efforts were not unfrequently directed against Liberia, are glad to welcome you, in behalf of the community, to these shores; recognizing, as they do in you, an ardent and devoted lover of the African race, and an industrious agent in promoting their interests. And they take this opportunity of expressing to you their most cordial sympathy with the enterprise which has brought you to these shores, sincerely praying that your endeavors may be crowned with complete success.

The undersigned, further, in the name and behalf of the members of this community, respectfully request that you would favor the citizens with a lecture to-morrow evening, or on any other evening you may choose to appoint, at half-past seven o'clock, on any subject you may be pleased to select.

On receiving your reply notices will be issued accordingly.

B. P. YATES	H. W. DENNIS
D. B. WARNER	URIAS A. McGILL
SAML. F. McGILL	H. A. JOHNSON
B. V. R. JAMES	EDW. W. BLYDEN
SAML. MATTHEWS	

Residence of the United States Consular Agent,
Monrovia, July 13th, 1859

GENTLEMEN—Your note of to-day has been received, for the honor of which I thank you, and beg to say that numerous engagements prevent me from complying with your request on to-morrow evening.

You are mistaken, gentlemen, in supposing that I have ever spoken directly 'against Liberia,' as wherever I have been I have always acknowledged a unity of interests in our race wherever located; and any seeming opposition to Liberia could only be constructively such, for which I am not responsible.

Should it be your pleasure, I will do myself the honor of serving you on Monday evening next, or any other evening during the week, by a discourse on the 'Political Destiny of the African Race,' and assure you of the pleasure with which I have the honor to be,

Your most obedient servant,

M. R. DELANY

Col. B. P. Yates; Hon. D. B. Warner; S. F. McGill, M.D.; Hon. B. V. R. James; Rev. Saml. Matthews; Urias McGill, Esq.; Rev. Edw. W. Blyden; H. W. Dennis, Esq.; H. A. Johnson, Esq., District Attorney.

———

M. R. Delany, Esq.:   Monrovia, July 14, 1859

SIR—We have the honor to acknowledge your note of to-day in reply to an invitation of yesterday from us requesting that you would favor us, with many others, with an address on to-morrow evening, or at any other time agreeable to yourself. Having signified to us that next Monday evening you would be pleased to comply with the request, we tender you our thanks and will be happy to listen to a discourse on the 'Political destiny of the African Race.'

We have the honor to be, very respectfully, &c., yours,

B. V. R. JAMES
SAML. MATTHEWS
And others

Reception

On Monday evening, the 19th of July, having addressed a crowded audience in the Methodist Episcopal Church, Ex-Governor McGill in the chair, T. M. Chester, Esq., Secretary; Ex-President Roberts rose and in a short speech, in the name of the Liberians, welcomed me to Africa. By a vote of thanks and request to continue the discourse on a subsequent evening, this request was complied with on the following Tuesday evening.

Dr. M. R. Delany: Monrovia, July 28, 1859
DEAR SIR—The undersigned citizens of Monrovia having been much edified by listening to two very interesting lectures delivered by you in the Methodist church, avail themselves of this method to express their appreciation of the same, and to respectfully request that you will favor the community with a popular lecture on 'Physiology' on Friday evening, the 29th inst.

HENRY J. ROBERTS   HENRY W. DENNIS
SAML. F. McGILL   EDWD. W. BLYDEN
B. P. YATES

Public Lecture

The reply to this polite invitation of Doctors Roberts and McGill, and others, having been mislaid, I simply remark here that the request was complied with on the evening of August 3d, in the Methodist Church, to a crowded house of the most intelligent citizens of Monrovia, of both sexes and all ages.

Departure from Monrovia. Coasting, Cape Palmas

On the evening of August 5th, I left Monrovia in the bark Mendi, stopping at Junk, Little Bassa, Grand Bassa mouth of St. John's River, Sinou, arriving at Cape Palmas Sabbath noon, August 20th.

Half an hour after my arrival, I was called upon by the Rev. Mr. Hoffman, Principal of the Female Orphan Asylum, at the residence of John Marshall, Esq., whose hospitality I was then receiving, and in the name of the white Missionaries welcomed to that part of Liberia. Before Mr. Hoffman left I was honored by a visit also from Rev. Alexander Crummell, Principal of Mount Vaughan High School, where, after partaking of the hospitality of Mr. Marshall during that day and evening, I took up my residence during a month's stay in this part of Liberia.

Missionary Greeting

Having taken the *acclimating fever* on the 5th of the month, the day I left Monrovia, and besides regularly a dessert spoonful of a solution of the sulphate of *quinia* three times a day, and the night of my arrival two eight grain doses of Dover's Powder, the reference to "the state of my health" in the following correspondence, will be understood:

Correspondence

To Dr. M. R. Delany:

DEAR SIR—We, the undersigned citizens of the county of Maryland, Liberia, beg to tender you a heartfelt welcome to our neighborhood, and to assure you of our warmest interest in the important mission which has called you to the coast of Africa. Perhaps you will consent, should your health permit, to favor us with a public interview before you leave. We would be most happy to hear your views concerning the interest of our race in general, and of your mission in particular. Moreover, by so doing, you will afford us an opportunity of paying you that respect which your reputation, talents, and noble mission command, and which it is our sincere desire to pay you.

If Thursday or Friday will suit your convenience it will be agreeable to us; but we leave the character of the meeting to be designated by yourself.

Aug. 23, 1859

	ALEX. CRUMMELL
D. R. FLETCHER	THOS. FULLER
B. J. DRAYTON	RICHD. W. KNIGHT
J. T. GIBSON	JOHN MARSHALL
C. H. HARMON	GILES ELEM
S. B. D'LYON	T. S. DENT
L. R. HAMILTON	A. WOOD
BENJAMIN COOK	J. W. WILLIAMS

H. W. Moulton

Ansburn Tubman

James M. Moulton

N. Jackson, Jun.

Jno. E. Moulton

Wm. W. Pearce

R. A. Gray

Jas. Adams

J. W. Cooper

Mount Vaughan, near Harper, Cape Palmas
August 27th, 1859

Gentlemen—Your note of the 23rd inst., requesting me, should my health permit, to appear before the citizens of your county, is before me, and for the sentiments therein expressed I thank you most kindly.

As I have reason to believe that I am now convalescent from my second attack of native fever, should my health continue to improve I shall start on an exploration for the head of Kavalla river on Monday next ensuing, to return on Friday evening.

Should it be your pleasure, gentlemen, and my health will permit, I will meet you on Monday, the 5th of September, the place and hour to be hereafter named according to circumstances.

I assure you of the pleasure, Gentlemen, with which I have the honor to be,

Your most obedient servant,

M. R. Delany

Gen. Wood; Judge Drayton; Rev. Alex. Crummell; John Marshall, Esq.; Hon. J. T. Gibson; C. H. Harmon, Esq.; J. W. Cooper, Esq.; Dr. Fletcher; Giles Elem, Esq.; Jas. M. Moulton, Esq.; Benjamin Cook, Esq.; S. B. D'Lyon, M.D., and others, Committee, &c., &c.

Reception Meeting at Palmas

On the evening of the 14th, this request was complied with in the Methodist Church at Latrobe, an out-village of Harper, by addressing a crowded assemblage of both sexes and all ages of the most respectable people of the Cape, on the part of whom I was most cordially welcomed by Rev. Alexander Crummell.

SECTION V
LIBERIA—CLIMATE, SOIL, PRODUCTIONS, ETC.

Territory, Climate

Liberia extends from a point north of Grand Cape Mount, about 7 deg. 30 min. north lat., on sea shore, northeasterly to the western extremity of the most southern range of the Kong Mountains, lat. 4 deg. 30 min. The climate is generally salubrious, and quite moderate. But it is frequently somewhat oppressive, though mild and genial, and the high hills and mountain ranges sometimes enervating to strangers or foreigners from temperate climates, in consequence of the "air being freighted with *fragrance*" from the *flowers* and *aroma* of the exuberant, rich, rank growth of vegetable matter, as trees, shrubbery, and other herbage.

The temperature is seldom or never great, the average being 85 deg. Fahr.* This, it will be perceived, is but 5 deg. above *summer* temperature in the temperate *zone* of America, according to Fahrenheit's scale. *Temperature*

It is worthy of observation that, by a natural law, we are enabled to compare the temperature in many parts of Africa satisfactorily with that of some other countries. There are parts of India, and also Central and South America, where it is said that *bees* cannot propagate, in consequence of their inability to build their cells because of the heat, the cera or wax melting in their hive or habitation. While in Africa such is not the case, there being no part known to civilized travelers where bees are not seen ever busy on every blossom, gathering their store, leaving laden with the rich delicacies of the blooming flowers; and Doctor Livingstone not only speaks most *Comparative Temperature Bees*

---

* This day, August 2, 1861, while revising this Report, the thermometer Fahr. stands in the most favorable shade in the town of Chatham, Kent county, C. W., 96 deg. (98 is the general test of this day) and in the sun 113—being one degree above *fever heat.* A fact to which my attention was called by an intelligent Liberian—and which science may hereafter account for—that the nearer the approach to the equator, the more moderate is the heat. Has the sun the same effect upon the general bulk of the earth that it has upon particular locations—the greater the elevation the cooler—or is it because of the superior velocity of this part, that a *current* is kept up by its passage through the *atmosphere* surrounding it? It is a settled fact that the earth is "elevated at the equator and depressed at the poles," and hills are cool, while valleys and plains are hot, because of their peculiar property of attracting and reflecting heat.

frequently of the profusion of honey in the extensive country through which he traveled, but says that, while near the coast in Loango, he encountered many persons laden with "tons of *beeswax*," carried on their heads exposed to the sun, on their way to the trading posts. And during our stay at Abbeokuta, Mr. Campbell my colleague, had two swarms of bees; the first taken by him when in *transitu* (swarmed) and hived, which bred a new swarm in the hive at the Mission House where we resided.

Soil, Stone, Minerals, Productions

The soil is very rich, which, like that of other parts of Africa through which I traveled, rates from a sandy loam to a rich alluvial, resting on strata of granite, limestone, and quartz with a large percentage of mica, profusely incorporated with iron, and doubtless other rich minerals not yet discovered. Palm oil and camwood are abundant, comprising the principal articles of native products for exportation; a good deal of ivory from the interior through the Golah country, but not so much as formerly; palm nuts, which principally go to France; ginger, arrowroot, pepper, coffee, sugar and molasses, to which three latter articles (as well as pepper, ginger and arrowroot,) the industrious citizens of Liberia have, during the last six years, turned their attention.

Domestic Animals, Fowls, Goats, Sheep, Swine, Cattle

The stock consists of fowls of various kinds—as chickens, ducks, common and Muscovy; Guinea fowls in abundance; turkeys, and on one farm—the *Gaudilla farm* of William Spencer Anderson, Esq., sugar planter, on the St. Paul River—geese. Neither are the cows so small as supposed to be from the general account given of them by travelers. Those which are common to, and natives of this part of Africa, which I shall classify as the *Bassa* (pronounced *Bassaw*) cattle, are handsome and well-built, comparing favorably in size (though neither so long-legged nor long-bodied) with the small cattle in the interior counties of Pennsylvania, U.S., where no attention is paid scientifically to the breeding of cattle; though the Liberia or Bassa are much the heaviest, and handsomely made like the *Golah,* or *Fulatah,* hereafter to be described, resembling the Durham cattle of England in form. Also swine, goats, and sheep are plentiful.

I saw but one horse in Liberia, and that on the Gaudilla farm of Mr. Anderson; and though, as the Liberians
themselves informed me, they have been taken there by
the Mandingo and Golah traders, they never lived. And
why—if they live in other parts of Africa, on the western
coast, which they do, even near the *Mangrove swamps,*
as will hereafter be shown—do they not live in Liberia,
the civilized settlements of which as yet, except on the
St. Paul and at Careysburg, are confined to the coast?
There are certainly causes for this, which I will proceed
to show.

Horses, none. Why?

In the first place, horses, like all other animals,
must have feed naturally adapted to their sustenance. This
consists mainly of grass, herbage, and grains, especially
the latter when the animal is domesticated. Secondly,
adequate shelter from sun and weather, as in the wild
state by instinct they obtain these necessary comforts for
themselves.

Horse Feed, Pasturage, hay

Up to the time, then, when the Liberians ceased the
experiment of keeping horses, they had not commenced
in any extensive manner to cultivate farms, consequently did not produce either maize (Indian corn), Guinea
corn (an excellent article for horses in Africa, resembling
the American broom corn both in the stock, blade, and
grain, the latter being larger and browner than those of
the broom corn, and more nutricious than oats); peas,
nor any other grain upon which those animals are fed,
and the great, heavy, rich, rank, pseudo reed-grass of the
country was totally unfit for them, there being no grass
suited either for pasturage or hay. Again, I was informed
by intelligent, respectable Liberians, that to their knowledge there never had been a stable or proper shelter prepared for a horse, but that they had, in one or more instances, known horses to be kept standing in the sun the

*No culti-
vated Farms
—No shelter
for Horses*

55

entire day, and in the open air and weather during the entire night, while their owners had them.

It is very evident from this, that horses could not live in Liberia, and since the *tsetse* fly introduced to the notice of the scientific world recently by Doctor Livingstone the African Explorer, has never been seen nor heard of in this part of the continent, nor any other insect that tormented them, those must have been the prime causes of fatality to these noble and most useful domestic creatures. I have been thus explicit in justice to Liberia, even in opposition to the opinion of some very intelligent and highly qualified gentlemen in that country (among whom is my excellent friend, Doctor Roberts, I think,) because I believe that horses can live there as well as in other parts of Africa, when fairly and scientifically inquired into and tested. Proper feed and care, I have no doubt, will verify my opinion; and should I but be instrumental, by calling the attention of my brethren in Liberia to these facts, in causing them *successfully* to test the matter, it will be but another evidence of the fact, that the black race should take their affairs in their own hands, instead of placing them in the hands of others.

My explorations in Liberia extended to every civilized settlement in the Republic except Careysburg, and much beyond these limits up the Kavalla River. There is much improvement recently up the St. Paul River, by the opening up of fine, and in some cases, extensive farms of coffee and sugar; also producing rice, ginger, arrowroot, and pepper, many of which have erected upon them handsome and well-constructed dwellings; also sugar mills and machinery for the manufacture of sugar and molasses, which articles manufactured, compare favorably with the best produced in other countries. There has, as yet, been no improvement introduced in the hulling and drying of coffee, there being probably not enough produced to induce the introduction of machinery. I am informed that there have also been commenced several good farms on the Junk River, which district, farther than the settlement at the mouth, I did not visit. The people are willing and anxious for improvement, and on introducing to many of the farmers the utility of cutting off the centre of each young coffee-tree so soon as it grew above the reach of a man of ordinary height, I had the satisfaction of seeing them immediately commence the execution of the work. The branches of the tree spread, in proportion to the checking of the height; hence, instead of eight feet apart, as some of the farmers have done, the trees should be planted at least twenty feet apart, thus leaving ample space between for the spreading of the branches. The tree should never be permitted to grow too high to admit of the berry being picked from the ground, or at least from a stand which may be stepped upon without climbing.

Schools

The schools are generally good, every settlement being amply accommodated with them; and in Monrovia and at Cape Palmas the classics are being rigidly prosecuted.*

Churches
Missionaries

Churches are many and commodious, of every Christian denomination—except, I believe, the Roman Catholic. The Missionaries seem to be doing a good work, there being many earnest and faithful laborers among them of both sexes, black and white, and many native catechists and teachers, as well as some few preachers.

Business,
Professions,
Theology,
Medicine,
Law

The principal business carried on in Liberia is that of trading in native and foreign produce, the greater part being at the Capital. The greater part of merchants here are Liberians; but there are also three white houses —two German and one American. And along the coast

* The "Liberia College" has been fully established since my visit there, by the erection of a fine stone edifice, and the choice of the Hon. Ex-President Joseph Jenkins Roberts, President and Professor of Jurisprudence and International Law; Rev. Alexander Crummell, A.B., Professor of Intellectual and Moral Philosophy and English Literature; Rev. Edward Welmot Blydon, Professor of Greek and Latin Languages and Literature. This is a grand stride in the march of African Regeneration and Negro Nationality.

there are a number of native trading-posts, the proprietors of which are white foreigners, with black agents. Many of the Liberian Clergy of all denominations are well educated gentlemen; and the Medical Profession is well represented by highly accomplished Physicians; but of all the professions, the Law is the most poorly represented—there being, as I learnt when there, but one young gentlemen at the bar who had been bred to the profession; and not a Judge on the bench who was learned in the law. This I do not mention in disparagement of the gentlemen who fill those honorable positions of presiding over the legal investigations of their country, as many—indeed, I believe the majority of them—are clergymen, who from necessity have accepted those positions, and fill their own legitimate callings with credit. I sincerely hope that the day is not far distant when Liberia will have her learned counsellors and jurists—dispensing law, disseminating legal opinions, and framing digests as well as other countries, for the benefit of nations.

Council

At Grand Bassa I held a Council with some of the most eminent Liberians, among whom were several members of the National Legislature—the venerable Judge Hanson in the chair. Several able speeches were made— the objects of my mission and policy approved; and I shall never forget the profound sensation produced at that ever-memorable Council, and one of the most happy hours of my life. When the honored old judge and sage, sanctioning my adventure, declared that, rather than it should fail, he would join it himself, and with emotion rose to his feet; the effect was inexpressible, each person being as motionless as a statue.

Public Affairs, Municipal and Public Improvements

The laws of Liberia seem to be well constructed, and framed to suit the wants of the people, and their public affairs are quite well and creditably conducted. But there is a great deficiency in public improvements, and, as I learned—and facts from actual observation verified until

58

comparatively recent—also in public spirit. There are no public buildings of note, or respectable architectural designs; no harbor improvements, except a lighthouse each on the beautiful summit rock-peaks of Cape Messurado and Cape Palmas—not even a buoy to indicate the shoal; no pier, except a little one at Palmas; nor an attempt at a respectable wharfage for canoes and lighters (the large keels owned by every trading vessel, home and foreign, which touches there.) And, with the exception of a handsome wagon-road, three and a half miles out from Harper, Cape Palmas, beyond Mount Vaughan, there is not a public or municipal road in all Liberia. Neither have I seen a town which has a paved street in it, although the facilities for paving in almost all the towns are very great, owing to the large quantities of stone everywhere to be had.

And what is surprising, Monrovia, although the capital, has not a city municipality to give it respectability as such; hence, there is neither mayor nor council (city council I mean) to give character to any public occasion, but His Excellency the President, the Chief Executive of the nation, must always be dragged down from his reserved and elevated position, and made as common as a common policeman, to head every little petty affair among the people. The town was once, by the wisdom of some legislators, chartered into a city, and Dr. T. F. M'Gill (ex-governor) chosen mayor, who, by his high intelligence and fitness for the office, had commenced the most useful and commendable improvements; but the wisdom of other legislators, after a year's duration, in consequence of the heavy expenses incurred to "make Monrovia, where big folks lived, a fine place," repealed the act, degrading their Capital to a town. That is the same as declaring that a court shall not have a judge—the nation a President or Executive, or there shall be no head at all; hence, to reduce the judge to the grade of a lawyer, the lawyer to that of the clerk of the court,

The Capital no City

the President of the nation to that of the county magistrate, and the county magistrate to that of a constable. How much respect would a people be entitled to who would act thus? They must understand that nothing is greater than its head, and the people of a nation cannot rise above the level of the head of their nation any more than the body of the individual in its natural position can be raised above the head. It is just so with a town population. A villager is a villager, a citizen is a citizen, and a metropolitan is a metropolitan—each of which is always expected to have a standing commensurate with his opportunities.

Self-reliance, Ways and Means

One word as a suggestion in political economy to the young politician of Liberia: Always bear in mind, that the fundamental principle of every nation is *self-reliance,* with the *ability to create their own ways and means:* without this, there is no capacity for *self-government.* In this short review of public affairs, it is done neither to disparage nor under-rate the gentlemen of Liberia with whom, from the acquaintance I have made with them in the great stride for black nationality, I can make common cause, and hesitate not to regard them, in unison with ourselves, a noble band of brothers.

Executive Munificence

There has been much progress made in the various industrial vocations within a few years past by the munificence of President Benson, aided by the wisdom of the Legislature, through the agency of a national agricultural fair, with liberal premiums on samples exhibited in a spacious receptacle prepared each season for the purpose, in the Public Square in front of the President's mansion, called Palm Palace. Like his predecessor President Roberts, in pressing the claims of his country before the nations of Europe, President Benson has spared no authority which he possessed in developing the agricultural resources of his country. Every man has his *forte,* and in his turn probably becomes a *necessity* for the time being, according to his faculty. Consequently my opinion is, that the *forte* and mission of President Roberts for the time being were the establishment of a Nationality, and that of President Benson the development of its resources, especially the agricultural. Neither of these gentlemen, therefore, might be under-rated, as each may have been the instrument which God in his wisdom appointed to a certain work.

To John Moore, Esq., Government Surveyor; the Hon. B. P. Yates, ex-Vice-President of the Republic; Hon. John Seys, U.S. Agent for Re-captured Africans, and Consular Agent, I am much indebted for acts of kindness in facilitating my Explorations in Liberia. The Hon. Mr. Seys and Mr. Moore, for personally accompanying me up the St. Paul River; and Colonel Yates, for the loan of his fine canvas-covered boat for my use. Also to Dr. Henry J. Roberts, for remedies and medicines for my own use; Dr. Thomas F. M'Gill, for offering to make advances on articles of merchandise which I took out on trade to bear expenses, much beyond the market price; and to those excellent gentlemen, Messrs. Johnson, Turpin, and Dunbar, also for large advances made above market price in cash for my commodity, as well as other favors, especially on the part of Mr. Johnson, who, having for years been a resident in Monrovia, did everything to advance my mission and make my duty an agreeable one.

Official and personal favors

To the Rev. Alexander Crummell, who accompanied me up the Kavalla, above the Falls, making my task an easy one; to Drs. Fletcher and D'Lyon, who rendered me professional aid, and also to our excellent, faithful, and reliable guide, Spear Mehia, a native civilized Christian Prince, the son of the old friend of the missionaries, Nmehia, the deceased King of Kavalla, I here make acknowledgments. And I cannot close this section without an acknowledgment that, wherever I went, the people of the country generally did everything to make me happy—Esquire Wright at Junk, Dr. Smith at Grand

Bassa, and the Hon. Mr. Priest at Sinou, whose guest I was, all here will receive my thanks for their aid in facilitating my mission.

Settlement and Sites of Towns

I conclude this section by remarking, that Monrovia is one of the handsomest and most eligible sites for a city that I ever saw, and only lacks the population and will of the people to make it a most beautiful place; and how much it is to be regretted that the charter was repealed, and Mayor M'Gill and the City Council cut off in the beginning of the first steps towards a national pride, which was to have a Capital City in reality as well as name.* How unsightly to a stranger, as he steps from the boat at the mouth of Stockton Creek, on the Messurado River, is the rude and rugged steep, leading by simple pathways in true native style, from the warehouses up to the town, which, if improved as it might and should be, would be one of the most pleasing as well as attractive approaches to any city in the world. Not even is there a respectable public market-house or market space in town. But wisdom decreed it otherwise, and for the present it must be so. "Wisdom" in this case "hath" *not* "built her house" neither "hath she hewn out" the stone "pillars" leading from the beach.

Another good site for a city is Edina, on the northeast side of the St. John River, opposite Buchanan, Grand Bassa, which doubtless in time Buchanan will include. This is also a handsome plàce, from the gradually rising elevation. Edina is the residence of that great-hearted, good old gentleman, Judge Hanson. Junk, Little Bassa, and Sinou, are also good, but each of these are low, and consequently not so imposing.

* I am happy to learn by advices recently received from Liberia, that Monrovia has again been created and organized a City Municipality, ex-Judge James, Mayor; and I should have named in connection with the public spirit of Liberia, three newspapers—the *Liberia Herald, Star of Liberia,* and *Christian Advocate*—the last, a religious journal, under the auspices of that excellent Christian gentleman, Bishop Burns the Methodist Missionary-Bishop of Liberia.

Next to Monrovia is Cape Palmas for beauty of location and scenery, and a stranger will more readily be pleased at first sight with Harper than the Capital. A beautiful city will in time occupy the extensive Cape for several miles back, including Mount Vaughan and the country around; and it may be remarked, that this place presents greater evidences of public improvement than any town in Liberia, and the only place in the country which has a regular wagon road with ox-teams running upon it.

The private buildings in Liberia are generally good and substantial, and especially those of Monrovia, built of brick. Many of them are handsome and quite extensive mansions, the warehouses mostly being built of stone. The wooden houses generally are well-built frames, and "weatherboarded," and not, as some romancers and wonder-vendors would have it, being either log, bamboo, or mud huts. To take the settlers generally, there cannot be much fault found with their style of living, except perhaps in some instances, rather a little too much extravagance. Caldwell, Clay-Ashland, and Millsburg on the St. Paul, are pleasant and prospectively promising villages, and deserve a notice in this place. Clay-Ashland is the residence of Judge Moore, to whom I am indebted for personal favors and much useful information when examining the land over his extensive sugar and coffee farms. And to my excellent friend Dr. Daniel Laing, of the same place, for similar acts of courtesy and kindness, I am much indebted.

Buildings

I addressed the citizens in a very large political meeting in the Methodist church, on the evening of my visit there.

Public Meeting

SECTION VI

DISEASES—CAUSE—REMEDY

*First
Symptoms*

The first sight and impressions of the coast of Africa are always inspiring, producing the most pleasant emotions. These pleasing sensations continue for several days, more or less, until they gradually merge into feelings of almost intense excitement, not only mentally, but the entire physical system share largely in it, so that it might be termed a hilarity of feeling almost akin to approaching intoxication; or as I imagine, like the sensation produced by the beverage of champagne wine. Never having enjoyed the taste of it, I cannot say from experience.

*Second stage
of Symptoms*

The first symptoms are succeeded by a relaxity of feelings, in which there is a disposition to stretch, gape, and yawn, with fatigue.

*Third stage
of Symptoms*

The second may or may not be succeeded by actual febrile attacks, with nausea, chills, or violent headache; but whether or not such symptoms ensue, there is one most remarkable, as almost (and I think quite) a necessary affection, attendant upon the acclimation at this incipient stage: *a feeling of regret that you left your native country for a strange one; an almost frantic desire to see friends and nativity; a despondency and loss of the hope of ever seeing those you love at home again.*

These feelings, of course, must be resisted, and *regarded as a mere morbid affection of the mind* at the time, arising from an approaching disease, which is not necessarily serious, and may soon pass off; which is really the case.

Its Effects

It is generally while laboring under this last-described symptom, that persons send from Africa such despairing accounts of their disappointments and sufferings, with horrible feelings of dread for the worst to come.

Recovery

When an entire recovery takes place, the love of the country is most ardent and abiding. I have given the symptoms *first,* to make a proper impression first.

I have thought it proper to give a section in my Report entirely to the diseases of Liberia, which are the same as those in other parts of Africa, with their complication with diseases carried from America by the settlers.

Diseases

The native diseases are mainly the native fever, which is nothing but the *intermittent fever* of America, known in different parts as *ague, chills and fever, fever and ague,* with its varied forms of *bilious, intermittent, remittent, continued,* and it is worst form of *inflammatory,* when it most generally assumes the *congestive* type of the American Southern States. In this condition, the typhoid symptoms with *coma,* give unmistakeable evidence of the character of the malady. The native fever which is common to all parts of Africa, in Liberia while to my judgment not necessarily fatal (and in by far the greater per centage of cases in the hands of an intelligent, skilful physician, quite manageable), is generally much worse in its character there than in the Yoruba country, where I have been. The symptoms appear to be much more aggravated and the patient to suffer more intensely.

Native Diseases

Peculiar character in Liberia

The density and rankness of the vegetable growth, the saturation of the air continually with fragrance, and other *miasma,* and the *malaria* from the mangrove swamps, I assign as the cause of difference in the character of the same disease in different parts of the continent. The habits also of the settlers, have much to do with the character of the disease. A free indulgence in improper food and drink, which doubtless is the case in many instances, are exciting causes to take the malady, and aggravating when suffering under it.

Causes

There are several other diseases that might be named, which I reserve for a section on another part of Africa, and confine my remarks simply to the complication of the native with foreign. All *scorbutic, scrofulous,* or *syphilitic* persons, where the affection has not been fully suppressed, may become easy victims to the fever in

Complication

Liberia, or lingering sufferers from *ulcers, acute rheumatism,* or *elephantiasis*—a frightful enlargement of the limbs. *Ulcerated opthalmia* is another horrible type, that disease in such chronically affected persons may assume. But any chronic affection—especially lung, liver, kidney, and rheumatic—when not too deeply seated, may, by favorable acclimation, become eliminated, and the ailing person entirely recover from the disease.

Remedies, Natural and Artificial

The natural remedy for the permanent decrease of the native fever, is the clearing up and cultivation of the land, which will be for some time yet to come, tardy; as emigration to Liberia is very slow, and the natives very unlike those of Yoruba—cultivate little or nothing but rice, cassaba, and yams, and these in comparative small patches, so that there is very little need for clearing off the forest. Neither have they in this part of Africa any large towns of substantial houses, all of which would necessitate a great deal of clearing; but instead, they consist of small clusters of reed or bamboo huts in a circle, always in the densest of the forest, which can scarcely ever be seen (except they be situated on a high hill) until you are right upon them. The clearing away of the mangrove swamps—which is practicable—will add greatly to the sanitary condition of Liberia; but this also will take time, as it must be the work of a general improvement in the country, brought about by a populating and civilizing progress.

Treatment

The treatment of the native fever must be active and prudential. But the remedies are simple and easily obtained, being such as may be had at any well-kept apothecary's shop. The *sulphate of quinia,* in moderate doses, three or four times a day, with the usual attention to the febrile changes, gentle *aperients, effervescent* and *acidulous* drinks, taking care to prevent acridness in the stomach. In my advice to persons going to Africa, I shall speak more pointedly of the domestic or social customs to be avoided.

I observed that all elevated places, as Monrovia and Freetown, subject to severe visitations of disease, are situated near mangrove swamps; consequently, from the *rising* of the *malaria,* they are much more unhealthy than those in low plains, such as Lagos and many other places, *above* which the *miasma* generally rises for the most part passing off harmlessly.

I left Cape Palmas, Liberia, on Thursday, 2 P.M. the 15th of Sept., on the British Royal Mail African steamer, "Armenian," Captain Walker, to whom and his officers, I make acknowledgments for acts of kindness.

SECTION VII

THE INTERIOR—YORUBA

Thursday, the 20th of September, about noon, after stopping at Cape-Coast Castle for twelve hours, on the Coast of Benin, the steamer made her moorings in the roadstead, Bight of Benin, Gulf of Guinea, off Lagos. I disembarked, going ashore with the mail-boat managed by natives; from whence, by the politeness of the gentlemanly young clerk (a native gentleman) of Captain Davies', a native merchant, I was taken in a sail-boat, also manned by natives, up the bay, and landed at the British Consulate; whence I was met by Mr. Carew, the native agent of the Rev. J. M. Harden, a most excellent man, Missionary, and conducted to the Baptist Mission House.

After a stay of five weeks, visiting almost every thing and place worthy of note, being called upon by many of the most noted persons, among whom were several chiefs, having several interviews with the authorities, and meeting the most active, intelligent, Christian young men, in several of their associated gatherings, I was waited on by the messenger of the king; when after several interchanges of "words" between us, the following instrument of writing was "duly executed, signed, sealed, and delivered," I and Mr. Harden being present, and witnessing the measurement of the land, according to the present custom in that place:

TITLE DEED

Dr. M. R. Delany

Lagos, October 25th, 1859

Know all Men by these Presents:

That I DOCEMO, King of Lagos and the Territories thereunto belonging, have this day granted, assigned, and made over, unto Doctor Martin R. Delany, for his use and the use of his Heirs and Assigns forever, All that Piece of Ground, situated on the South of the Premises and Ground occupied by Fernando, in the field at Okai Po, Po, measuring as follows, Three Hundred and Thirty Feet square.

Witness my Stamp hereunto affixed, and the Day and Year above written.

KING
DOCEMO
OF LAGOS.

BRITISH CONSULATE,
Lagos, October 28th, 1859

I CERTIFY that the Circular Stamp, as above, with KING DOCEMO, OF LAGOS in the centre, is the Official Stamp of Docemo, King of Lagos, and is used by him as his signature to all Letters, Deeds, and Documents.

 SEAL

EDWD. F. LODDER
Acting Consul.

The Deed of Land above, granted to Doctor Martin R. Delany, by King Docemo of Lagos, has this 18th day of October, 1859, been registered in the Registry Book of the British Consulate, and numbered.

JOHN P. BOYLE, *Clerk*

On the 30th of October, I left Lagos, proceeding *via* Ogun river, to Abbeokuta, which I reached on Saturday, the 5th of November.

*Explor-
ations.
Abbeokuta*

Here I met for the first time with my colleague and Assistant Commissioner, Mr. Robert Campbell, from whom, at Lagos, I found a letter waiting for my arrival in the hands of Acting Consul, Lieut. Edward F. Lodder, of Her Majesty's war vessel "Brun," which continually lies in the harbor, directly opposite and near to the Consulate. Consul Campbell (since deceased), had paid an official visit to England, and Lieut. Lodder was supplying his place.

From Abbeokuta, population 110,000, we proceeded to Ijaye, population 78,000, reckoned by the white missionaries and officers of the Niger Expedition of Her Majesty's service, who passed through once, at 80,000; Oyo, population, 75,000; Ogbomoso, population 70,000; Illorin, population 120,000; returning back, *via* Ogbomoso to Oyo: when by arrangement, Mr. Campbell leaving me at Oyo, returned to Abbeokuta by a new route through Isen and Biolorin-Pellu, small places: whence I, a week later, also by another strange route, returned, passing through Iwo, population 75,000; and Ibaddan, population 150,000, an immense city, the estimated number of inhabitants by the Civil Corps who passed through, being 250,000. It will be seen that I have made a liberal deduction of two-fifths, or 100,000 from this estimate; still, the population is immense and the city extensive, the walls embracing an outline of at least twenty-three miles.

Towns from Abbeokuta

From Abbeokuta, the water being very low, it was thought advisable that Mr. Campbell take charge of all our luggage, and proceed by way of the Ogun to Lagos, (he having disposed of his horse at Abbeokuta) whilst I, on horseback, with William Johnson our cook, the only servant we retained—a civilized native—as guide and attendant, proceeded by land, both reaching Lagos three days after, in the same hour of the same day.

Return to Lagos

SECTION VIII

TOPOGRAPHY, CLIMATE, ETC.

Topography, Climate

The whole face of the country extending through the Aku region or Yoruba, as it is laid down on the large missionary map of Africa, is most beautifully diversified with plains, hills, dales, mountains, and valleys, inter-lined with numerous streams, some of which are merely temporary or great drains; whilst the greater part are perennial, and more or less irrigating the whole year, supplying well the numerous stocks of cattle and horses with which that country is so well everywhere provided. The climate is most delightful.

First Plateau

Second Plateau, or Table Lands

The first plateau or low land from Lagos, extends about thirty-five or forty miles interiorly, with but occasionally, small rugged or rocky elevations breaking the surface, when it almost abruptly rises into elevated lands, undulating and frequently craggy, broken often by deep declivities of glens and dales.

Soil

The soil of the first plateau, for ten or fifteen miles, is moist and sandy, more or less, gradually incorporating with a dark rich earth, which, extending quite through the second plateau, continually varies in quality, consistence, and color, from a sandy loam and clay-red iron pyrite appearance to a potter's-clay, and rich alluvial color and quality, the whole being exceedingly fertile and productive; as no district through which we traveled was without cultivation more or less, and that always in a high degree, whatever the extent of ground under cultivation or the produce cultivated.

Stone Formation

The stone formation throughout these regions consist of primitive dark-gray granite, quartz, and conglomerates, with, occasionally, strata of felspar and mica, which are found mainly in the beautiful mountain regions (which are detailed extensions of the great mountains of Kong), having in these sections always beautiful gaps or passes of delightful valleys.

The minerals consist of iron in the greatest abundance, which at present is smelted by the natives from the clay, and every town of any note or size has not only its blacksmiths' shops, but the largest all have iron smelting works. At Ijaye there is quite an extensive and interesting establishment of the kind. And, as they manufacture *brass*, there must be also zinc and copper found there—indications of the last-named metal being often seen by the color of certain little water surfaces. The stone formation bears the usual indications of aqueous and igneous deposits, but more of the former than the latter.

Minerals, Iron, Copper, Zinc

The timber is numerous, and for the following classification I am indebted to my learned friend the Rev. Alexander Crummell, Episcopal missionary and Principal of the Mount Vaughn High School at Cape Palmas: Teak, ebony, lignum vitae, mahogany, brimstone, rosewood, walnut, hickory, oak, cedar, unevah, and mangrove.

Productions Timber

Gum Yoruba (the same as gum Arabic), acacia or senna, castor oil, croton oil, rhubarb root, colomba-root, ipecacuanha, quasia, nux-vomica, cubebs, tobacco, and many others.

Medical Productions

All the fruits common to the tropics are found in these regions; in fact, so redundant is Africa with these productions, that she combines the whole within herself; that is, there are some fruits found in the tropical parts of Asia, South America, the Asiatic and West India Islands, common or peculiar to one which may not be found in the other, but all of which, it may safely be said, can be found in Africa. Pineapples the most delicious in flavor and taste conceivable oranges the same, bananas the finest, plantains equally so, mangrove plums (a peculiar but delightful and wholesome fruit, said by the natives to be a *febrifuge*), guavas, and "soursops," a delightful *febrifuge* of pure *citric acid,* without the least acridness, as well as a hundred others which I cannot now

Fruits

name. The papaw or tree-melon also grows very finely here, and is a very useful and wholesome fruit. When green, "stewed and mashed," and well-flavored with the usual culinary spices, it cannot be distinguished from the best green apple-sauce—for which reason it makes excellent pies. When fully ripe, it cannot be told from the finest muskmelon or cantelope.

Agricultural Products

The Agricultural labor of this part of Africa is certainly very great, and merits the attention of every intelligent inquirer; from the simple fact that, so far as it exhibits the industry of the inhabitants, it shows the means which may be depended upon for a development of the commercial resources of the country.

Palm Oil

Palm oil is produced in great abundance, as a staple commodity among themselves, as well as for exportation since the common light for houses consists of palm oil burnt in native manufactured lamps, some constructed of iron and others of earthenware. The oil of the nut is the most general in use among the natives, both for light and cooking, because it is the richest, being the most unctuous. This use of the nut-oil is certainly an antiquated custom among the people of this region, whilst those contiguous to Liberia have recently learned that the kernels could be put to commercial use, by the discovery or rather practical application by Mr. Herron, of Grand Bassa, Liberia, and subsequent demand by the French traders. The fact that the Yorubas generally produce their charcoal from the hull of the palm nut, is an evidence of the long-continued and abundant use of the latter article for the manufacture of oil. They have regular establishments for the manufacture of the palm oil, with vats and apparatus (simple though they be), places and persons for each process: as bruising the fruit from the nut, boiling, carrying the pulp to a vat, where it is pressed and washed to extract the oil; one to skim it off from the top of the liquid—another to carry off the fiber of the pulp or bruised fruit, which fiber is also appropriated to kindling and other uses. There is no such method of extracting the oil, as the mistaken idea so frequently reported by African traders from Europe and America, that the natives bruise the nut with stones in holes made in the ground, thereby losing a large per centage of the oil. Even among the crudest they know better than this, and many use shallow troughs, made of wood in some parts of Africa, as the Grebo, Golah, and some other peoples on the western coast, adjacent to Liberia.

All through the Yoruba country the palm tree is cultivated, being regularly trimmed and pruned, and never cut down in clearing a farm, except when from age the tree has ceased to bear, or is of the male species, when it is cut down for the wine, which is the sap, extracted from the trunk, in a horizontal position, by boring a hole near the top and catching it in a vessel, when it is drunk either before, during, or after fermentation.

Palm trees cultivated. Camwood. Ivory

Camwood is also very plentiful, but owing to its great weight and the inconvenience at present of transportation, it does not enter extensively into the commerce of these parts, except as dyestuffs in the native markets. Gum elastic or India rubber is plentiful.

Ivory enters largely into commerce, being brought by "middle men" from the distant interior.

Indian corn, the finest in the world (usually white) is here raised in the greatest quantities, we having frequently passed through hundreds of acres in unbroken tracts of cultivated land, which is beginning to enter into foreign commerce; Guinea corn in great abundance—an excellent article for horses, spoken of in another place; also peas, such as are raised for horse and cattle feed in Canada and other parts of America; white beans in great quantities, as well as those of all colors; black-eye peas; horse beans; in fact, all of the pulse vegetables; also ginger, arrowroot, red pepper in pods (the cayenne of com-

Indian corn or Maize, Peas, Beans, Ginger, Pepper, Arrowroot, &c

merce), and black pepper, all of which are articles of commerce; indigo; they also produce salt, and pea-nuts.

Yams, cassaba, sweet potatoes, onions, cucumbers, and many other culinary roots and vegetables; and I am certain that beets, parsnips, and carrots, which we did not see under cultivation, could be successfully raised, if desired. Cabbage grows freely in all parts of Africa, if planted in the right season.

Whether or not the common potato of America and Europe can be propagated here has not been tested, but such is the excellence of the yam, that served up in the same manner, there is little or no difference between them and potatoes; and I am certain that when well cooked, "mashed" and seasoned, the best judge could not tell them from good potatoes. I mean good yams, because they differ in quality like potatoes.

Crockeryware is manufactured very extensively, of almost every conceivable size and kind of vessel, for various purposes. Some of them are quite handsome, and all nearly of the ancient oriental mould. The largest earthen vessels I ever saw are made by these people, some of them being large enough for small cisterns. Iron implements for agricultural and military, as well as other domestic purposes, are made by them in every large city. They make excellent razors, which shave quite well, as also other steel-bladed knives, which prove that they have the art of tempering iron. Brass as well as glass ornaments and trinkets are made in considerable quantities.

The people are of fine physical structure and anatomical conformation, well and regularly featured; not varying more in this particular from the best specimen of their own race than the Caucasian or Anglo-Saxon from that of theirs. They are very polite—their language abounding in vowels, and consequently euphonious and agreeable—affable, sociable, and tractable, seeking information with readiness, and evincing willingness to be taught. They are shrewd, intelligent, and industrious, with high conceptions of the Supreme Being, only using their images generally as mediators. "So soon," said an intelligent missionary, "as you can convince them that there is a mediator to whom you *may talk, but cannot see,* just so soon can you make Christians of them"; their idea being that God is too great to be directly approached; therefore there must be a mediator to whom they must talk that they can see, when God will listen and answer if pleased.

After my arrival at Abbeokuta, not going out for two days, they expecting me through information from Mr. Campbell, the third day the Chief Atambala called upon me, inviting me in turn to call and see him. In a few days after, the king had a popular religious festival in the great public space, where there were assembled many chiefs and elders; but, on our approach, the old king sent his messenger to escort us to the porch of the piazza upon which he was seated, eagerly grasping me by the hand, bidding me welcome to Abbeokuta and his court; telling me, pointing to Mr. Campbell, that he was acquainted with him, and had heard of me through him.

How received by them

In December, a meeting of the native cotton-traders, chiefs, and others, was held at the residence of the great chief Ogubonna concerning the price of cotton. On the meeting assembling, and finding that we were not present, the chief at once despatched a messenger, requesting our immediate attendance, as "we knew how things ought to be done." On going down, we found a large assemblage waiting, among whom were Messrs. Samuel and Josiah Crowther, H. Robbing, J. C. During, F. Rebeiro, and C. W. Faulkner, civilized native gentlemen; also Mr. J. G. Hughes, an English gentleman. By a motion from myself, seconded by J. Crowther, the chief Ogubonna was chosen chairman, and, upon a motion by Mr. Campbell, seconded by J. G. Hughes, Mr. Robbing was chosen vice-chairman. The meeting went off well, we making

Native estimate of civilized educated men

many suggestions during the proceedings, which were always received with approbation.

The following from the native minister, being his own writing and composition, will explain itself:

ABBEOKUTA, Igbore, 23rd Dec., 1857

M. R. DELANY, Esq.:

DEAR SIR—A meeting of the Wesleyan Missionary Society will be held at the Wesleyan Chapel, on Monday next, the 26th instant, at ten o'clock, A.M., precisely. You are sincerely and respectfully solicited to be the Chairman on the occasion.

The object of the Meeting is to offer Thanksgiving to Almighty God for the past years' success; and to pray for an outpouring of the Holy Spirit's influence upon the Church, for a further success, &c.

Collection will be made at the close of the above.

Yours respectfully and affectionately,

EDWD. BICKERSTETH
Wesleyan Minister

P.S. An early answer will be much obliged.

I replied in the affirmative to this kind invitation (the copy of reply is now mislaid), when, at the appointed time, a crowded house was assembled.

Influence of civilization— Native demonstration

In a simple and comprehensive address made to them (being interpreted by the minister as I proceeded), such was the effect that it not only produced their unanimous applause, but aroused Mr. During (a native civilized merchant, who had never before spoken in public) to his feet, who approved of what I had said, with such an appeal of native eloquence, that when he ceased, sixty bags of cowries (£54, or $270, estimating them at 18s. or $4.50 a bag, the then current value of cowries) were paid down on the spot, to aid the spread of civilization through the gospel and education. Many, very many were the thanks given me that day by these, my native kinsmen and women. Several other gentlemen, among them Surgeon Samuel Crowther, the Pastor, Mr. Rebeiro, and Mr. Campbell my colleague, also addressed them.

Many had been the social, friendly, and official interchanges between us and the king and chiefs during our stay in Abbeokuta, when, on the twenty-seventh, the day after the missionary meeting, the following document was duly executed, with the express understanding that no heterogeneous nor promiscuous "masses" or companies, but select and intelligent people of high moral as well as religious character were to be induced to go out. And I am sure that every good and upright person in that region, whether native or foreign missionary, would exceedingly regret to see a reckless set of religion-spurning, God-defying persons sent there—especially by disinterested white societies in America, which interferingly came forward in a measure which was originated solely by ourselves (and that, too, but a few of us), as our only hope for the regeneration of our race from the curse and corrupting influences of our white American oppressors.

TREATY

This Treaty, made between His Majesty, OKUKENU, Alake; SOMOYE, Ibashorun; SOKENU, OGUBONNA, and ATAMBALA, Chiefs and Balaguns, of Abbeokuta, on the first part; and MARTIN ROBISON DELANY, and ROBERT CAMPBELL, of the Niger Valley Exploring Party, Commissioners from the African race, of the United States and the Canadas in America, on the second part, covenants:

ART. 1.   That the King and Chiefs on their part, agree to grant and assign unto the said Commissioners, on behalf of the African race in America, the right and privilege of settling in common with the Egba people, on any part of the territory belonging to Abbeokuta, not otherwise occupied.

ART. 2.   That all matters, requiring legal investigation among the settlers, be left to themselves, to be disposed of according to their own custom.

ART. 3.   That the Commissioners, on their part, also agree that the settlers shall bring with them, as an equivalent for the privileges above accorded, Intelligence, Education, a Knowledge of the Arts and Sciences, Agriculture, and other Mechanical and Industrial Occupations, which they

77

shall put into immediate operation, by improving the lands, and in other useful vocations.

ART. 4. That the laws of the Egba people shall be strictly respected by the settlers; and, in all matters in which both parties are concerned, an equal number of commissioners, mutually agreed upon, shall be appointed, who shall have power to settle such matters.

As a pledge of our faith, and the sincerity of our hearts, we each of us hereunto affix our hand and seal this Twenty-seventh day of December, ANNO DOMINI, One Thousand Eight Hundred and Fifty-nine.

His Mark,	+	OKUKENU, Alake
His Mark,	+	SOMOYE, Ibashorum
His Mark,	+	SOKENU, Balagun
His Mark,	+	OGUBONNA, Balagun
His Mark,	+	ATAMBALA, Balagun
His Mark,	+	OGUSEYE, Anaba
His Mark,	+	NGTABO, Balagun, O. S. O.
His Mark,	+	OGUDEMU, Ageoko
		M. R. DELANY
		ROBERT CAMPBELL

Witness—SAMUEL CROWTHER, Jun.
Attest—SAMUEL CROWTHER, Sen.

———

Executive Council, and Ratification of the Treaty

On the next evening, the 28th, the king, with the executive council of chiefs and elders, met at the palace in Ake, when the treaty was ratified by an unanimous approval. Such general satisfaction ran through the council, that the great chief, his highness Ogubonna, mounting his horse, then at midnight, hastened to the residence of the Surgeon Crowther, aroused his father the missionary and author, and hastily informed him of the action of the council.

Native confidence; Hopes in educated blacks; Princess Tinuba

On our return from the interior, having previously made the acquaintance of, and had several interviews with, and visits to and from the Princess Tinuba, being called upon by her, I informed her that during our tour I learned that she had supplied the chief of Ijaye with the means and implements for carrying on the war, which that chief was then waging against Oyo and Ibaddan.

I had previous to that, obtained her fullest confidence as an adviser, a person of integrity, a friend of my race and of Africa. She had previously expressed to a friend of mine, that she had more hope of a regeneration of Africa through me than ever before. She had promised to place the entire management of her extensive business in my hands, as much advantage was taken of her by foreigners. She has attached to her immediate household about sixty persons, and keeps constantly employed about three hundred and sixty persons bringing her in palm-oil and ivory. She had come with a private retinue of six or seven persons, her secretary, a man and several maid-servants, to counsel and give me a written statement of what she desired me to do. Having conversed for some time, after receiving my admonition concerning the part which I had learned she had taken with Arie of Ijaye, she sat some time after, positively negativing the accusation, when, bidding me farewell, and saying that she would "*send* me a letter," retired. In the course of the afternoon, her secretary, "Charles B. Jones," a native, came to the house, and presenting his mistress's compliments, with her final adieu, handed me a written paper, from which I take the following extracts, simply to show the general feeling and frankness of these people, as well as the hopes and confidence they have in our going there:

DR. MARTIN R. DELANY: Abbeokuta, April 3rd, 1860

SIR—This is to certify you, that it is with a willing mind I come to you for help; and I trust you will do according to your promise. * * I return you my sincere gratitude for your kind information gave me while at your house, and can assure you that all what you heard is false respecting my sending guns and powder to Arie, the Chief of Ijaye. * * * I beg to say, you must not forget to find the Clerk who will stop at Lagos to ship my cargo. * * * and make agreement with him before you send him here. * * * I need not say much more about the affairs, as you yourself have known my statements. With hopes that you are well, I am, dear Sir,

Your humble servant,

TINUBA

P.S. You must not forget to send the two guage-rods. I beg you * * * Yours, &c.,—TINUBA

Per Charles B. Jones.

I have preferred to give these extracts just as they were written, without correcting the composition in any way.

Royal deference to black men

The liberality which is here accorded to the people of Abbeokuta may be also accorded to most other places. The king of Illorin sat in his court exposed to our view, because, he said, we were "his people"; a privilege which he never allowed "a strange white man," who was never permitted to look upon his royal black face publicly. He also sent with us an escort of a horseman and five footmen, with sword and spear, as a guard of honor, sending us cowries to pay the expenses. The king of Oyo paid us distinguished honors through his great Arie Kufu, calling me a relative, and sending the chief to inquire after our health. On my leaving Oyo finally, he sent with me a very large escort, at the head of whom was his commander-in-chief Kufu, as a guard of honor, and three native gentlemen, high in rank, as my special carriers. These gentlemen complained to the missioners, Mr. and Mrs. Hinderer at Ibaddan, that I was quite mistaken as to their true social position at home. To this I plead guilty, as they were quite right.

Domestic Animals; Fowls, Chickens, Ducks, Muscovy, Turkeys Swine; common, Guinea

Chickens (and eggs plentifully) the sweetest and tenderest, ducks and turkeys; also Guinea fowls, as well as the fine Muscovy, are abundant.

The swine consist of two distinct classes; the common, descended from the wild—a long, lean, gaunt, long-eared, long-nosed, sharp-featured, hungry-looking brute, like the American hog; and the Guinea, a short-legged, heavy-bodied, short-nosed, short-eared, fat-jawed, full-headed, jolly-looking animal, closely resembling the Berkshire of English breeding.

The goats are the most beautiful, shiny, plump, active, saucy creatures, the mutton being most excellent flesh; and the sheep, though hairy instead of woolly, in every other particular are like other sheep, and the mutton frequently equaling English mutton in flavor and sweetness. I suspect the common sheep of this country to be of another genus, as there are some very fine woolly sheep in the interior. We intend testing the woolly sheep when we get settled there.

Goats, Sheep

The cattle are of two classes, and merit particular attention. The windward or Mandingo, a tall, long-horned, beautiful animal, the type of the Herefordshire; and the leeward or Golah, a short-legged, short-horned, heavy-bodied, broad-backed ox, the exact conformation of the splendid English Durham beeves.

Cattle—Mandingo and Golah

The horses are of two distinct classes, and not only merit much attention here, but must be regarded as among the most surprising evidences (as well as the cattle and improved breed of swine) of the high degree of intelligence and heathen civilization attained by the people.

Horses; Aku, Bornou

The Aku or Yoruba, is a small, well-built, generally sprightly animal, equal in size to the largest American-Indian pony. They are great travelers, and very enduring, and when broke to the shafts or traces will be excellent in harness as family hackneys.

Aku, or Yoruba horse

The Bornou, a noble horse, from twelve to seventeen hands high, finely proportioned and symmetrically beautiful, and the type of the description of the sire of the great first English blood horse, Godolphin, is exceedingly high-spirited, and fleet in the race or chase. These noble animals abound in all this part of Africa; are bred in Bornou, where great attention is paid to the rearing of them, from whence they are taken by the

Bornou, or Soudan horse

Ishmaelitish traders, in exchange for their commodities, to Arabia; from thence they are sent to Europe as their own production; just as, a few years since, and probably up to the present day, mules were reared in great numbers in Mexico, purchased by Ohio and Kentucky muleteers, who sold them in the eastern and northern States of America, where for years the people supposed and really believed that they were bred in the western States, from whence they were purported to come. The fine Bornou, known as the Arabian horse, is a native of Africa, and raised in great numbers. Denham and Clapperton, as long ago as thirty-five or forty years, wrote, after visiting that part of Africa, "It is said that Bornou can muster fifteen thousand Shonaas in the field mounted. They are the greatest breeders of cattle in the country, and annually supply Soudan with from two to three thousand horses." These animals are used for riding, and well exercised, as the smallest boys are great riders, every day dashing at fearful speed along the roads and over the plains.

Game; quadrupeds

Game is also very plentiful. Deer, antelopes, wild hogs, hedge hogs, porcupines, armadillos, squirrels, hares and rabbits, raccoons and opossoms, are among the most common quadruped game.

Wild Fowl

Wild turkey, wild ducks of various kinds, wild pigeons, ocpara (a very fine quail, much larger, fatter and plumper than the American pheasant), and the wild Guinea fowl, are among the most common biped game.

Markets, and Domestic Habits of the People

The markets are also worthy of note, and by their regular establishment and arrangement indicate to a certain extent the self-governing element and organized condition of the people. Every town has its regular market-place or general bazaar, and everything to be had in the town may be found, in more or less quantities, in these market-places. In describing the large cities through which Mr. Campbell my colleague, and I passed, and those through which I passed alone (none of which were under seventy thousand of a population), there were numerous smaller places of various sizes, from very small villages of one hundred to two thousand inhabitants, which were not mentioned in the enumerated towns. Of these market-places I may mention that Illorin has five, the area of the largest comprising about ten acres, and the general market of Abbeokuta comprising more than twelve altogether, whilst that of Ijaye contains fully twenty acres or more, in which, like the markets generally, everything may be obtained. These markets are systematically regulated and orderly arranged, there being parts and places for everything, and "everything in their places," with officially appointed and excellent managing market-masters. The cattle department of the Abbeokuta and Ijaye markets, as well as Illorin are particularly attractive, there being as many as eight hundred sheep at one time in either of the two former, and horses and mules, as well as sheep and goats exhibited in the latter. When approaching the city of Ibaddan, I saw at a brook, where they had been let out of their cages or coops to drink and wash themselves, as many as three thousand pigeons and squabs going to the Ibaddan market.

The following description of the Illorin market, extracted from "Bowen's Central Africa," is truthful as far as it goes, and will give a general idea of markets in the great cities of Africa:

The most attractive object next to the curious old town itself—and it is always old—is the market. * * * Here the women sit and chat all day, from early morn till nine o'clock at night, to sell their various merchandise. Some of the sheds however, are occupied by barbers, who shave people's heads and faces; and by leather dressers, who make charms like Jewish phylacteries, and bridle reins, shoes, sandals, &c.; and by dozens and scores of men, who earn an honest living by dressing calabashes, and ornamenting them with various neat engravings. * * * The principal market hour, and proper time to see all the wonders, is in the evening.† * * * * * As

† Lagos is an exception to this, the market commencing early in the day, and closing at night.

the shades of evening deepen, if the weather allow the market to continue and there is no moon, every woman lights her little lamp, and presently the market presents, to the distant observer, the beautiful appearance of innumerable stars.

The commodities sold in market are too tedious to mention, even if all could be remembered. Besides home productions, there are frequently imported articles from the four quarters of the globe. Various kinds of meat, fowls, sheep, goats, dogs, rats, tortoises, eggs, fish, snails, yams, Indian corn, Guinea corn, sweet potatoes, sugar-cane, ground peas, onions, pepper, various vegetables, palm-nuts, oil, tree-butter, seeds, fruits, firewood, cotton in the seeds, spun cotton, domestic cloth, imported cloth, as calico, shirting, velvets, &c., gunpowder, guns, flints, knives, swords, paper, raw silk, Turkey-red thread, needles, ready-made clothing, as trowsers, caps, breeches, shirts without sleeves, baskets, brooms, and no one knows what all.

This description was given by Mr. Bowen in his (in many respects) admirable work, published in 1857, after a missionary residence and tour of seven years, from 1850 to the time of writing, among the people of whom he wrote.

Native houses and cities

The houses are built of unburnt clay which hardens in the sun, covered with a beautiful thatch—long, peculiar grass—exhibiting only the walls to the streets, the doors all opening inside of these walls, which are entered by a gate or large doorway; the streets generally irregular and narrow, but frequently agreeably relieved by wider ones, or large, open spaces or parks shaded with trees; all presenting a scene so romantic and antiquated in appearance, that you cannot resist the association with Babylon, Nineveh, Tyre, and Thebais. The buildings are heavy and substantial for their kind, many of which are very extensive. These towns and cities are all entrenched and walled; extending entirely around them; that of Abbeokuta with the new addition being twenty-seven miles, though the population is less by forty thousand than Ibaddan, which embraces about twenty-three miles.

Great affection exists between husband and wife, the women being mostly restricted to household work, trading, and gathering in the fields, and aiding in carrying, whilst the men principally do the digging, planting, chopping, and other hard work. The children are also passionately beloved by their parents, sometimes with too much indulgence. They are very active, and every day some of them of all sizes may be seen dashing along a road or over a plain at fearful speed on horseback. They are great vaulters and ankle-springers, and boys may frequently be seen to spring from the ground whirling twice—turning *two* summersets—before lighting on their feet.

Conjugal and filial affection. Activity of Children

It may not be out of place here to add, that the population of the capital of Liberia is certainly not above three thousand, though they claim for it five thousand. And what has been said of the lack and seeming paucity of public improvement may be much extenuated when it is considered that the entire population of settlers only number at present some 15,000 souls; the native population being 250,000, or 300,000, as now incorporated.

Population of Monrovia and the State

As the enquiry has been frequently made of me as to "whether there are really dogs and cats in Africa," and if so, "whether they are like other dogs and cats;" and since a very intelligent American clergyman said to me that he had read it somewhere as a fact in natural history, that dogs in Africa could not bark; I simply here inform the curious enquirer, that there are dogs and cats plentifully in Africa, which "look like other dogs and cats," and assure them that the dogs bark, eat, and *bite,* just like "other dogs."

Canine and Feline

A word about slavery. It is simply preposterous to talk about slavery, as that term is understood, either being legalized or existing in this part of Africa. It is nonsense. The system is a patriarchal one, there being no actual difference, socially, between the slave (called

Slavery

by their protector *son* or *daughter*) and the children of the person with whom they live. Such persons intermarry, and frequently become the heads of state: indeed, generally so, as I do not remember at present a king or chief with whom I became acquainted whose entire members of the household, from the lowest domestic to the highest official, did not sustain this relation to him, they calling him *baba* or "father," and he treating them as children. And where this is not the case, it either arises from some innovation among them or those exceptional cases of despotism to be found in every country. Indeed, the term "slave" is unknown to them, only as it has been introduced among them by whites from Europe and America. So far from abject slavery, not even the old feudal system, as known to exist until comparatively recent in enlightened and Christian Europe, exists in this part of Africa.

Criminals and prisoners of war are *legally sold* into slavery among themselves, just as was the custom in almost every civilized country in the world till very lately, when nothing but advanced intelligence and progressive Christianity among the people put a stop to it. There is no place, however, but Illorin, a *bona fide* Mohammedan kingdom, where we ever witnessed any exhibition of these facts.

How slaves are obtained

Slaves are abducted by marauding, kidnapping, depraved natives, who, like the organized bands and gangs of robbers in Europe and America, go through the country thieving and stealing helpless women and children, and men who may be overpowered by numbers. Whole villages in this way sometimes fall victims to these human monsters, especially when the strong young men are out in the fields at work, the old of both sexes in such cases being put to death, whilst the young are hurried through some private way down to the slave factories usually kept by Europeans (generally Portuguese and Spaniards) and Americans, on some secluded part of the coast. And in no instances are the parents and relatives known to sell their own children or people into slavery, except, indeed, in cases of base depravity, and except such miserable despots as the kings of Dahomi and Ashantee; neither are the heads of countries known to sell their own people; but like the marauding kidnapper, obtain them by war on others.

SECTION IX

DISEASES OF THIS PART OF AFRICA, TREATMENT, HYGIENE, ALIMENT

The diseases in this part of Africa are still more simple *Diseases* than those of Liberia; and even the *native fever,* for known causes, generally is much less severe. In Liberia, and all that part of Africa, the entire country (except the cleared farms in the republic and the limited rice-fields of the natives) is a dense, heavy-wooded, *primitive* forest, *Face of the* rank with the growth and putrified vegetation of a thou- *country* sand ages. But the entire Aku country, throughout the second plateau, presents a very different phase. Here, one is struck with the beautiful clear country which continu- ally spreads out in every direction around; and (except the thickets or forests left as defences, ambuscades, and arbors of rest, rugged hilltops, and gullies), there is noth- ing but recent timber to be found growing on the lands. Timber in Africa is reproduced very speedily; hence may be found in some parts designedly left very heavy timber; but the greatest unbroken forest through which we passed at any one time, of this description, never ex- ceeded, I think, ten miles. All the spring (shallow wells generally) and other living water, as perennial streams, is both good-tasted, and if the constant use of running stream water be a fair test, I would decide as wholesome. *Spring water* There are some good springs in Africa, and good water doubtless may everywhere be obtained by digging suitable wells.

Drinking water in the tropics should always be kept in large vessels of crockery ware (usually termed "stone" and "earthen ware") and smaller bottle or decanter-shaped jugs or vessels for table convenience. If earthen or crockery ware cannot be obtained for table use, by all means use glass bottles—the more globular, or ballon-shaped, the better.

To make and keep water cool in any crockery or glass vessel, wrap around it a cloth or any kind, but especially *woolen*—flannel or blanket being the best—which keep simply *wet,* and the water in the vessel, by *evaporation* from the *cloth,* can be made or kept almost ice cool.

A most simple method by which the cloth may be kept wet, and evaporation thereby kept up, is to have a large vessel, with the water in for common use, so placed that a small vessel with water can be suspended over it in such a manner that a *drip* can be kept constantly on the cloth. The cloth being first saturated, it will readily be seen that a very small drip is required to keep up the dampness. The drip may be arranged, where convenient, with a small *faucet* so as to regulate the drop, or the more primitive method of a little *spiggot* or *sharpened stick* put into a hole made in the vessel, so regulated as to keep up a sufficient dripping to keep the cloth of sufficient dampness. Simple as this may appear to the reader, it is an important sanitary measure, besides adding greatly to the immediate comfort of the traveler or resident in those regions.

The atmosphere in this region of the continent is much purer than that of Liberia and the region round about; and, although incorporated with odors, these are pleasant and seem familiar to the sense, and not obnoxious with the rich rank fragrance so sensibly experienced in that country. There is little, comparatively, of the decayed vegetation, which sends up malaria from the surface in Liberia; and the immense fields and plains of grass not under cultivation at the time, are burnt down during the dry season, thereby bringing to bear, though probably unawares to them, a sanitary process throughout that extensive country at least once every year.

Intermittent fever, as described in section VI., page 65, on Liberia, though generally of a mild type, *diarrhoea, dysentery* (neither of which is difficult to subdue by a little rational treatment), *opthalmia,* and *umbilical hernia,* and sometimes, but not frequently, *inguinal hernia,* are the principal diseases. The opthalmia I suspected as originating from taint, probably having been primarily carried from the coast, as it was not so frequently met with as to warrant the idea of its being either a contagion or the effects of poisonous sands or winds, as supposed to exist. The hernia is caused by the absence of proper *umbilical attention* and *abdominal support* to the child after *parturition.* Umbilical hernia is fearfully common all through Africa, I having frequently seen persons, especially females, with the hernial tumor as large as their own head, and those of little children fully as large as the head of an infant a month old.

Kinds of disease

A singular disease affects some persons, though I have never seen this upon a native, and believe it to be peculiar to the region round about Liberia. The person whose case I examined had formerly resided in Liberia, where, doubtless, the disease commenced, but for the last three years previously had resided at Ijaye, in the capacity of cook, for the American Baptist Missionaries, Revs. A. D. Phillips and J. R. Stone and lady, and then resided at Abbeokuta. This is a peculiar ulceration of the leg, immediately above the ankle-bone, where they say it usually commences; the edges of the ulcer, and the cuticle quite up to the edge, and all the surrounding parts, having a healthy appearance, as though a portion of the flesh had been recently torn out, leaving the cavity as it then was. The most peculiar feature of this singular disease is a *white fiber,* which, coming out from the integuments of the muscles of the leg above, hangs suspended in the

Guinea Worm

cavity (ulcer) the lower end loose, and somewhat inclined to coil (and when *straightened* out, resuming again the serpentine curves, of course from the *elasticity* with *motion*), is supposed to be a *worm*; hence its name—*Guinea worm*. The fibre seems in color and texture to be in a normal condition; indeed, there appear to be little or no pathological symptoms about the parts at all, except a slight appearance of *vermillion* inflammation over the surface of the ulcer, which is more apparent sometimes than others.

What is Guinea Worm?

I have examined closely this fibre, and from its appearance, color, size, and texture, especially as it is sensibly felt high up in the leg near the tuberosity of the tibia, when pulled by the dangling end, my own impression is that the so-called "Guinea worm" is nothing more than the *external saphenus* or *communis tibiae* (nerve) exposed in a peculiar manner, probably by a disease, which, by a curious pathological process, absorbs away the muscular parts, leaving the bare nerve detached at its lower extremity, suspended loose in this unnatural space. I have never seen but this one case of Guinea worm, but had frequent opportunities of examining it; indeed, the patient consulted me concerning it, and by the advice and consent of the very clever native gentleman, Samuel Crowther, Esq., who received his professional education at the Royal College of Surgeons, Lincoln's Inn Fields, London, insisted on my taking the case, which I declined, partly for the want of time to do justice to the patient, and aside from courtesy and equity to the surgeon who had the case in hand, mainly because I *knew nothing about it*—the best reason of all. The patient was an American quadroon, black nearly in complexion, of one-fourth white blood, from North Carolina. This, of course was a black quadroon.

I should add, that the fiber at times entirely *disappears* from the cavity (by *contraction,* of course), when again it is seen suspended as before. This is one reason why it is believed to be a *worm,* and supposed to *creep* up and down in the flesh.

The treatment of fever in this part of Africa should be the same as that in Liberia, given on page 66. The best remedy which I have found for diarrhoea is: *Treatment of Diseases— Diarrhoea*

℞. Pulv. Rad. Rhei. ʒj.; Syr. Simp. f. ℥jv.; Spts. Terebinth. f. ʒj.; Tinct. Opii., gtt. x. M. ft.

Pulverized rhubarb, one drachm, (or one-eighth of an ounce); simple syrup, four ounces (or eight large table-spoonfuls); laudanum, ten drops; spirits of turpentine, one spoonful. Mix this well together to take.

For dysentery the recipe is: *Dysentery*

℞. Pulv. Rad. Rhei. Pulv. G. Catech. a. a., ʒj.; Syr. Simp. f. ℥jv.; Spts. Terebinth. Spts. Ammon. Arromat., a. a. f. ʒj.; Tinct. Opii. gtt. x. M. ft.

Pulverized rhubarb and pulverized gum catechu, each, one-eighth of an ounce; simple syrup, eight large table-spoonfuls; spirits of turpentine and aromatic spirits of ammonia, of each one teaspoonful; laudanum, ten drops. Mix this well together to take. Of this take one teaspoon-ful (if very bad, a dessert spoonful) every three hours, or four times a day (always beginning at least one hour before breakfast), till the symptoms cease.

During the presence of febrile symptoms, in the absence of all diarrhoea and dysenteric symptoms, even when the person is not complaining, an excellent simple antidote to be taken at discretion, not oftener than once every hour during the day, is: *Fever Antidote*

℞. Syr. Simp., ℥jv.; Spts. Ammon. Arromat. ʒjss. M. ft. —

Simple syrup, eight large tablespoonfuls; aromatic spirits of ammonia, one and a-half teaspoonfuls. Mix this well together. Take a teaspoonful of this preparation in a little cold water, or a glass of lemonade if preferred, and the condition of the bowels will admit, as often as thought advisable under the circumstances.

I have thus thought proper to simplify this treatment, that it may be in the reach of every person going to the tropics, as I am certain that there has been a great deficiency in the treatment and discovery of remedies in diseases of that continent especially. These prescriptions, as compounded, are entirely new, originating with the writer, who has only to add that he is in hopes that they prove as advantageous and successful in other hands as they have been in his.

Regimen

Persons laboring under fever should eat moderately of such food as best agrees with their appetite; but frequently, if required or desired, that the system may be well supported. When there is *diarrhoea* or *dysentery* present, there should be no solid food taken, but the patient or ailing person should be confined strictly to a thin milk porridge of fine Guinea-corn flour, which is always obtainable in Africa, crumbled crackers or soda biscuits, light (leavened) wheat bread if to be had, or well-done rice boiled to a pulp. The soda-biscuit as a porridge with milk rather aggravates the bowels of most persons; therefore, whenever it is found to have this effect, its use should be immediately abandoned. In many instances, where there is either diarrhoea or dysentery present, without other prominent symptoms, I have found the mere use of cooked milk (merely "scalded," as women usually term it—being heated to the boiling point without permitting it to boil), taken as food alone, to be the only remedy required.

Hygiene—
Eating

The laws of health should be particularly observed in going to Africa. In respect to eating, there need be no material change of food, but each individual observing those nourishments which best agree with him or her. When there is little inclination to eat, eat but little; and when there is none, eat nothing. I am certain that a large percentage of the mortality which occurs may be attributed to too free and too frequent indulgence in eating, as was the case with the Lewis family of five at Clay-Ashland, in Liberia—all of whom died from that cause; as well as others that might be mentioned.

So soon as you have taken your bath and put on your morning wrapper, even before dressing, you may eat one or more sweet oranges, then take a cup of coffee, creamed and sweetened, or not, to your taste. Make your toilet, and walk out and take the cool air, always taking your umbrella or parasol, because no foreigner, until by a long residence more or less acclimated, can expose himself with impunity to a tropical sun. If preferred, coffee should always be taken with cream or milk and sugar, because it is then less irritating to the stomach. One of the symptoms of native fever is said to be *nervous irritability of the stomach;* hence, all exciting causes to irritation of that part should be avoided as much as possible. Such fruits as best agree with each individual should be most indulged in; indeed, all others for the time should be dispensed with; and when it can be done without any apparent risk to the person, a little fruit of some kind might be taken every day by each new comer. Except oranges, taken as directed above, all fruits should be eaten *after,* and *not* before breakfast. The fruits of the country have been described in another place.

Let your habits be strictly temperate, and for human nature's sake, abstain from the erroneous idea that some sort of malt or spirituous drink is necessary. This is not the case; and I am certain that much of the disease and dire mortality charged against Africa, as a "land of pestilence and death," should be charged against the Christian lands which produce and *send bad spirits* to destroy those who go to Africa. Whenever wine, brandy, whisky, gin, rum, or pure alcohol are required as a medical remedy, no one will object to its use; but, in all cases in which they are used as a beverage in Africa, I have no

Coffee. Air Fruits—

Drinks

hesitation in pronouncing them deleterious to the system. The best British porter and ale may, in convalescence from fever, be used to advantage as a tonic, because of the bitter and farinoceous substances they contain—not otherwise is it beneficial to the system in Africa. Water, lemonade, effervescent drinks—a teaspoonful of super-carbonate of soda, to a glass of lemonade—all may be drunk in common, when thirsty, with pleasure to the drinker as well as profit. Pure ginger-beer is very beneficial.

Bathing

Bathing should be strictly observed by every person at least once every day. Each family should be provided with a large sponge, or one for each room if not for each person, and free application of water to the entire person, from head to foot, should be made every morning.

*Early
Rising—
Breezes*

Every person should rise early in Africa, as the air is then coolest, freshest, and purest; besides the effect upon the senses, the sight and song of the numerous birds to be seen and heard, produce a healthful influence upon the mental and physical system. The land and sea-breezes blow regularly and constantly from half-past three o'clock P.M. till half-past ten o'clock A.M., when there is a cessation of about five hours till half-past three again.

Never sultry

The evenings and mornings are always cool and pleasant, *never sultry* and oppressive with heat, as frequently in temperate climates during summer and autumn. This wise and beneficent arrangement of Divine Providence makes this country beautifully, in fact, delightfully pleasant; and I have no doubt but in a very few years, so soon as scientific black men, her own sons, who alone must be more interested in her development than any other persons, take the matter in hand, and produce works upon the diseases, remedies, treatment, and sanitary measures of Africa, there will be no more contingency in going to Africa than any other known foreign country. I am certain, even now, that the native fever of Africa is not more trying upon the system, when properly treated, than the native fever of Canada, the Western and Southern States and Territories of the United States of America.

Dress should be regulated according to the feeling, with sometimes more and sometimes less clothing. But I think it advisable that adults should wear flannel (thin) next to their person always when first going to Africa. It gradually absorbs the moisture, and retaining a proper degree of heat, thus prevents any sudden change of temperature from affecting the system. Avoid getting wet at first, and should this accidentally happen, take a thoroughly good bath, rub the skin dry, and put on dry clothes, and for two or three hours that day, keep out of the sun; but if at night, go to bed. But when it so happens that you are out from home and cannot change clothing, continue to exercise until the clothes dry on your person. It is the abstraction of heat from the system by evaporaion of water from the clothing, which does the mischief in such cases. I have frequently been wet to saturation in Africa, and nothing ever occurred from it, by pursuing the course here laid down. Always sleep in clean clothes.

Dress

Avoid getting wet

I am sure I need inform no one, however ignorant, that all measures of cleanliness of person, places, and things about the residences, contribute largely to health in Africa, as in other countries.

Sanitary Measures

All dwellings should be *freely ventilated* during the *night,* as well as day, and it is a great mistake to suppose, as in Liberia (where every settler sleeps with every part of his house closely shut—doors, windows, and all) that it is deletereous to have the house ventilated during the evening, although they go out to night meetings, visit each other in the evening, and frequently sit on their porches and piazzas till a late hour in the night, conversing, without any injurious effects whatever. Dr. Roberts, and I think Dr. McGill and a few other gentlemen, informed me that their sleeping apartments were excep-

Ventilation of houses

tions to the custom generally in Liberia. This stifling custom to save themselves does not prevail among the natives of Africa anywhere, nor among the foreigners anywhere in the Yoruba country, that I am aware of, and I am under the impression that it was the result of fear or precaution, not against the night air, but against the imaginary (and sometimes real) creeping things—as insects and reptiles—which might find their way into the houses at night.

Test of night air

While in Liberia, I have traversed rivers in an open boat at night, slept beyond the Kavalla Falls in open native houses, and at the residence of Rev. Alexander Crummel, Mount Vaughan, Cape Palmas, I slept every evening while there with both window and door as ventilators. The window was out and the door inside. In Abbeokuta, Ijaye, Oyo, and Ogbomoso, we slept every night with ventilated doors and windows, when we slept at all in a house. But in Illorin we always slept out of doors by preference, and only retired to repose in-doors (which were always open) when it was too cool to sleep out, as our bedding consisted only of a native mat on the ground, and a calico sheet spread over us. And I should here make acknowledgments to my young colleague, Mr. Campbell, for the use of his large Scotch shawl when I was unwell, and indeed almost during our entire travel—it being to me a great accommodation, a comfort and convenience which I did not possess.

Test of exposure

I have started two and three hours before daybreak, laying on my bed in an open canoe, ascending the Ogun river, at different times during the six days' journey up to Abbeokuta; Mr. Campbell and myself have frequently slept out in open courts and public market-places, without shed or piazza covering; and when journeying from Oyo to Ibaddan, for three successive evenings I lay in the midst of a wilderness or forest, on a single native mat without covering, the entire night; and many times during our travels we arose at midnight to commence our journey, and neither of us ever experienced any serious inconvenience from it.

That houses in Africa may be properly ventilated during the night without annoyance, or, what is equally as bad, if not worse, the continual fear and imagination of the approach of venomous insects, creeping things, and reptiles, the residents should adapt them to the place and circumstances, without that rigid imitation of European and American order of building. Every house should be well ventilated with windows on opposite sides of the rooms, when and wherever this is practicable, and the same may be said of doors. And where the room will not admit of opposite windows, or windows at least on two sides of a room, whether opposite or otherwise, a chimney or ventilating flue should be constructed on the opposite side to the window—which window should always be to the windward, so as to have a continual draught or current of fresh air. Persons, however, should always avoid sitting in a *draught,* though a free circulation of air should be allowed in each room of every house.

Improved window and door ventilation

Instead of window-sashes with glass, as in common use, I would suggest that the windows have a sash of four, or but two (if preferred) panels, to each window (two upper and two lower, or one upper and one lower—or one lower and two upper, which would make a neat and handsome window), each panel or space for panes being neatly constructed with a sieve-work, such as is now used as screens during summer season in the lower part of parlor windows. To prevent too great oxydization or too rapid decay of so delicate a structure as the wire must be, it should be made of brass, copper, or some composition which would not readily corrode. Inside or outside doors of the same material, made to close and open like the Venetian jalousies now in use in civilized countries, would be found very convenient, and add much to the comfort and health of dwellings as a sanitary measure. The frames of the panels or sashes should be constructed of maple, cherry, walnut, or mahogany, according to the means of the builder and elegance of the building—as these articles seasoned are not only more neat and durable, but, from their solidity, are less liable to warp or shrink. This would afford such a beautiful and safe protection to every dwelling against the intrusion of all and every living thing, even the smallest insect—while a full and free circulation of fresh air would be allowed—that a residence in Africa would become attractive and desirable, instead of, as now (from imagination), objectionable.

Sanitary effects of Ants—Termites, and Drivers

A word about ants in Africa—so much talked of, and so much dreaded—will legitimately be in place here, regarding them as a sanitary means, provided by Divine Providence. The *termites,* bug-a-bug or white double ant, shaped like two ovals somewhat flattened, joined together by a cylinder somewhat smaller in the middle, with a head at one end of one of the ovals, is an herbivorous insect, and much abused as the reputed destroyers of books, papers, and all linen or muslin clothing. They feed mainly on such vegetable matter as is most subject to decay—as soft wood, and many other such, when void of vitality—and there is living herbage upon which they feed, and thereby prove a blessing to a country with a superabundance of rank vegetable matter. It is often asserted that they destroy whole buildings, yet I have never seen a person who knew of such a disaster by them, although they may attack and do as much mischief in such cases at times as the wood-worms of America; and, in regard to clothing, though doubtless there have been instances of their attack upon and destruction of clothing, yet I will venture to assert that there is no one piece of clothing attacked and destroyed by these creatures, to ten thousand by the moths which get into the factories and houses in civilized countries, where woolen goods are kept. In all my travels in Africa, I never had anything attacked by the termite; but during my stay of seven months in Great Britain, I had a suit of woolen clothes completely eaten up by moths in Liverpool.

Drivers, as every person already knows, are black ants, whose reputation is as bad for attacking living animals, and even human beings, as the termites' for attacking clothing. This creature, like its white cousin, is also an instrument in the hands of Providence as a sanitary means, and to the reverse of the other is carnivorous, feeding upon all flesh whether fresh or putrified. Like the white, for the purpose of destroying the superabundance of vegetable, certainly these black ants were designed by Providence to destroy the excess of animal life which in the nature of things would be brought forth, with little or no destruction without them; and although much is said about their attacking persons, I will venture the opinion that there is not one of these attacks a person to every ten thousand musquitoes in America, as it is only by chance, and *not by search after it*, that drivers attack persons.

They usually go in search of food in narrow rows, say from half an inch to a hand's breadth, as swiftly as a running stream of water, and may in their search enter a house in their course—if nothing attract them around it—when, in such cases, they spread over the floor, walls, and ceiling; and finding no insect or creeping thing to destroy, they gather again on the floor, and leave the premises in the regular order in which they entered. Should they encounter a person when on these excursions, though in bed, does he but lie still and not disturb them, the good-hearted negro insects will even pass over the person without harm or molestation; but if disturbed, they will retaliate by a sting as readily as a bee when the hive is disturbed, though their sting, so far from being either dangerous or severe, is simply like the severe sting of a musquito. An aged missionary gentleman, of twenty-five years' experience, informed me that an

Drivers

How they travel

entire myriad (this term is given to a multitude of drivers, as their number can never be less than ten thousand—and I am sure that I have seen as many millions together) passed over him one night in bed, without one stinging him. Indeed, both the black and white ants are quite harmless as to personal injury, and very beneficial in a sanitary point.

How to Drive them out of the Houses

There is much more in the imagination than the reality about these things; and one important fact I must not omit, that, however great the number of drivers, a simple *light set in the middle of the floor* will clear the room of them in ten minutes. In this case they do not form in column, but go out in hasty confusion, each effecting as quick retreat and safe escape for himself as possible, forming their line of march outside of the house, where they meet from all quarters of their points of escape.

How to Destroy them

Chloride of sodium or common salt (fine), slightly damped, will entirely destroy the termites; and *acetum* or vinegar, or *acetic acid* either, will destroy or chase off the drivers. These means are simple, and within the reach of every person, but, aside from this, both classes or races of these creatures disappear before the approach of civilization. In a word, moths, mice, roaches, and musquitoes are much greater domestic annoyances, and certainly much more destructive in America and Europe than the bug-a-bug or driver is in Africa.

Their Pugnacious and Martial Character

I cannot endorse the statement from personal knowledge of the desperate hostility which the drivers manifest towards the termites, as given by Dr. Livingstone, who, calling them "black rascals," says "they stand deliberately and watch for the whites, which, on coming out of their holes, they instantly seize, putting them to death." Perhaps the whites were *kidnappers,* in which case they served the white *rascals* right. Though I have never seen an encounter, it is nevertheless true, that the blacks do subdue the whites whenever they meet. In fact, they go, as do no other creatures known to natural science, in immense incalculable numbers—and I do not think that I exaggerate if I say that I have more than once seen more than six hogsheads of them traveling together, had they been measured—and along the entire line of march, stationed on each side of the columns, there are warriors or soldiers to guard them, who stand sentry, closely packed side by side with their heads towards the column, which passes on as rapidly as a flowing stream of water. I have traced a column for more than a mile, whose greatest breadth was more than a yard, and the least not less than a foot. It is inconceivable the distance these creatures travel in a short time. Should anything disturb the lines, the soldiers sally out a few feet in pursuit of the cause, quickly returning to their post when meeting no foe. The guards are much larger than the common drivers, being about the length of a barley-corn, and armed with a pair of curved horns, like those of the large American black beetle, called "pinching bug." There are no bed-bugs here.

One important fact, never referred to by travellers as such, is that the health of large towns in Africa will certainly be improved by the erection of *cesspools,* whereas now they have none. With the exception of the residences of missionaries and other civilized people, there is no such thing in Africa. Every family, as in civilized countries, should have such conveniences. Our senses are great and good faculties—seeing, hearing, tasting, smelling, and feeling—God has so created them, and designed them for such purposes; therefore, they should neither be perverted nor marred when this can be avoided. Hence, we should beautify, when required, and make pleasing to the sight; modify and make pleasant to the hearing; *cleanse* and *purify* to make *agreeable* to the smelling; improve and make good to the taste; and never violate the feelings whenever any or all of these are at our will or control.

Cesspools

Wild Beasts and Reptiles

A single remark about these. The wild beasts are driven back before the march of civilization, I having seen none, save one leopard; and but four serpents during my entire travels, one three and a half feet long (a water snake); one fourteen inches long; and another ten inches long; the two last being killed by natives—and a tame one around the neck of a charmer at Oyo. During the time I never saw a centipede, and but two tarantulas.

SECTION X

MISSIONARY INFLUENCE

To deny or overlook the fact, the all-important fact, that the missionary influence had done much good in Africa, would be simply to do injustice, a gross injustice to a good cause.

Protestant Missionaries

The advent of the Protestant Missionaries into Africa, has doubtless been effective of much good, though it may reasonably be expected that many have had their short comings. By Protestant, I mean all other Christian denominations than the Roman Catholic. I would not be regarded either a bigot or partialist so far as the rights of humanity are concerned, but facts are tenable in all cases, and whilst I readily admit that a Protestant monarch granted the first letters-patent to steal Africans from their homes to be enslaved by a Protestant people, and subsequently a *bona-fide* Protestant nation has been among the most cruel oppressors of the African race, my numerous friends among whom are many Roman Catholics—black as well as white—must bear the test of truth, as I shall apply it in the case of the Missionaries, as my object in visiting my father-land, was to enquire into and learn every fact, which should have a bearing on this, the grandest prospect for the regeneration of a people, that ever was presented in the history of the world.

In my entire travels in Africa, either alone or after meeting with Mr. Campbell at Abbeokuta, I have neither seen nor heard of any Roman Catholic Missionaries; but the most surprising and startling fact is, that every slave-trading point on the coast at present (which ports are mainly situated South and East) where the traffic is carried on, are either Roman Catholic trading-ports, or native agencies protected by Roman Catholics; as Canot, formerly at Grand Cape Mount, Pedro Blanco, and Domingo at Wydah in Dahomi. And still more, it is a remarkable and very suggestive reality that at all of those places where the Jesuits or Roman Catholic Missionaries once were stationed, the slave-trade is not only still carried on in its worst form as far as practicable, but slaves are held in Africa by these white foreigners at the old Portuguese settlements along the Southern and Eastern coasts, of Loango and Mozambique for instance; and although some three years have elapsed since the King of Portugal proclaimed, or pretended to proclaim "Liberty to all the people throughout his dominions," yet I will venture an opinion, that not one in every hundred of native Africans thus held in bondage on their own soil, are aware of any such "Proclamation." Dr. Livingstone tells us that he came across many ruins of Roman Catholic Missionary Stations in his travels—especially those in Loando de St. Paul, a city of some eighteen or twenty thousand of a population—all deserted, and the buildings appropriated to other uses, as storehouses, and the like. Does not this seem as though slavery were the legitimate successor of Roman Catholicism, or slave-traders and holders of the Roman Catholic religion and Missionaries? It certainly has that appearance to me; and a fact still more glaring is, that the only professing Christian government which in the light of the present period of human elevation and national reform, has attempted such a thing, is that of Roman Catholic Spain, (still persisting in holding Cuba for the wealth accruing

Influence of Roman Catholic Religion in favor of Slavery

103

from African Slaves stolen from their native land) which recently expelled every Protestant Missionary from the African Island of Fernando Po, that they might command it unmolested by Christian influence, as an export mart for the African Slave-Trade. To these facts I call the attention of the Christian world, that no one may murmur when the day of retribution in Africa comes—which come it must—and is fast hastening, when slave-traders must flee.

Influence of Protestant Religion against Slavery, and in favor of civilization

Wherever the Protestant Missionaries are found, or have been, there are visible evidences of a purer and higher civilization, by the high estimate set upon the Christian religion by the natives, the deference paid to the missionaries themselves, and the idea which generally obtains among them, that all missionaries are opposed to slavery, and the faith they have in the moral integrity of these militant ambassadors of the Living God. Wherever there are missionaries, there are schools both Sabbath and secular, and the arts and sciences, and manners and customs, more or less of civilized life, are imparted. I have not as yet visited a missionary station in any part of Africa, where there were not some, and frequently many natives, both adult and children, who could speak, read, and write English, as well as read their own language; as all of them, whether Episcopalian, Wesleyan, Baptist, or Presbyterian, in the Yoruba country, have Crowther's editions of religious and secular books in the schools and churches, and all have native agents, interpreters, teachers (assistants) and catechists or readers in the mission. These facts prove indisputably great progress; and I here take much pleasure in recording them in testimony of those faithful laborers in that distant vineyard of our heavenly Father in my fatherland. Both male and female missionaries, all seemed much devoted to their work, and anxiously desirous of doing more. Indeed, the very fact of there being as many native missionaries as there are now to be found holding responsible positions, as elders, deacons, preachers, and priests, among whom there are many finely educated, and several of them authors of works, not only in their own but the English language, as Revs. Crowther, King, Taylor, and Samuel Crowther, Esq., surgeon, all show that there is an advancement for these people beyond the point to which missionary duty can carry them.

I am indebted to the Missionaries generally, wherever met with, whether in Liberia or Central Africa, for their uniform kindness and hospitality, among whom may be named: Rev. J. M. Harden and excellent wife, (a refined highly educated native Ibo lady at Lagos), Revs. H. Townsend, C. H. Gollmer, J. King, E. Bickersteth and ladies in Abbeokuta; A. D. Phillips, J. A. Stone and lady, Ijaye; T. A. Reid, and Mr. Mekin, Oyo; and Rev. D. Hinderer and lady, Ibaddan. I am indebted to the Baptist Missionaries for the use of their Mission House and furniture during our residence at Abbeokuta: Rev. John Roberts and lady, Miss Killpatrick, Reverend Bishop Burns and lady, Rev. Mr. Tyler, Rev. Mr. Gipson, Rev. Edward W. Blyden and others, Rev. Mr. Hoffman and lady, and Rev. Mr. Messenger and lady, all of Liberia, I am indebted for marks of personal kindness and attention when indisposed among them, and my kind friends, the Reverend Alexander Crummell and lady, whose guest I was during several weeks near the Cape, and who spared no pains to render my stay not only a comfortable, but a desirable one.

Kindness of Missionaries and personal acknowledgments

I would suggest for the benefit of missionaries in general, and those to whom it applies in particular, that there are other measures and ways by which civilization may be imparted than preaching and praying—temporal as well as spiritual means. If all persons who settle among the natives would, as far as it is in their power and comes within their province, induce, by making it a rule of their house or family, every native servant to sit on a stool or chair; eat at a table instead of on the ground; eat with a

Hints to those to whom they apply

knife and fork (or *begin* with a spoon) instead of with their fingers; eat in the house instead of going out in the yard, garden, or somewhere else under a tree or shed; and sleep on a bed, instead of on a bare mat on the ground; and have them to wear some sort of a garment to cover the entire person above the knees, should it be but a single shirt or chemise, instead of a loose native cloth thrown around them, to be dropped at pleasure, at any moment exposing the entire upper part of the person—or as in Liberia, where that part of the person is entirely uncovered—I am certain that it would go far toward impressing them with some of the habits of civilized life, as being adapted to them as well as the "white man," whom they so faithfully serve with a will. I know that some may say, this is difficult to do. It certainly could not have been with those who never tried it. Let each henceforth resolve for himself like the son of Nun, "As for me and my house, we will serve the Lord."

Changing names

I would also suggest that I cannot see the utility of the custom on the part of Missionaries in *changing* the names of native children, and even adults, so soon as they go into their families to live, as though their own were not good enough for them. These native names are generally much more significant, and euphonious than the Saxon, Gaelic, or Celtic. Thus, Adenigi means, "Crowns have their shadow." This was the name of a servant boy of ours, whose father was a native cotton trader. It is to be hoped that this custom among Missionaries and other Christian settlers, of changing the names of the natives, will be stopped, thereby relieving them of the impression, that to embrace the Christian faith, implies a loss of name, and so far loss of identity.

SECTION XI

WHAT AFRICA NOW REQUIRES

From the foregoing, it is very evident that missionary duty has reached its *ultimatum*. By this, I mean that the native has received all that the missionary was sent to teach, and is now really ready for more than he can or may receive. He sees and knows that the white man, who first carried him the Gospel, which he has learned to a great extent to believe a reality, is of an entirely different race to himself; and has learned to look upon everything which he has, knows and does, which has not yet been imparted to him (especially when he is told by the missionaries, which frequently must be the case, to relieve themselves of the endless teasing enquiries which persons in their position are subject to concerning all and every temporal and secular matter, law, government, commerce, military, and other matters foreign to the teachings of the gospel; that these things he is not sent to teach, but simply the gospel) as peculiarly adapted and belonging to the white man. Of course, there are exceptions to this. Hence, having reached what he conceives to be the *maximum* of the black man's or African's attainments, there must be a re-action in some direction, and if not progressive it will be retrogressive.

What Missionary labor has done

The missionary has informed him that the white man's country is great. He builds and resides in great houses; lives in great towns and cities, with great churches and palaver-houses (public and legislative halls); rides in great carriages; manufactures great and beautiful things; has great ships, which go to sea, to all parts of the world, instead of little canoes such as he has paddling up and down the rivers and on the coast; that the wisdom, power, strength, courage, and wealth of the white man and his country are as much greater than him and his, as the big ships are larger and stronger than the little frail canoes;

How it was done

all of which he is made sensible of, either by the exhibition of pictures or the reality.

He at once comes to a stand. "Of what use is the white man's religion and 'book knowledge' to me, since it does not give me the knowledge and wisdom nor the wealth and power of the white man, as all these things belong only to him? "Our young men and women learn their book, and talk on paper (write), and talk to God like white man (worship), but God no hear 'em like He hear white man! Dis religion no use to black man." And so the African *reasonably* reasons when he sees that despite his having yielded up old-established customs, the laws of his fathers, and almost his entire social authority, and the rule of his household to the care and guardianship of the missionary, for the sake of acquiring his knowledge and power—when, after having learned all that his children can, he is doomed to see them sink right back into their old habits, the country continue in the same condition, without the beautiful improvements of the white man—and if a change take place at all, he is doomed to witness what he never expected to see and dies regretting—himself and people entangled in the meshes of the government of a people foreign in kith, kin, and sympathy, when he and his are entirely shoved aside and compelled to take subordinate and inferior positions, if not, indeed, reduced to menialism and bondage. I am justified in asserting that this state of things has brought missionary efforts to their *maximum* and native progress to a pause.

Religion has done its work, and now requires temporal and secular aid to give it another impulse. The improved arts of civilized life must now be brought to bear, and go hand in hand in aid of the missionary efforts which are purely religious in character and teaching. I would not have the standard of religion lowered a single stratum of the common breeze of heaven. No, let it rather be raised, if, indeed, higher it can be. Christianity certainly is the most advanced civilization that man ever attained to, and wherever propagated in its purity, to be effective, law and government must be brought in harmony with it—otherwise it becomes corrupted, and a corresponding degeneracy ensues, placing its votaries even in a worse condition than the primitive. This was exemplified by the Author of our faith, who, so soon as he began to teach, commenced by admonishing the people to a modification of their laws— or rather himself to condemn them. But it is very evident that the social must keep pace with the religious, and the political with the social relations of society, to carry out the great measures of the higher civilization.

Christianity and Law or Government must harmonize, to be effective of good

Of what avail, then, is advanced intelligence to the African without improved social relations—acquirements and refinement without an opportunity of a practical application of them—society in which they are appreciated? It requires not the most astute reformer and political philosopher to see.

Like seeks like

The native sees at once that all the higher social relations are the legitimate result and requirements of a higher intelligence, and naturally enough expects, that when he has attained it, to enjoy the same privileges and blessings. But how sadly mistaken—what dire disappointment!

Natives desire higher social relations

The habits, manners, and customs of his people, and the social relations all around him are the same; improvements of towns, cities, roads, and methods of travel are the same; implements of husbandry and industry are the same; the methods of conveyance and price of produce (with comparative trifling variation) are the same. All seem dark and gloomy for the future, and he has his doubts and fears as to whether or not he has committed a fatal error in leaving his native social relations for those of foreigners whom he cannot hope to emulate, and who, he thinks, will not assimilate themselves to him.

Native doubts respecting the eventual good effects of Missionary labor

The proper element as progressive Missionary agencies

It is clear, then, that essential to the success of civilization, is the establishment of all those social relations and organizations, without which enlightened communities cannot exist. To be successful, these must be carried out by proper agencies, and these agencies must be a *new element* introduced into their midst, possessing all the attainments, socially and politically, morally and religiously, adequate to so important an end. This element must be *homogenous* in all the *natural* characteristics, claims, sentiments, and sympathies—the *descendants of Africa* being the only element that can effect it. To this end, then, a part of the most enlightened of that race in America design to carry out these most desirable measures by the establishment of social and industrial settlements among them, in order at once to introduce, in an effective manner, all the well-regulated pursuits of civilized life.

Precaution against error in the first steps

That no mis-step be taken and fatal error committed at the commencement, we have determined that the persons to compose this new element to be introduced into Africa, shall be well and most carefully selected in regard to moral integrity, intelligence, acquired attainments, fitness, adaptation, and, as far as practicable, religious sentiments and professions. We are serious in this; and, so far as we are concerned as an individual, it shall be restricted to the letter, and we will most strenuously oppose and set our face against any attempt from any quarter to infringe upon this arrangement and design. Africa is our fatherland and we its legitimate descendants, and we will never agree nor consent to see this—the first voluntary step that has ever been taken for her regeneration by her own descendants—blasted by a disinterested or renegade set, whose only object might be in the one case to get rid of a portion of the colored population, and in the other, make money, though it be done upon the destruction of every hope entertained and measure introduced for the accomplishment of this great and prospectively glorious undertaking. We cannot and will not permit or agree that the result of years of labor and anxiety shall be blasted at one reckless blow, by those who have never spent a day in the cause of our race, or know nothing about our wants and requirements. The descendants of Africa in North America will doubtless, by the census of 1860, reach five millions; those of Africa may number two hundred millions. I have outgrown, long since, the boundaries of North America, and with them have also outgrown the boundaries of their claims. I, therefore, cannot consent to sacrifice the prospects of two hundred millions, that a fraction of five millions may be benefitted, especially since the measures adopted for the many must necessarily benefit the few.

Africa, to become regenerated, must have a national character, and her position among the existing nations of the earth will depend mainly upon the high standard she may gain compared with them in all her relations, morally, religiously, socially, politically, and commercially.

National character essential to the successful regeneration of Africa

I have determined to leave to my children the inheritance of a country, the possession of territorial domain, the blessings of a national education, and the indisputable right of self-government; that they may not succeed to the servility and degradation bequeathed to us by our fathers. If we have not been born to fortunes, we should impart the seeds which shall germinate and give birth to fortunes for them.

SECTION XII

TO DIRECT LEGITIMATE COMMERCE

As the first great national step in political economy, the selection and security of a location to direct and command commerce legitimately carried on, as an export and import metropolis, is essentially necessary. The

First steps in political economy

facilities for a metropolis should be adequate—a rich, fertile, and productive country surrounding it, with some great staple (which the world requires as a commodity) of exportation. A convenient harbor as an outlet and inlet, and natural facilities for improvement, are among the necessary requirements for such a location.

The Basis of a great Nation— national wealth

The basis of great nationality depends upon three elementary principles: first, territory; second, population; third, a great staple production either natural or artificial, or both, as a permanent source of wealth; and Africa comprises these to an almost unlimited extent. The continent is five thousand miles from Cape Bon (north) to the Cape of Good Hope (south), and four thousand at its greatest breadth, from Cape Guardifui (east) to Cape de Verde (west), with an average breadth ot two thousand five hundred miles, any three thousand of which within the tropics north and south, including the entire longitude, will produce the staple cotton, also sugar cane, coffee, rice, and all the tropical staples, with two hundred millions of *natives* as an industrial element to work this immense domain. The world is challenged to produce the semblance of a parallel to this. It has no rival in fact.

Advan- tageous location

Lagos, at the mouth of the Ogun river in the Bight of Benin, Gulf of Guinea, 6 deg. 31 min. west coast of Africa, 120 miles north-west of the Nun (one of the mouths of the great river Niger) is the place of our location. This was once the greatest slave-trading post on the west coast of Africa, and in possession of the Portuguese—the slavers entering Ako Bay, at the mouth of the Ogun river, lying quite inland, covered behind the island till a favorable opportunity ensued to escape with their cargoes of human beings for America. Wydah, the great slave-port of Dahomi, is but 70 or 80 miles west of Lagos. This city is most favorably located at the mouth of a river which during eight months in the year is a great thoroughfare for native produce, which is now brought down and carried up by native canoes and boats, and quite navigable up to Aro the port of Abbeokuta, a distance of eighty or a hundred miles, for light-draught steamers, such as at no distant day we shall have there. Ako Bay is an arm of the gulf, extending quite inland for three and a half miles, where it spreads out into a great sea, extending north ten to fifteen miles, taking a curve east and south, passing on in a narrow strip for two or three hundred miles, till it joins the Niger at the mouth of the Nun. It is the real harbor of Lagos, and navigable for light-draught vessels, as the Baltimore clippers and all other such slavers, formerly put into it; and Her Majesty's war-steamer Medusa has been in, and H. M.'s cruiser Brun lies continually in the bay opposite the Consulate.

Metropolis

This is the great outlet of the rich valley of the Niger by land, and the only point of the ocean upon which the intelligent and advanced Yorubas are settled. The commerce of this part is very great, being now estimated at ten million pounds sterling. Besides all the rich products, as enumerated in another section, palm oil* and ivory are among the great staple products of this rich country. But as every nation, to be potent must have some great source of wealth—which if not natural must be artificial—so Africa has that without which the workshops of Great Britain would become deserted, and the general commerce of the world materially reduced; and Lagos must not only become the outlet and point at which all this commodity must centre, but the great metropolis of this quarter of the world.

Trade of Lagos

The trade of this port now amounts to more than two millions of pounds sterling, or ten millions of dollars, there having been at times as many as sixty vessels in the roadstead.

The merchants and business men of Lagos are prin-

* Nine-tenths of all the Palm Oil of commerce goes from this point.

cipally native black gentlemen, there being but ten white houses in the place—English, German, French, Portuguese, and Sardinian—and all of the clerks are native blacks.

Buoys in the roadstead, lighthouses (two) and wharf improvements at the city in the bay, with steam-tugs or tenders to tow vessels over the Ogun bar-mouth or inlet, are all that we require to make Lagos a desirable seaport, with one of the safest harbors in the world for light-draught vessels.

The fish in these waters are very fine, and Ako is one of the finest natural oyster bays in the world. The shell-fish are generally of good size, frequently large, and finely flavored.

As a religious means, such a position must most largely contribute, by not only giving security to the Missionary cause, but by the actual infusion of a religious social element permanently among the natives of the country; and as a philanthropic, by a permanent check to the slave-trade, and also by its reflex influence on American slavery—not only thus far cutting off the supply, but also by superseding slavery in the growth and supply of those articles which comprise its great staple and source of wealth—thereby rendering slave labor *unprofitable and worthless,* as the succeeding section will show.

As to the possibility of putting a stop to the slave-trade, I have only to say, that we do not leave America and go to Africa to be passive spectators of such a policy as traffic in the flesh and blood of our kindred, nor any other species of the human race—more we might say— that we will not live there and permit it. "Self-preservation is the first law of nature," and we go to Africa to be *self-sustaining;* otherwise we have no business there, or anywhere else, in my opinion. We will bide our time; *but the Slave-trade shall not continue!*

Another important point of attention: that is, the

slave-trade ceases in Africa, wherever enlightened Christian civilization gains an influence. And as to the strength and power necessary, we have only to add, that Liberia, with a coast frontier of seven hundred miles, and a sparse population, which at the present only numbers fifteen thousand settlers, has been effective in putting a stop to that infamous traffic along her entire coast. And I here record with pleasure, and state what I know to be the fact, and but simple justice to as noble-hearted antagonists to slavery as live, that the Liberians are uncompromising in their opposition to oppression and the enslavement of their race, or any other part of the human family. I speak of them as a nation or people and ignore entirely their Iscariots, if any there be. What they have accomplished with less means, we, by the help of Providence, may reasonably expect to effect with more—what they did with little, we may do with much. And I speak with confidence when I assert, that if we in this new position but do and act as we are fondly looked to and expected—as I most fondly hope and pray God that, by a prudent, discretionate and well-directed course, dependant upon Him, we may, nay, I am certain we will do—I am sure that there is nothing that may be required to aid in the prosecution and accomplishment of this important and long-desired end, that may not be obtained from the greatest and most potent Christian people and nation that ever graced the world. There is no aid that might be wanted, which may not be obtained through a responsible, just, and equitable negotiation.

Means of doing it

There is some talk by Christians and philanthropists in Great Britain of subsidizing the King of Dahomi. I hope for the sake of humanity, our race, and the cause of progressive civilization, this most injurious measure of compensation for wrong, never will be resorted to nor attempted.

Subsidizing the King of Dahomi

To make such an offering just at a time when we are about to establish a policy of self-regeneration in Africa, which may, by example and precept, effectually check forever the nefarious system, and reform the character of these people, would be to offer inducements to that monster to continue, and a license to other petty chiefs to commence the traffic in human beings, to get a reward of subsidy.

SECTION XIII

COTTON STAPLE

Natural elements to produce cotton

Cotton grows profusely in all this part of Africa, and is not only produced naturally, but extensively cultivated throughout the Yoruba country. The soil, climate, and the people are the three natural elements combined to produce this indispensible commodity, and with these three natural agencies, no other part of the world can compete.

Africans the only reliable producers

In India there is a difficulty and great expense and outlay of capital required to obtain it. In Australia it is an experiment; and though it may eventually be obtained, it must also involve an immense outlay of capital, and a long time before an adequate supply can be had, as it must be admitted, however reluctantly by those desirous it should be otherwise, that the African, as has been justly said by a Manchester merchant, has in all ages, in all parts of the world, been sought to raise cotton wherever it has been produced.

Serious contingencies and uncertainty in American cotton supply

In America there are several serious contingencies which must always render a supply of cotton from that quarter problematical and doubtful, and always expensive and subject to sudden, unexpected and unjust advances in prices. In the first place, the land is purchased at large prices; secondly, the people to work it; thirdly, the expense of supporting the people, with the contingencies of sickness and death; fourthly, the uncertainty of climate and contingencies of frost, and a backward season and consequent late or unmatured crop; fifthly, insubordination on the part of the slaves, which is not improbable at any time; sixthly, suspension of friendly relations between the United States and Great Britain; and lastly, a rupture between the American States themselves, which I think no one will be disposed now to consider impossible. All, or any of these circumstances combined, render it impossible for America to compete with Africa in the growth and sale of cotton, for the following reasons:

Superior advantages of Africa over all other countries in the production of cotton

Firstly, landed tenure in Africa is free, the occupant selecting as much as he can cultivate, holding it so long as he uses it, but cannot convey it to another; secondly, the people all being free, can be hired at a price less than the *interest* of the capital invested in land and people to work it—they finding their own food, which is the custom of the country; thirdly, there are no contingencies of frost or irregular weather to mar or blight the crop; and fourthly, we have two regular crops a year, or rather one continuous crop, as while the trees are full of pods of ripe cotton, they are at the same time blooming with fresh flowers. And African cotton is planted only every seven years, whilst the American is replanted every season. Lastly, the average product per acre on the best Mississippi and Louisiana cotton plantations in America, is three hundred and fifty pounds; the average per acre in Africa, a hundred per cent more, or seven hundred pounds. As the African soil produces two crops a year to one in America, then we in Africa produce fourteen hundred pounds to three hundred and fifty in America; the cost of labor a hand being one dollar or four shillings a day to produce it; whilst in Africa at present it is nine hundred per cent less, being only ten cents or five pence a day for adult labor. At this price the native lives better on the abundance of produce in the country, and has more money left at the end of a week than the European or free American laborer at one dollar a day.

Cotton, as before stated, is the great commodity of the world, entering intimately into, being incorporated with almost every kind of fabric of wearing apparel. All kinds of woollen goods—cloths, flannels, alpacas, merinoes, and even silks, linen, nankin, ginghams, calicoes, muslins, cordages, ship-sails, carpeting, hats, hose, gloves, threads, waddings, paddings, tickings, every description of book and newspaper, writing paper, candle wicks, and what not, all depend upon the article cotton.

Importance of the African Race in the Social and Political Relations of the world

By this it will be seen and admitted that the African occupies a much more important place in the social and political element of the world than that which has heretofore been assigned him—holding the balance of commercial power, the source of the wealth of nations in his hands. This is indisputably true—undeniable, that cotton cannot be produced without negro labor and skill in raising it.

The African Race sustains Great Britain

Great Britain alone has directly engaged in the manufacture of pure fabrics from the raw material, five millions of persons; two-thirds more of the population depend upon this commodity indirectly for a livelihood. The population (I include in this calculation Ireland) being estimated at 30,000,000, we have then 25,000,000 of people, or five-sixths of the population of this great nation, depending upon the article cotton alone for subsistence, and the black man is the producer of the raw material, and the source from whence it comes. What an important fact to impart to the heretofore despised and underrated negro race, to say nothing of all the other great nations of Europe, as France, for instance, with her extensive manufactures of muslin delaines—which simply mean *cotton and wool*—more or less engaged in the manufacture and consumption of cotton.

The Negro race sustains the whites—able to sustain themselves

If the negro race—as slaves—can produce cotton as an *exotic* in foreign climes to enrich white men who oppress them, they can, they must, they will, they shall, produce it as an *indigene* in their own-loved native Africa

118

to enrich themselves, and regenerate their race; if a faithful reliance upon the beneficence and promise of God, and an humble submission to his will, as the feeble instruments in his hands through which the work is commenced, shall be available to this end.

The Liberians must as a policy as much as possible, patronise home manufactured, and home produced articles. Instead of using foreign, they should prefer their own sugar, molasses, and coffee, which is equal to that produced in any other country; and if not, it is the only way to encourage the farmers and manufacturers to improve them. The coffee of Liberia, is equal to any in the world, and I have drunk some of the native article, superior in strength and flavor to Java or Mocca, and I rather solicit competition in judgment of the article of coffee. And singular as it may appear, they are even supplied from abroad with spices and condiments, although their own country as also all Africa, is prolific in the production of all other articles, as allspice, ginger, pepper black and red, mustard and everything else. *Home Trade*

They must also turn their attention to supplying the Coast settlements with sugar and molasses, and everything else of their own production which may be in demand. Lagos and the Missionary stations in the interior, now consume much of these articles, the greater part of which—sugar and molasses—are imported from England and America. This trade they might secure in a short time without successful competition, because many of the Liberia merchants now own vessels, and the firm of Johnson, Turpin and Dunbar, own a fine little coasting steamer, and soon they would be able to undersell the foreigners; whilst at present their trade of these articles in America is a mere *favor* through the benevolence of some good hearted gentlemen, personal *friends* of theirs, who receive and dispose of them—sugar and molasses—at a price much above the market value, to encourage them. This can only last while these friends *Coast Trade* continue, when it must then cease. To succeed as a state or nation, we must become self-reliant, and thereby able to create our own ways and means; and a trade created *in* Africa *by* civilized Africans, would be a national rock of "everlasting ages."

Domestic Trade. Corn meal, Guinea corn and Yam flour

The domestic trade among the natives in the interior of our part of Africa—Yoruba—is very great. Corn meal, Guinea corn flour very fine, and a fine flour made of yams is plentiful in every market, and cooked food can always be had in great abundance from the women at refreshment stands kept in every town and along the highway every few miles when traveling.

Candy

Molasses candy or "taffy," is carried about and sold by young girls, made from the syrup of sugar cane, which does not differ in appearance and flavor from that of civilized countries.

Soap

Hard and soft soap are for sale in every market for domestic uses, made from lye by percolation or dripping of water through ashes in large earthen vessels or "hoppers."

Coloring and Dying. Making Indigo

Coloring and dying is carried on very generally, every woman seeming to understand it as almost a domestic necessity; also the manufacturing of indigo, the favorite and most common color of the country. Red comes next to this which is mostly obtained of camwood, another domestic employment of the women. Yellow is the next favorite color. Hence, blue, red, and yellow may be designated as the colors of Yoruba or Central Africa.

Weaving and cloth manufacturing; Leather

The manufactory of cotton cloth is carried on quite extensively among them; and in a ride of an hour through the city of Illorin, we counted one hundred and fifty-seven looms in operation in several different establishments. Beautiful and excellent leather is also manufactured, from which is made sandals, shoes, boots, bridles, saddles, harness-caparisons for horses, and other ornaments and uses. They all wear clothes of their own manufacture. The inhabitants of Abbeokuta are called

Egbas, and those of all the other parts of Yoruba are called Yorubas—all speaking the Egba language.

Our policy must be—and I hazard nothing in promulging it; nay, without this design and feeling, there would be a great deficiency of self-respect, pride of race, and love of country, and we might never expect to challenge the respect of nations—*Africa for the African race, and black men to rule them.* By black men I mean, men of African descent who claim an identity with the race.

So contrary to old geographical notions, Africa abounds with handsome navigable rivers, which during six or eight months in the year, would carry steamers suitably built. Of such are the Gallinos, St. Paul, Junk, and Kavalla of Liberia; the Ogun, Ossa, the great Niger and others of and contigious to Yoruba; the Gambia, Senegambia, Orange, Zambisi and others of other parts. The Kavalla is a beautiful stream which for one hundred miles is scarcely inferior to the Hudson of New York, in any particular; and all of them equal the rivers of the Southern States of America generally which pour out by steamers the rich wealth of the planting States into the Mississippi. With such prospects as these; with such a people as the Yorubas and other of the best type, as a constituent industrial, social, and political element upon which to establish a national edifice, what is there to prevent success? Nothing in the world.

The Governments in this part are generally Patriarchial, the Kings being elective from ancient Royal families by the Council of Elders, which consists of men chosen for life by the people, for their age, wisdom, experience, and service among them. They are a deliberative body, and all cases of great importance; of state, life and death, must be brought before them. The King as well as either of themselves, is subject to trial and punishment for misdemeanor in office, before the Council of Elders.

Lagos is the place of the family residence of that

excellent gentleman, Aji, or the Rev. Samuel Crowther, the native Missionary; and also his son-in-law Rev. T. B. Macaulay, who has an excellent school, assisted by his wife an educated native lady.

"Princes shall come out of Egypt; Ethiopia shall soon stretch out her hands unto God."—Ps. lxviii. 31. With the fullest reliance upon this blessed promise, I humbly go forward in—I may repeat—the grandest prospect for the regeneration of a people that ever was presented in the history of the world. The disease has long since been known; we have found and shall apply the remedy. I am indebted to Rev. H. H. Garnet, an eminent black clergyman and scholar, for the construction, that "soon," in the Scriptural passage quoted, "has reference to the period ensuing *from the time of beginning.*" With faith in the promise, and hope from this version, surely there is nothing to doubt or fear.

SECTION XIV

SUCCESS IN GREAT BRITAIN

Departure from Africa and arrival in England

Mr. Campbell and myself left Lagos on the 10th of April, per the British Royal Mail steam-ship Athenian, commander Lowrie, arriving in Liverpool May 12th, and in London on the 16th, having spent four days in the former place.

First Meeting

On Thursday, the 17th, by a note of invitation, we met a number of noblemen and gentlemen, interested in the progress of African Regeneration, in the parlour of Dr. Hodgkin, F.R.G.S., among whom were the Lord Alfred S. Churchill, Chairman; Right Hon. Lord Calthorpe; Hon. Mr. Ashley, brother of the Earl of Shaftesbury; Colonel Walker; Charles Buxton, Esq., M.P.; Rev. J. Baldwin Brown, A.B.; Rev. Samuel Minton, M.A.; Dr. Hodgkin, and others. By request of the noble chairman, I made a statement of our Mission to Africa, imparting to the first of their knowledge, our true position as independent of all other societies and organizations then in existence. Mr. Campbell also made some remarks.

Many subsequent meetings were held in various places, private and public, several of which were presided over by the Lord Alfred S. Churchill and Rt. Hon. Lord Calthorpe, at which I and Mr. Campbell both spoke; when in June an invitation was received by each of us from the "Committee of the National Club," to attend a "Company," on "Wednesday evening, June 27th, 1860, when information will be given on the Condition and Prospects of the African Race." The invitation (being the same as sent to all other persons) went on to state that, "Among others, Dr. Delany, of Canada West, and R. Campbell Esq., of Philadelphia, gentlemen of color, lately returned from an exploring tour in Central Africa, will take part in the proceedings."

Origin of the African Aid Society

This was the first great effective move in aid of our cause, though all other previous meetings were preliminary to it. At this, as at previous meetings, a full and thorough statement was made of our mission, several gentlemen taking part in the discussion.

Subsequently the following note was received—Mr. Campbell receiving a similar one—with the accompanying circular, referred to as the "enclosed paper":—
African Aid Society, 7, Adams Street, Strand, W.C.,

July 14th, 1860

DEAR SIR—The Provisional Committee of the above-named Society will feel obliged if you will kindly attend a meeting to be held at the Caledonian Hotel, Robert Street, Adelphi Terrace, on Thursday next, July 19th, to consider the enclosed paper, and to decide on a further course of action. Lord Alfred Churchill, M.P., will take the chair at half-past two o'clock.

I am, dear Sir, yours faithfully,

Dr. Delany.   WILLIAM CARDWELL, Hon. Sec.

At a meeting held at 7, Adams Street, on July 6th, 1860 (arising out of the proceedings of a *soiree*, which took place at the National Club, on the 27th of the previous month, when the subject of the "Condition and Prospects of the African Race" was discussed) present, Lord Alfred Churchill, M.P. in the chair; Lord Calthorpe; Sir C. E. Eardley, Bart; Joseph Ferguson, Esq., late M.P. for Carlisle; Rev. Mesac Thomas, Secretary of the Colonial Church and School Society; Rev. J. Davis; Rev. Samuel Minton, Minister of Percy Chapel; J. Lyons Macleod, Esq., late H.B.M.'s Consul at Mozambique; Rev. J. Baldwin Brown, Claylands Chapel; and Rev. W. Cardall, the following resolutions were unanimously passed:—

I. That it is desirable to form a Society, to be designated the 'African Aid Society.' II. That the noblemen now present be a Provisional Committee of such Society, with power to add to their number; and that Lord Alfred Churchill, M.P., be requested to be Chairman. III. That Sir C. E. Eardley, Bart., J. Lyons Macleod, Esq., the Rev. S. Minton, and the Rev. J. Baldwin Brown, be a Sub-Committee to prepare a draft statement of the proposed objects of the Society, and rules for its government.

At a subsequent meeting of the Committee, on a report of the Sub-Committee, the statement of objects and rules was adopted, which is given above.

What black men want

The contents of this paper had been fully and fairly discussed at a previous meeting to which myself and colleague were honored with an invitation, when I then and there, fully, openly, and candidly stated to the noblemen and gentlemen present what was desired and what we did not; that we desired to be dealt with as men, and not children. That we did not desire gratuities as such in the apportioning of their benevolence—nothing eleemosynary but means *loaned* to our people upon their *personal obligations, to be paid in produce or otherwise.* That we did not approve of *restriction* as to *where* such persons went (so that it was to some country where the population was mainly colored, as that was our policy) letting each choose and decide *for himself,* that which was *best for him.*

To these sentiments the noblemen and gentlemen all cordially and heartily agreed, establishing their society, as we understand it, expressly to aid the *voluntary* emigration of colored people from America in general, and our movement as originated by colored people in particular. Indeed, I here now say, as I did then and there, that I would give nothing for it, were it not a self-reliant project, originating with ourselves. The following completes the doings of the gentlemen in London. I should have remarked, that at many of these meetings, especially that at White Hall on the 27th day of June, and that of the 19th July, and the preliminary ones above referred to, the respected President of our Council, Wm. Howard Day, Esq., M.A., was present. For some of the important preliminary meetings, he and Rev. D'Arcy Irvine kindly made arrangements.

Primary objects of the African Aid Society

AFRICAN AID SOCIETY

7,* ADAMS STREET, STRAND, W.C., LONDON

PRESIDENT

VICE-PRESIDENTS

*The Right Hon. Lord Calthorpe.

The Rt. Rev. the Bishop of Sierra Leone.

COUNCIL

*The Lord Alfred Churchill, M.P., F.R.G.S., Chairman of the Executive Committee

Ashley, Hon. Wm., St. James's Palace.

Bagnall, Thomas, Esq., J. P., Great Barr, near Birmingham.

*Brown, Rev. J. Baldwin, B.A., 150, Albany Street.

Bullock, Edward, Esq., Handsworth, near Birmingham.

*Cardall, Rev. Wm., M.A., Sec., of the Evangelical Alliance.

Clegg, Thomas, Esq., Manchester.

*Davis, Rev. James, Sec. of the Evangelical Alliance.

* Now 8 Adolphi Terrace, Strand.

125

STATEMENT OF OBJECTS AND RULES

I. That the name of the Society be the "African Aid Society."

II. That its chief objects shall be to develop the material resources of Africa, Madagascar, and the adjacent Islands; and to promote the Christian civilization of the African races; as by these means the Society believes that the annihilation of the Slave Trade will ultimately be accomplished.

III. That for the attainment of these objects it will strive to employ the following and other suitable means:—

1. Encourage the production of cotton, silk, indigo, sugar, palm oil, &c., by the introduction of skilled labor, African or European, into those parts of the earth which are inhabited by the African race.

2. Assist, by loans or otherwise, Africans willing to emigrate from Canada and other parts to our West Indian Colonies, Liberia, Natal, and Africa generally, or to any countries that may offer a suitable field of labor.

3. Form Industrial Missions in harmony, where practicable, with the agency already established for the extension of Christianity in Africa.

4. Supply (as occasion may require) suitable Mechanical and Agricultural Implements for the use of the same.

5. Procure samples of every kind of native produce, for the purpose of submitting the same to the mercantile and manufacturing communities of this country, with a view to the promotion of legitimate commerce.

6. Encourage and assist exploring expeditions into the interior of Africa and Madagascar.

IV. That Subscribers of not less than Half a Guinea annually be Members of this Society, during the continuance of their subscriptions; that the subscriptions be payable in advance, and be considered due at the commencement of each year; that Donors of Ten Guineas and Collectors of Twenty Guineas be Life Members.

V. That the management of the Society be vested in a Patron, Vice-Patrons, President, Vice-Presidents, and a Council consisting of not less than Twenty Members.

VI. That a general Meeting of the Members of the Society be held in London in the spring of each year, when the financial statement shall be presented, and the Council elected for the year ensuing, who shall appoint an Executive Committee to conduct the business of the Society.

VII. That the Honorary and Corresponding Members may be nominated by the Council.

VIII. That any funded property of the Society be invested in the names of three Trustees, to be chosen by the Council, and that all orders for payments on account of the Society be signed by two Members of the Executive Committee and the Secretary.

IX. That the accounts of the Society be audited annually by a professional auditor, to be chosen by the General Meeting.

X. That the Council shall have power to appoint such officers and assistants as they shall deem necessary for the efficient conduct of the affairs of the Society, subject to the approval of the next Annual Meeting.

XI. That the Council shall have power to convene Special General Meetings of the Members of the Society when necessary.

XII. That no alteration shall be effected in the constitution of the Society, except at the Annual Meeting, or at a Special General Meeting convened for the purpose on the requisition of Twenty Members.

In furtherance of the objects of this Society, the Executive Committee, with the generous aid of friends to this movement, have already assisted Dr. Delany and Professor Campbell (two colored gentlemen from America) with funds to enable them to continue their labors and to lay before the colored people of America the reports of the Pioneer Exploration Expedition into Abbeokuta, in West Africa, from which they have lately returned.

A correspondence has already been opened with

Jamaica, Lagos in West Africa, Natal, the United States of America, and "The Fugitive-Aid Society"—which for the last *ten years* has been receiving and instructing fugitive Africans in agricultural and other pursuits on the Elgin settlement—at Buxton, Canada West.

The assistance of all friends to Christianity, Freedom, and lawful Commerce, as opposed to the Slave Trade and Slavery, is earnestly solicited.

"COTTON IS KING! IN AMERICA"
"COTTON IS BREAD! IN ENGLAND"

The free colored people of America are said to be looking forward to their ultimate removal from the United States, and are anxiously seeking for locations suitable for their final settlement in Africa or other intertropical regions; where they may obtain that freedom which is the inherent right of man, and by their industry acquire adequate independence.

The African Aid Society has been formed to assist this movement, and to annihilate the slave trade, by encouraging the development of the resources of those countries inhabited by the African races generally, as well as to cause African free labor to supersede African slavery and degradation.

In Canada West no less than 45,000 colored persons, flying from slavery, have now taken refuge; willing to meet the rigors of the climate, so that they are assured of personal freedom under the aegis of the British flag. From the enactments lately made in some States of the Union, for the purpose of compelling all the free people of color either to leave the country or to be again reduced to a state of slavery, a considerable addition will, no doubt, shortly be made to the number of those who have already found their way to Canada; while, from physical causes, Canada can be looked upon by the colored only as a "CITY OF REFUGE."

Great Britain has for half a century been employing physical force for the suppression of the slave trade, which after the expenditure of upwards of forty millions sterling, and the noble sacrifice of the lives of some of the best and bravest of her sons, still exists. It is but just to state that the exportation of slaves from Africa has been reduced from 150,000 to 50,000 per annum, by the persevering effort of those who are opposed to a traffic disgraceful to Christianity.

Is the ultimate object of those who are opposed to this traffic its suppression or its annihilation? The annihilation of the slave trade and slavery in Africa was unquestionably the aim of the philanthropists who originated this great movement.

The experience of half a century has proved that physical force cannot destroy the traffic while there is a demand for slave labor. Diplomacy must be baffled in its well-intentioned efforts to oppose this traffic while the profits for carrying each slave from the continent of Africa to the island of Cuba amount to the enormous return of fourteen hundred per cent.

It is a well-attested fact, that the same quality of cotton may be obtained from Africa for twenty millions of money for which Great Britain pays the slaveholders in America thirty millions per annum. If cotton can be sold in the Liverpool market at anything less than 4¾d. per lb., the slaveholders in America will cease to grow what, under altered circumstances, would be unprofitable. Cotton of middling quality (which is in the greatest demand) may be obtained in West and Eastern Africa at 4d. per lb.; and, already, cotton from Western Africa (Liberia) has been sent to Liverpool, there re-shipped, and sold at Boston, in the United States, at a less cost than cotton of a similar quality could be supplied from the Southern States of the Union.

The Executive Committee feel assured that the peaceful means adopted by this society for the Christian

civilization of the African races require only the advo-
cacy of *Christian Ministers* and the *Press* generally to
be responded to by the people of Great Britain.

The horrors of the slave trade, as perpetrated on the
continent of Africa and during the middle passage, can
only be put an end to by the establishment of a lawful
and a lucrative, a powerful and a permanent, trade between this country and Africa; which will have the effect
of destroying the slave trade, spreading the Gospel of
Christ, and civilizing the African races. For this purpose
the support of the mercantile class is earnestly solicited
for a movement which—commenced by the colored people
of America flying from oppression—bids fair to open new
cotton fields for the supply of British industry, and new
markets for our commerce, realizing the sublime promise
of Scripture, "Cast thy bread upon the waters, and after
many days it shall return unto thee."

Alarmists point to the sparks in the cotton fields of
America, while thoughtful men reflect that the commercial prosperity of this great country hangs upon a thread
of cotton, which a blight of the plant, an insurrection
among the slaves, an untimely frost, or an increased demand in the Northern States of the Union, might destroy; bringing to Lancashire first, and then to the whole
kingdom, a return of the Irish famine of 1847, which reduced the population of that portion of the kingdom
from eight to six millions.

The Southern States of the American Union are following the example of the infatuated Louis the Four-
teenth of France. As he drove into exile thousands of his
subjects engaged in manufactures and trade, who sought
refuge in England and laid the foundation of our manufacturing supremacy, so are the Slave States now driving
from their confines thousands of freed colored men.
Where are the exiles to go? The Free States are too

crowded, and Canada too cold for them. Can we not offer them an asylum in Jamaica and other colonies? They are the cream, the best of their race; for it is by long-continued industry and economy that they have been enabled to purchase their freedom, and joyfully will they seize the hand of deliverance which Great Britain holds out to them. We only want additional labor; give us that, and we shall very soon cultivate our own cotton.—*Slavery Doomed.*

FUGITIVE-AID SOCIETY IN CANADA

At a meeting held in the Town Hall, Manchester, on the 8th of August inst., the following remarks were made by Thomas Clegg, Esq., who presided on the occasion.

The Chairman said that they held but one opinion as to the horrors and evils of slavery; and he thought that most of them believed that one of the great benefits which would result from Africans trained in Canada being sent to Africa, would be that they could there, for the advantage of themselves and their country, grow cotton, sugar, and fifty other articles, which we much needed. During his first year's operations in getting cotton from Africa, all his efforts only purchased 235 lbs.; but in 1858, he got 219,615 lbs.; and he saw from one of the London papers of the previous day, that not less than 3,447 bales, or 417,087 lbs., were received from the West Coast during 1860. This rapid increase, in the early history of the movement, showed that Africa was the place that could grow cotton, and that Africans were the men who ought to grow it. (Hear, hear.) There was no part of Africa, of which he had heard, where cotton did not grow wild; there was no part of the world, except India, perhaps, in which cotton was cultivated, where it was not sought to obtain Africans as cultivators. Wild African cotton was worth from 1½d. to 2¼d. a pound more than the wild produce of India; cultivated cotton from the West Coast was worth, on an average, as much as New Orleans possibly could be. (Hear, hear.) He would undertake that good African cotton could be laid down free in Liverpool at 4¼d. per pound; that it should be equal to New Orleans; and at this moment such cotton was worth probably 6¼d. per pound. (Hear, hear.) He looked upon this question as affecting not only the success of missions, but as affecting also the eternal welfare of the Africans and the temporal welfare of our people.

HEATHEN AND SLAVE-TRADE HORRORS

At Lagos, communication between the town and the shipping had been suspended for ten days, in consequence of the high surf at the entrance of the river and along the beach, and great difficulty was experienced in getting off the mails. The war in the interior, between the chiefs of Ibadan and Ijaye, continued with unabated fury; the former district is said to contain 100,000 inhabitants, and the latter 50,000. Abbeokuta had taken side with Ijaye, but at the last battle, which took place on the 5th of June, his people are reported to have suffered severely. The King of Dahomey was about to make an immense sacrifice of human life to the memory of the late King, his father. The *West African Herald*, of the 13th ult., referring to this intention, says: His Majesty Badahung, King of Dahomey, is about to make the 'Grand Custom' in honor of the late King Gezo. Determined to surpass all former monarchs in the magnitude of the ceremonies to be performed on this occasion, Badahung has made the most extensive preparations for the celebration of the Grand Custom. A great pit has been dug which is to contain human blood enough to float a canoe. Two thousand persons will be sacrificed on this occasion. The expedition to Abbeokuta is postponed, but the King has sent his army to make some excursions at the expense of some weaker tribes, and has succeeded in capturing many unfortunate creatures. The young people among these prisoners will be sold into slavery, and the old persons will be killed at the Grand Custom. Would to God this might meet the eyes of some of those philanthropic Englishmen who have some feeling for Africa! Oh! for some man of eloquence and influence to point out to the people of England the comparative uselessness of their expensive squadron out here, and the enormous benefits that must result to this country, and ultimately to England herself, morally and materially, if she would extend her establishments on this coast! Take away two-thirds of your squadron, and spend one-half its cost in creating more stations on shore, and greatly strengthening your old stations.—*The Times,* August 13, 1860.

The following extract from the *Times,* August 11, 1860, shows that noble hearts across the Atlantic are ready to respond to our call:—

A NOBLE LADY.—Miss Cornelia Barbour, a daughter of the Hon. James Barbour, of Virginia, formerly Governor of that State, and a Member of President J. Q. Adams' Cabinet, has resolved to emancipate her numerous slaves, and locate them in a Free State, where they can enjoy liberty and (if they will) acquire property.—*New York Tribune.*

☞ *Contributions to the Funds of this Society may be paid to the Chairman, the Hon. Secretary, or to the Society's account at the London and Westminster Bank, 1, St. James's square. P.O. Orders to be made payable to the Honorary Secretaries at Charing-cross.*—AUGUST, 1860.

The subjoined paper has been issued by the African Aid Society, London, England, which I give for the benefit of those desirous of going out under its auspices, as it will be seen that the Society is determined on guarding well against aiding such persons as are objectionable to us, and likely to be detrimental to our scheme:

AFRICAN AID SOCIETY
PAPER FOR INTENDING SETTLERS IN AFRICA

1. Are you desirous to leave   and go to the Land of your Forefathers. 2. Name. 3. Age. 4. Married or Single. 5. What Children (state ages:) Boys   , aged   years; Girls   , aged   years. 6. How many of these will you take with you? 7. Of what church are you a member? 8. How long have you been so? 9. Can you read and write? 10. Will you strive to spread the truths of the Gospel among the natives? 11. What work are you now doing? 12. What other work can you do well? 13. Have you worked on a plantation? 14. What did you do there?   15. Will you, in the event of the African Aid Society sending you and your family to Africa, repay to it the sum of   Dollars, as part of the cost of your passage and settlement there   , as soon as possible, that the same money may assist others to go there also?

N.B.—It is expected that persons desiring to settle in Africa, under the auspices of this society, should obtain Certificates from their Minister, and if possible from their Employer, or other competent person, as to their respectability, habits, and character. These certificates should be attached to this paper.

I have every confidence in the sincerity of the Christian gentlemen who compose the African Aid Society, and for the information of those who are unacquainted with the names of those noblemen and gentlemen, would state that the Lord Alfred Churchill is the learned Oriental traveler and Christian philanthropist, brother to His Grace the Duke of Marlborough and son-in-law of Right Hon. Lord Calthorpe; Right Hon. Lord Calthorpe is the great Christian nobleman who does so much for Churches in Great Britain, and member of Her Majesty's Privy Council; Sir Culling Eardley Eardley is the great promoter of the Evangelical Alliance; George Thompson, Esq., is the distinguished traveler and faithful friend of the slave, known in America as a Garrisonian Abolitionist; and J. Lyons Macleod, Esq., the indefatigable British Consul who so praiseworthily exerted himself, and brought the whole of his official power to bear against the slave-trade on the Mozambique Channel. There are other gentlemen of great distinction, whose positions are not explained in the council list, and a want of knowledge prevents my explaining.

Before leaving England for Scotland, I received while at Brighton, the following letter, which indicates somewhat the importance of our project, and shows, in a measure, the superiority of the people in our part of Africa, and what may be expected of them compared with some in other parts; and how the Portuguese influence has ruined them. I may add, that the writer, Mr. Clarence, is a gentleman of respectability, brother-in-law to Edmund Fry, Esq., the distinguished Secretary of the London Peace Society. Mr. Clarence has resided in that part of Africa for twenty-five years, and was then on a visit to his relatives:

DR. DELANY: Brighton, August 28, 1860

MY DEAR SIR—I am sorry that I am obliged to leave Brighton before you deliver your lectures, and as we may not meet again, I thought I would write you a few lines just to revive the subject that was passing our minds yesterday. I cannot but think, if it were practicable for a few thousands, or even hundreds, of your West Coast men to come round to the East Coast, that is, to Port Natal, an immense amount of good would be derived therefrom; not only in assisting to abolish the barbarous customs of our natives in showing them that labor is honorable for man, but that the English population would appreciate their services, and that they would be able to get good wages. What we want is constant and reliable laborers; not those who come by fits and starts, just to work for a month and then be off. They must select their masters, and then make an engagement for twelve months; or it might be after a month on approval. Good laborers could get fifteen shillings per month, and as their services increased in value they would get twenty shillings, and their allowance of food, which is always abundant.

I have thought that some might work their passage down to the Cape of Good Hope in some of Her Majesty's Men-of-War, and from there they might work their passage in some of the coasting vessels that are continually plying backwards and forwards. My farm is only five miles from the Port. Should any ever come from your representations, direct them to me, and should I not require them myself I will give them such information as may lead them to find good masters. I have always said that Natal is the key to the civilization of South Africa; but, however, there are sometimes two keys to a door, and yours on the West, though a little north of the Line, may be the other; and, by God's blessing, I trust that the nations of the East and West may, before long, meet in Central Africa, not in hostile array, as African nations always have done, but in the bonds of Christian fellowship. Wishing you every success in your enterprize,

Believe me, dear Sir, yours most sincerely,

RALPH CLARENCE

NOTE.—Mr. Clarence is requesting to be sent some of our industrious natives from Western Africa, as he informed me that those in the East think it disreputable to work. The term "master" is simply English; it means employer. The "fifteen" and "twenty" referred to, means shillings sterling.

SECTION XV

COMMERCIAL RELATIONS IN SCOTLAND

I have only to add, as a finality of my doings and mission in Great Britain, that in Scotland I fully succeeded in establishing commercial relations for traffic in all kinds of native African produce, especially cotton, which businesses are to be done directly and immediately between us and them, without the intervention or agencies of any society or association whatever. The only agencies in the case are to be the producers, sellers, and buyers— the Scottish house dealing with us as men, and not children. These arrangements are made to facilitate, and give us the assurance of the best encouragement to prosecute vigorously commercial enterprises—especially, as before stated, the cotton culture—the great source of wealth to any people and all civilized nations. *Commercial relations*

The British people have the fullest confidence in our integrity to carry out these enterprises successfully, *Business integrity* and now only await our advent there, and commencement to do anything necessary we may desire, or that the circumstances justify. Each individual is regarded as a man in these new relations, and, as such, expected to make his own contracts according to business custom, discharging in like manner his individual obligations. It must here be expressly understood that there are to be nothing but *business relations* between us, their entire confidence and dependence being in the self-reliant, independent transactions of black men themselves. We are expected, and will be looked for, to create our own ways and means among ourselves as other men do.

Public endorsement

As an earnest of the estimate set upon our adventure, I subjoin the names of a number of the leading commercial British journals—the two first being English, and all the others Scottish, in the midst of manufacturing districts, and all speaking favorably of the project:

The Leeds Mercury, the Newcastle Daily Chronicle, the Glasgow Herald, the Glasgow Examiner, the Scottish Guardian, the North British Daily Mail, the Glasgow Morning Journal, the Mercantile Advertiser, and others. (For absence of these notices, see author's prefatory note.)

FROM THE DAILY CHRONICLE

Newcastle-on-Tyne, Monday, September 17th, 1860

DANGER AND SAFETY—* * * The cotton of the United States affords employment to upwards of three millions of people in England, and a famine of cotton would be far worse than a famine of bread; the deficiency of the latter could be supplied; but the destruction of the cotton crop in America would be an evil of unparalleled magnitude, and against which we have no present protection. * * From the district of Lagos on the Gold coast, near the kingdom of Dahomey, there comes amongst us Dr. Delany with promises of a deeply interesting exposition of the prospects of Africa, and the probabilities of the civilization and elevation of the black races. He is a *bona fide* descendant of one of the elite families of Central Africa, a highly educated gentleman, whose presence at the International Statistical Congress was noticed by Lord Broughham, and whose remarks in the sanitary section of the Congress upon epidemics were characterized by a great knowledge of the topic combined with genuine modesty. He is a physician of African blood, educated in America, who has revisted the lands of his ancestry, and proposes a most reasonable and feasible plan to destroy the slave trade, by creating a *cordon,* or fringe of native civilization, through which the kidnappers could not penetrate from without, and through which no slaves could be transported from within. Dr. Delany is one of the Commissioners sent out by the convention of the colored people of Canada and the United States. He has recently returned from the Yoruba country, adjoining the territory of the King of Dahomey, and desires to elicit a favorable consideration for the African Aid Society. His explorations have been productive of the most promising results, his fellow-blacks having everywhere received him with distinguished honors. His anecdotes are interesting, and his lectures are illustrated by specimens of native produce and manufactures highly curious. Of his lectures at Brighton and other places we have read lengthy reports, which represent the influence these addresses have produced, and which speak in eulogistic terms of Dr. Delany's matter and manner. The subject is one of vast importance to England, and we trust that we may witness ere long a proper appreciation of it.

FROM THE GLASGOW HERALD

All this betokens a considerable degree of intelligence. The towns had their market-places; in one of these, that of Ijaye, Dr. Delany saw many thousands of persons assembled, and carrying on a busy traffic. What a field might thus, in the course of time, be opened for European commerce.

FROM THE LEEDS MERCURY (ENGLAND)

Published by E. Baines, Esq., M.P., and Sons, December 8th, 1860

ELEVATION OF THE COLORED RACE, AND OPENING OUT OF THE RESOURCES OF AFRICA.—An important movement for opening out the resources of a vast portion of the continent of Africa has been made by some of the most intelligent colored people of the United States and Canada. Having formed a society with this object in view, among others, Dr. Delany and

Professor Campbell were commissioned to go out and explore a considerable portion of Western Africa, near to the mouths of the Niger, and not far from the equator. A report of this expedition is in progress by Dr. Delany, who is himself so fully convinced of the advantages which the rich resources of that part of Africa offer, that he has concluded to remove his family there immediately. A meeting of the Leeds Anti-Slavery Committee was held on Wednesday night, Wm. Scholefield, Esq., in the chair, when valuable information was communicated by Dr. Delany and William Howard Day, Esq., M.A., from Canada, who is connected with this movement. The following summary of their remarks will be found of deep interest:—

Wm. Howard Day, M.A., having been called upon, pointed out the necessity for an active anti-slavery organization in this country, as was so well expressed by the Chairman, to keep the heart of the English people warm upon the subject of human bondage. * * By the production of cotton slavery began to be a power. So that as the cotton interest increased the testimony of the Church decreased. Cotton now is three-fifths of the production of the South. So that the Hon. Amasa Walker, formerly Republican Secretary of State for the State of Massachusetts, at the meeting held in London, August 1, 1859, and presided over by Lord Brougham, really expressed the whole truth when he said—"While cotton is fourteen cents per pound slavery will never end." Now we propose to break the back of this monopoly in America by raising in Africa—in the African's own home—as well as in the West Indies, cotton of the same quality as the American, and at a cheaper rate. It had been demonstrated by Mr. Clegg, of Manchester, that cotton of superior quality could be laid down at Liverpool cheaper from Africa than America. We have sent my friend, Dr. Delany, to see what Africa is, and he will tell you the results—so very favorable—of his exploration. Then we feel that we have in Canada the colored men to pioneer the way—men reared among the cotton of the United States, and who have found an asylum among us. The bone and sinew is in Africa—we wish to give it direction. We wish thereby to save to England millions of pounds by the difference in price between the two cottons; we wish to ward off the blow to England which must be felt by four millions of people interested in the article to be produced if an untimely frost or an insurrection should take place—and, above all, to lift up Africa by means of her own children. After speaking of the organization among the colored people, which sent out Dr. Delany, and of which Mr. Day is president, he said one of the means to secure these ends was the establishment of a press upon a proper footing in Canada among the fugitive slaves; and to collect for that is now his especial work. It would aid powerfully, it was hoped, in another way. Already American prejudice has rolled in upon the borders of Canada—so that schoolhouse doors are closed in the faces of colored children, and colored men denied a place upon juries merely because of their color. It was with difficulty that last year even in Canada they were able to secure the freedom of a kidnapped little boy who was being dragged through the province to be sold in the slave-mart of St. Louis. In view of all these points. hastily presented, he asked the good will and active aid of all the friends of liberty.

Dr. M. R. Delany, whose name has become so celebrated in connection with the Statistical Congress, was invited to state what he had contemplated in going to Africa, and if he would kindly do so, what he had discovered there. Dr. Delany first dwelt upon the expectation which had been raised in his mind when a young man, and in the minds of the colored people of the United States, by the beginning of the anti-slavery work there by William Lloyd Garrison and his coadjutors. They had found, however, that all the anti-slavery people were not of the stamp of Mr. Garrison, who, he was proud to say, believed in giving to colored men just the same rights and privileges as to others, and that Mr. Garrison's idea had not, by the professed friends of the black man, been reduced to practice. And finding that self-reliance was the best dependence, he and others had struck out a path for themselves. After speaking of the convention of colored people, which he and others called in 1854, to consider this subject of self-help, and of the general organization which began then, and in which Mr. Day succeeded him as president, he said he went to Africa to find a locality suitable for a select emigration of colored people; if possible, a large cotton-growing region, and with a situation accessible by civilization. All this he had found, with, in addition, a well-disposed and industrious people. The facts which Dr. Delany grouped together as to the climate and soil; as to productions and trade; as to the readiness of the people to take hold of these higher ideas; and as to the anxiety of the people to have him and his party return, were new and thrilling. An interesting conversation ensued on the points brought forward, and the following minute, moved by Mr. Wilson

Armistead, and seconded by the Rev. Dr. Brewer, was unanimously passed:—

That the thanks of this meeting be tendered to Dr. Delany and Wm. Howard Day, Esq., for the valuable information received from them, with an ardent desire that their plans for the elevation of their race may be crowned with success, and it is the opinion of this meeting that they be made materially to hasten the extinction of the slave-trade and slavery.

Character of Commercial Relations

The commercial relations entered into in Scotland are with the first business men in the United Kingdom, among whom are Henry Dunlop, Esq., Ex-Lord Provost of Glasgow, one of the largest proprietors in Scotland; Andrew Stevenson, Esq., one of the greatest cotton dealers; and Messrs. Crum, Graham & Co., 111 Virginia Place, Glasgow, one of the heaviest firms in that part of the old world, which is the house with which I have negotiated for an immediate, active and practical prosecution of our enterprise, and whose agency in Europe for any or all of our produce, may be fully relied on. I speak from personal acquaintance with these extensively-known, high-standing gentlemen.

Reliable Arrangements

One of the most important parts of such an adventure as this, is to have reliable Foreign Agencies, and these have been fully secured; as whilst these gentlemen, as should all business men, deal with us only on business terms, yet they have entered into the matter as much as Christians and philanthropists, to see truth and right prevail whereby humanity may be elevated, as for anything else; because they are already wealthy, and had they been seeking after wealth, they certainly could and would have sought some more certainly immediate means.

I left Scotland December 3d, and sailed from Liverpool the 13th via Londonderry, arriving at Portland the 25th, the epoch of the Christian Era, and in Chatham the 29th.

SECTION XVI

THE TIME TO GO TO AFRICA

The best time for going to Africa is during "the rainy season," which commences about the middle or last of April, ending near or about the first of November. By going during this period, it will be observed that you have no sudden transition from cold to heat, as would be the case did you leave in cold weather for that country. But the most favorable time to avoid the *heavy surf* at Lagos, is from the first of October to the first of April, when the surges in the roadstead are comparatively small and not imminently dangerous. And I here advise and caution all persons intending to land there, not to venture over the heavy-rolling surf of the bar in one of those native canoes.

Yet persons can land with safety at any season of the year; but for this there must be a proper boat. Any person going there at present ought not to land if the surf is high, without *Captain Davies' large sail-boat,* which is as safe as a tug, and rides the sea like a swan. Send him word to send his *largest boat at the best hour for landing.* The Captain is a native merchant, and most obliging gentleman.

So soon as we get a Tender (called in America, steam-tug and tow-boat), which will be one of the first things done so soon as we get to Lagos, landing will be as safe at any and all times there as in the harbor at New York or Liverpool. For the information of many intelligent persons who are not aware of it, I would state that a pilot or tender has to take vessels into both of these great seaports on account of shoal water.*

The rainy season usually thought by foreigners to be "wet, muddy, and disagreeable weather," so far from

* I have received information from London, that an iron steam Tender has already been sent out to Lagos by an English house.

Caution against danger

Safety in Landing

A Tender

Rainy Season

The Niger Valley

this, is the most agreeable season of the year. Instead of steady rains for several days incessantly, as is common during "rainy weather" in the temperate zones, there is seldom or never rain during a whole day. But every day to a certainty during this season it rains, sometimes by showers at intervals, and sometimes a heavy rain for one, two, or three hours at a time—but seldom so long as three hours—when it clears up beautifully, leaving an almost cloudless sky. The rains usually come up very suddenly, and as quickly cease when done.

Drizzling rain, sudden showers

There is seldom or never such a thing in this part of Africa as a "drizzling" or mizzling rain, all suddenly coming on and as suddenly passing off; and should one be out and see indications of an approaching rain, they must hurry to a near shelter, so suddenly does the shower come on.

Tornadoes

Tornadoes are sudden gusts or violent storms of wind and rain, which are more or less feared, but which may always be known from other storms on their aproach, by the blackness of the clouds above, with the *segment of a circle* of *lighter cloud* just beneath the dark, and above the horizon.

Summer

The entire *wet* season may be justly termed the *summer* instead of "winter," as the old writers have it; and it is observable that at the commencement of Spring in the temperate zones (March) vegetation starts forth in Africa with renewed vigor.

Winter

Winter is during the *dry* season, and not the "wet," for the above reason; and it is also worthy of remark, that during autumn in the temperate zone (from October to the last of November) the foliage in Africa begins to fade and fall from the trees in large quantities.

Harmattans

It is during this season that the *harmattans* prevail, (from two to three weeks in December) which consist of a *dry cold* and *not* a "dry hot" wind as we have been taught; when furniture and wooden-ware *dries* and *cracks* for want of moisture, and the thermometer frequently rates as low as 54 deg. Fahr. in the evening and early in the morning; when blankets on the bed will not be out of place, and an evening and morning fire may add to your comfort.

———

SECTION XVII

CONCLUDING SUGGESTIONS

Native mariners

It may not be generally known as a fact, which is of no little importance in the industrial economy of Africa, that vessels of every class, of all foreign nations, are manned and managed by native Africans, so soon as they enter African waters.

The Krumen are the watermen or marines generally of Africa, going in companies of greater or less numbers, with one in the lead called "headman," who, hiring all the others, makes contracts with a vessel, which is met outside of the roadsteads or harbors, to supply a certain number of men to manage it during her coasting voyage. They usually bring with them the recommendations of all the commanders whose vessels they have managed on the coast. These are generally carried in the hat to prevent getting wet, and sometimes in calabashes, stopped up like a bottle, or in a tin can or case, (when such can be obtained,) suspended by a string like a great square medal around the neck.

So expert have these people become in marine affairs, that, with the exception of navigation, a vessel at sea might be managed entirely by many of those companies of Krumen. Everything that is to be done as the common work of seamen, is done by them during their engagement on the coasting vessels. The agility with which they scale the shrouds and rigging, mounting frequently to the very pinnacle of the main-mast head, or going out to the extreme end of the yard arms, is truly surprising. In these feats, they are far more dextrous than the white civilians.

The Fever—
Stages of
In cases of real intermittent fever—fever and ague or chills and fever—there are usually three distinct stages when the attack comes on—on what is usually termed *fever day:* the *cold* or shivering stage, the *hot* or burning stage, succeeded by the *sweating.*

Cold stage

So soon as there are symptoms of a chill, a cup of quite hot ginger or cinnamon tea—not too strong—may be taken, the person keeping out of the sun, and, if inclined, going to bed and covering warmly. He should always undress, putting on a night-shirt or gown, for the convenience of changing when required. A hot cup of tea, of any kind, is better than nothing, when neither cinnamon nor ginger is convenient.

Kneading or
Friction-
bath. Hot
stage

During the hot stage, the person must be kept as cool as possible, and when the fever is at its height—and, indeed, it is well to commence long before this—the entire person, from head to foot, should be continually bathed by a free application of cold water, used *plentifully* and *frequently changed* during the application, with a large sponge, napkin, or cloth of some kind.

Lime-bath

An excellent addition to the water is the juice of limes or lemons, and *less* of the first (lime) than the last is required, because of the superior strength of the one to the other.

Soda

Soda may also be used in the bath as an adjuvant to the water—not with the lime juice, of course, because they would effervesce or disagree. When lime or lemon juice is used, care should be taken, in the use of it, that it be not too strong: say, use two lemons, or one and a half limes if large, to a pail of water—as it will produce irritation on all of the tender parts of the person, and even over the general surface. A lime bath once or twice a week, in the absence of all fever, is said to be an excellent hygeian or prophylactic treatment. But, by all means, don't neglect the cold water application during the hot stage.

So soon as the sweating commences, the patient must *Sweating* have sufficient covering to prevent taking cold, which is *stage* then very readily done, in consequence of the general relaxation of the system and open state of the pores. When the sweating ceases, the shirt or gown must be immediately taken off, the entire person sponged off in clear lukewarm or air-cold water, fresh clean clothes put on, the sheets and wet bed-clothes removed by clean ones supplying their places; and in no case must a person ever be permitted to keep on the same clothes after the sweating stage, as the *virus* or fever-poison is expelled through the medium of the sweat and pores, and consequently absorbed by the clothing. The clothes should be changed *every day,* whether there be perspiration or not.

Either of these symptoms is to be treated as advised, *All the stages* independently of the other in the order of arrangement.

Persons should be careful not to sleep in sweaty *Fatigue-* clothes, especially those in which they have traveled; *clothes—* and they should be cautious not to sleep in the same *Caution* clothes worn on any day, as before but slightly alluded to. Clean, unsoiled night-clothes should be put on every evening, and those which may be worn again should be well aired and sunned during the day.

The Colonization Society has committed a great *Colonization* error in its philanthropic arrangements of providing *—an error in* for *six months' passiveness* after going to Africa. The *philanthropy* *provisions, for those who require them,* I do not object to, but the *passiveness* is fatally injurious.

Instead of going to Africa and quietly sitting down *Activity con-* in utter idleness, in anticipation *waiting in anxious ex-* *ducive to* *pectation for the fever to come*—in which cases the per- *health* son becomes much more susceptible—did they go directly about some active employment, to keep both mind and body properly exercised, I am certain that there would not be one-fourth of the mortality that there is even now, which is comparatively little.

147

The Niger Valley

Evidences of the fact

This will account for the reason that, among the numerous travelers and explorers who visit such countries, there is so much less, nay, so seldom any mortality from disease, compared with the missionaries, whose lives are rather easy and inactive, except the really energetic ones, who generally are they who survive. And I have the testimony of my friends Professor Crummell of Liberia College, late of Mount Vaughn High School, a most industrious, persevering gentleman, and W. Spencer Anderson, Esq., the largest sugar and coffee grower in Liberia, also a most energetic industrious gentleman—who corroborate my opinion on this important subject. Indeed, the people generally seem to have been long conscious of this fact, since among them they have an adage: "The *more* work, the *less* fever." But no one should infer that it meant that they should exercise without regard to care and judgment, with all the precautions and observations on health laid down in the preceding pages. I return of course, to Africa, with my family.

148

𝕬 𝕻𝖎𝖑𝖌𝖗𝖎𝖒𝖆𝖌𝖊 𝖙𝖔 𝕸𝖞 𝕸𝖔𝖙𝖍𝖊𝖗𝖑𝖆𝖓𝖉

AN

ACCOUNT
OF A JOURNEY

AMONG

THE EGBAS AND YORUBAS
OF CENTRAL AFRICA
In 1859-60

·

BY
ROBERT CAMPBELL

One of the Commissioners of the Niger Valley Exploring Party; late in
charge of the Scientific Department of the Institute for
Colored Youth, Philadelphia; and Member of the International
Statistical Congress, London

Preface

The intention was to prepare only a small pamphlet, containing those points of general information respecting the Egbas and Yorubas, as persons interested in the objects of my visit to those people would wish to learn; but in spite of efforts to be brief, the work has attained its present dimensions, with the length of which, however, as a book, there is certainly no cause of complaint. The narrative is, as far as possible, confined to personal observations, though this has perhaps deprived the casual reader of some details otherwise interesting. Much error, particularly in ference to Africa, has been propagated in consequence of writers generally not confining the subject of their books to their own observations. In my own case, I presume, the sources of information being equally accessible, that the intelligent reader can obtain for himself, as easily as I can for him, whatever information he desires about the early history of Africa, its ancient races, and the efforts of the Portuguese, British and Dutch to circumnavigate and colonize the continent.

Several items of information are omitted, partly because they are not of general interest, and partly because my worthy colleague and brother, Dr. M. R. Delany, will include them in the Report of our Expedition, the labor of which he has kindly assumed.

After what is written in the context, if I am still asked what I think of Africa for a colored man to live and do well in, I simply answer, that with as good prospects in America as colored men generally, I have determined, with my wife and children, to go to Africa to live, leaving the inquirer to interpret the reply for himself.

R. C.

Contents

CHAPTER I

LIVERPOOL TO LAGOS

Bathurst — Sierra Leone — Malignant Fever — Cape Palmas
— Cape Coast Castle — Acra, English and Dutch   157

CHAPTER II

ARRIVAL AT LAGOS

Bar bar — Landing mails under difficulties — Magnificent
Spectacle — Dexterous Canoemen — Offering to the Water-
demon — Sharks — Mr. Turner — The Consulate — Lieut.
Lodder — Disgusting Spectacle — Lagos — Alcoholic Stimulants and Fever — Emigrants — Cowries — King Docemo —
Kosoko, ex-king — A Visit to the Palace — Unfortunate Adventure — The Lesson   160

CHAPTER III

JOURNEY TO ABBEOKUTA

The Crowthers — River Ogun — Ogboi Creek — Nymphaea
— Rhizophora Mangle — Villages in the Swamp — Steam
Navigation on the Ogun — Fish-Snares — Current — Rocky
Bed — Crossing on Calabashes — "Agayen" — Subterranean
Streams — Aro — Orange Cottage   166

CHAPTER IV

ABBEOKUTA

Introduction to the "Alake" — Royal Attire — Wives, over
one hundred — Ogboni Elders — Native Game, *Wari* —
Visit to the Chiefs   170

CHAPTER V

NATIVE AUTHORITIES

Peculiarity of Government — "Ibashorun" or Prime Minister
— Shukenu — "His Highness Ogubonna," Friend of Civilization — "You are of my own Kindred" — Atambala — Agé —
Mr. Crowther and the Doctors — Order of Succession — Departments of Government — Shodeke   176

A Pilgrimage

CHAPTER VI

MISCELLANEOUS

African Cities — Forms of "Compounds" — Native Food —
Clothing — Industry — Percolator — Blacksmiths — Iron-
smelting — Weaving — Farming Implements — Indigo —
Palm-oil Factories — "Taffi" — Traders — Personal Habits —
Cola-nuts — Native Affability — Onoshoko, "Father of the
King" — Polygamy — Slavery — African Honor — Symmetry
of Form — Calisthenics — Archery — Native Games of Skill
— Stray Fact — Wild Bees — An Adventure — Funeral —
Processions — Discovery of Abbeokuta   181

CHAPTER VII

RELIGION

Shango exorcised — Existence of Spirits — Ifa — Agugu —
Oro — Aspect of a City on Oro-day — Gymnastic Sports —
Pugilistic Encounters — Missions   202

CHAPTER VIII

JOURNEY TO YORUBA

Our Caravan — Atadi — Extortion of Carriers — Ilugun —
Peter Elba — Open Air Accommodation — Articles left by the
roadside for sale — Ijaye — Kumi — Telegraphic Drums —
Interviews with Chief — "Palaver with the water" — Great
Market — The Drivers — Carriers — Value of a Shirt — Departure for Oyo — Fever Again — Visit to King Adelu — Exchange of Presents — Tax collecting — Snake-Charmer —
Adeneji — Small Pox — Ogbomishaw — Dr. Delany, Fever
still again — Scarcity of Water   207

CHAPTER IX

ILORIN

Magnificent Conflagration — Grassy Plains and Forests —
Freedom of the Country from Beasts and Reptiles; why —
Extravagant Welcome — Nasamo the Executioner, and his
Dwelling — Wifeless — Royal Present of Food — Prisoners —
Interview with the King — Schools — Arabians — Mulatto —
Musical Instruments — Banjo — Beggars — Looms — Gambari
Market — Escort   218

154

CHAPTER X

RETURN

"Two Horsemen," and their Adventure — Exchange Horses — What about Vaughn — Progress Arrested — New Route — Voices in the Bush — Village in Ashes — Isehin — A Hunting Party — Dead Man by the Roadside — Ibadan Soldiers, another Adventure — "Enough, Enough, white man, go on!" — A City on a Hill — Berecadu, and its Defenses — Night Travel in Africa — Abbeokuta again — "The Dahomians are Coming" — Deputation — The Doctor is come, and how he did it — Final Departure for the Coast — The Carrier Nuisance once more — Troubles — Heroic Woman — Safe at Lagos — Departure —Krumen — A Slaver   224

CHAPTER XI

CONCLUSION

Willingness of Natives to receive Settlers — Comparative Healthiness of Coast and Interior — Expense of Voyage — Protection — How to procure Land — Commercial and Agricultural Prospects — Time of Arriving at Lagos — The Bar — Extent of Self-Government — Climate — African Fever and Treatment — Cotton Trade — Domestic Animals — Agricultural Products — Minerals — Timber — Water — African Industry — Expense of Labor — Our Treaty — *Finis*   242

CHAPTER I

Liverpool To Lagos

Bathurst — Sierra Leone — Malignant Fever — Cape Palmas
— Cape Coast Castle — Acra, English and Dutch.

On the 24th June, 1859, I departed from Liverpool on
board the African S.S. "Ethiope," Capt. French. On the
2d of July we arrived at Funchal, Madeira; the 4th was
spent at Santa Cruz, Teneriffe, four days after leaving
which we came in sight of Cape Verda, Africa; the next
day we anchored in the port of Bathurst on the Gambia.
This little town is built on one of those great deposits of
sand commonly found on the Deltas of large rivers. It is
said to be surrounded by very unhealthy influences, although the American Consul, with whom I enjoyed an
hour's conversation, assured me that he had not known a
case of fever among the white inhabitants of the place for
six months. The trade is chiefly in ground-nuts, (*Arachis
Hypogaea*). Except perhaps Freetown, there is not a better looking place on the West Coast. The largest houses
are built along the river-side, and present a handsome appearance, heightened by some fine large trees growing
before them, and a fine avenue is left between the trees
and houses. The streets are wide and regularly intersect
at right angles, with sewers for draining; the town, which
from being low would otherwise be swampy, is thus kept
dry. The white inhabitants, including the officers of the
garrison and the missionaries, comprise about thirty persons. There is another small town about one hundred and
fifty miles up the Gambia, called Macarthy's Island. The
settlements on this river are British, and are garrisoned

by African soldiers from the W. I. Regiment. The natives are chiefly Jolofs and Mandingas. Many of the latter, who are Mohammedans, read and write Arabic; both comprise some very active and successful traders.

On the 12th we were at anchor in the harbor of Freetown, Sierra Leone, lat. 8° 29′ N., long. 13° 14′ W., said to be the best harbor on the West Coast of Africa. Affairs were in a bad condition, the yellow fever, or as some say, a malignant form of bilious fever had appeared there, and swept off more than a third of the white inhabitants, while the small pox was busy among the natives. During the two days that the ship continued in the port I had frequent opportunities of conversing with several of the natives, men of respectability, and in some instances of education; they complain bitterly of some of the Europeans, on account of their laxity of morals and unblushing disregard of the demands of decency. It is fortunate that the number of this class of persons is small compared with the number of high-minded, worthy men who are deservedly much esteemed.

On the 17th, Sunday, we arrived at Cape Palmas. Our stay there was short. I contrived to spend about three hours on shore, and was fortunate in meeting the Reverend Alex. Crummell, who conducted me to the two or three places of interest which could be visited in that time; amongst the rest he took me to the church in which he sometimes officiates. I was much gratified to witness more than one hundred natives, including an old chief, listening with deep attention to the word of God. I regret exceedingly not being able to accompany my Reverend friend to Mount Vaughn, his school and dwelling a little way from the town, where he is doing efficient service in training some promising native boys, a few of whom I met in his company. Here I received intelligence of the arrival of the barque "Mendi" at Monrovia, with my colleague Dr. Delany on board.

On the 19th July we arrived off Cape Coast Castle,

situated in lat. 5° 6′, N., long. 1° 5′ W. The town is not
so low as either Bathurst or Lagos, but at the same time
not more healthy than either. It was originally founded
by the Portuguese; the British became its owners in 1672.
The immediate site of the town wears a very rugged and
barren aspect, but there are some beautiful green hills in
the background where Indian corn and other products are
cultivated. Gold dust is the principal article of export—
the gold is chiefly brought from the Ashantee country in
the interior, but the women procure small quantities after
rain by washing the black sand scraped from the sea-beach
and water-courses. The landing is bad, although the
native canoe-men manage so well as seldom to wet their
passengers. The inhabitants experience great want of
water, relying for their supply on wells and pools which
are frequently dry, and the latter sometimes muddy and
unwholesome. The natives are very industrious, and
manufacture tolerably fine articles of jewelry. The women
both of this place and of Acra wear a strange-looking
appendage to their dress immediately at the base of the
lumbar region. Bustle would be hardly an appropriate
term for it, as, although worn in about the same position,
the appearance is different; and though used as a support for infants, which African women universally
carry on their backs, it is evidently not intended solely
for that purpose, as the women in other sections of Africa
carry their children without such support, and many use
it who have no children to carry. The women are generally very tastefully attired, displaying about their persons
many trinkets of pure gold.

Early in the morning of the 20th we found ourselves
anchored in the roads off Acra. This place is remarkable
for being both British and Dutch; it is in fact simply two
forts, one owned by each party, and the people's alle-
giance being thus divided, there is considerable confusion in collecting taxes, etc. There were some distur-
bances at the time of my visit, growing out of this cause.

CHAPTER II

Arrival At Lagos

Bad bar — Landing mail under difficulties — Magnificent Spectacle — Dexterous Canoemen — Offering to the Water-demon — Sharks — Mr. Turner — The Consulate, Lieut. Lodder — Disgusting Spectacle — Lagos — Alcoholic Stimulants and Fever — Emigrants — Cowries — King Docemo — Kosoko, ex-King — A Visit to the Palace — Unfortunate Adventure — The Lesson.

On the 21st July, early in the afternoon, our ship anchored off Lagos.

Our arrival was at the most unpropitious season of the year, the bar being then and during all June, July, and August more dangerous than at any other time; we found it impossible to effect any communication except by signals. The next day some natives were persuaded to come off from the beach; the bar being still very unsafe, they carried off the mails secured in a cask, and I, leaving my packages in charge of a man who accompanied me from Manchester, ventured to go on shore in their boat, which, however, I would not have done had I been aware of the great risk I incurred.

Could one but have divested himself of the sense of danger, the scene was magnificent—the huge "swells" chasing each other, and our little bark now riding victoriously on the crest of one, than engulfed in a deep chasm between two others, rising high on both sides. It is perhaps impossible for men to evince more dexterity than these natives in the control of their canoes, especially on approaching the beach. There were twelve men paddling with two others, one steering and the other in the prow watching the approaching surges and directing according- ly. When near the beach, the last, who is their head man, with much ceremony pours a few drops of rum on the water, and a great deal more down his throat, after which he very vehemently harangues, first I suppose the demon of the water to whom the rum was offered, and then his crew, cheering them for their work. There was another native on the beach who gave directions of some sort to the steersman by strange gesticulations; his appearance, as he stood above a group of companions, himself mounted on an inverted surf-boat with his loose garments waving in the air, presented a subject which would have de- lighted an artist, and was indeed wildly picturesque. It is necessary to watch carefully the regular successive rise and fall of the waves in order to prevent them breaking over the boat. Within a few yards of the beach they stop, "backing water" and watching intently their leader, then at a signal from him, they dash on vigorously on the top of a wave. As soon as the canoe touches, simultaneously they are in the water, and seizing their frail craft, in an instant bear her high and dry on the beach.

The bar of Lagos is dangerous chiefly on account of the large number of sharks which are always ready to make a repast on the bodies of the unfortunate occu- pants of any boat capsizing there.

The difficulties of the bar are not, however, insuper- able: small vessels can always easily sail over it into the fine bay within, where they can load or unload with little trouble and without risk. It is not so easy to go out again, however, for then it would be necessary to "beat" against the wind; but a small steamboat could at once take them out in tow with perfect safety. I was informed that slavers used always to enter the bay: they could of course afford to wait for a favorable wind with which to get out. On landing I was kindly received by a Mr.

Turner, a re-captured slave, educated at Sierra Leone by the British, and now a respectable merchant at Lagos.

After partaking of some refreshments provided by my hospitable friend, I was conducted to the house of Lieut. Lodder, the acting Consul, to whom I brought a letter from Lord Malmesbury, British Minister for Foreign Affairs in the late Derby Administration. My reception was cordial, and I was afforded convenient accommodation at the Consulate all the time I continued at Lagos.

A disgusting spectacle presented itself at the entrance of the river: on the right margin stood two bodies, transfixed by poles passing through their mouths. They were nearly dry, and strange to say were not disturbed by buzzards, although a great number of these birds—fortunately very abundant in Africa—were flying about them. They were two of five men who were executed for robbery: one of them was the son of a chief, and his connection with the party gave rise to a great "palaver," his friends contending that in consequence of his birth he should not suffer a malefactor's death, while others contended that his crime had degraded him to the position of other men, like whom he should answer for his offenses.

Lagos is a small island about six miles in circumference, located on the west coast of Africa, in the Bight of Benin, Gulf of Guinea, lat. 6° 24′ N., long. 3° 22′ E. Like Bathurst, on the Gambia, it is very low, and formed by an accumulation of sand. In some places lower than the surface of the river, it is very swampy from the infiltration of water. Like many localities on the coast of tropical countries, it is unhealthy. The prevailing disease is fever with chills; with common prudence, however, there is nothing to fear in this disease; but if the person suffering from it will blindly persist in the use of alcoholic stimulants, the consequence might be serious. I am sorry to say that Europeans and others, generally indulge far too freely in these beverages. In too many instances, I believe the climate is blamed for the evils thus created. After passing through what is called the acclimating process, which lasts during twelve or fifteen months, one is seldom troubled again with fever.

The population of Lagos is estimated at about thirty thousand: there are about fifteen hundred emigrants from Sierra Leone, the Brazils and Cuba. All these are themselves native Africans, brought from the interior and sold on different parts of the coast. Those from Sierra Leone are recaptured, and the others redeemed slaves. Few are more than half civilized. The white inhabitants number about twenty-five, and include English, Germans, French, Italians, and Portuguese. A few very fine houses have been erected near the water-side, and others were being built at the time of our departure. They use as money small shells *(Cyproea Moneta)* called cowries by the English, *owu* by the natives, this being also the general term for money. The value of the dollar and its fractions, as well as English currency, is well understood and appreciated: it is fast getting to be the same at Abbeokuta.

The present King of Lagos is call Docemo. He was placed in the position by the late Consul Campbell, after his brother Kosoko was deposed for warring against the English, and for his participation in the slave-trade. Kosoko has still a few adherents, particularly among the Europeans: only the guns of H. M. gun-boat "Brune," lying always in the river, preserve the present King his position. Kosoko lives not far from Lagos: he is said to be cruel and tyrannical, and still claims to be the legitimate King of the place.

On the morning of the first of August I made a visit to his Majesty King Docemo. Lieut. Lodder, the acting Consul, sent a messenger to his Majesty, informing him of the intended visit, and asking his permission, which being obtained, a party, consisting of the Commander of the "Brune," the Paymaster of H.M.S.S. "Medusa," the acting Consul and myself, proceeded. We were received in the reception-room, and some chairs, intended solely for such occasions, (for neither the King nor the members of his household sit on chairs,) were offered us. After waiting a few minutes, his Majesty, tastefully arrayed in a cloth of plaid velvet, and gold embroidered slippers, presented himself, and was introduced to his visitors respectively. The interview lasted about an hour. I told him briefly, through the interpreter, our object in visiting Africa, which seemed to give him much pleasure: so far as his dominions extended, he said, emigrants might select land suitable to their purpose, and he would gladly give it. I thanked him for his offer, and then spoke for a few minutes of the great results which must flow from the development of a country like his, so blessed with resources. In reference to an American emigrant who came with me from Manchester, he inquired whether he understood using oxen for agricultural purposes: when answered in the affirmative, he seemed rather incredulous. The other gentlemen had also business to transact with the King, which rendered our conversation rather brief.

When I had been a few days at Lagos, Mr. Williams, a somewhat intelligent native, interpreter to the Consul, invited me to see his farm on the mainland, a few miles across the river. Accompanied by two other persons, we left early in the morning before breakfast, expecting to return in two hours at most. Reaching the land, it was still necessary to journey a few miles to the farm: though yet early, it was warm, and the walk tiresome, so that I was obliged to rest myself on a stump while my companions proceeded to a little distance to plant some seed. Seeing a bird which I wanted to preserve, alight a few yards off, I tried to come within shot of it: before able to do so, it pursued its flight. I followed and eventually shot it, but in attempting to return I unfortunately took a direction leading away from my first position. I wandered about for more than two hours, shouting all the time at the top of my voice to attract attention, for my ammunition being in the possession of my companions, I could not fire my gun for that purpose. I soon found myself in the midst of an almost impenetrable jungle, the shrubbery and vines so thickly interlacing, that it was with the greatest difficulty I could break through: the ground too was swampy, and I sometimes sunk nearly to my knees. By this time my friends were as busy seeking me. I never felt more joyful than when I heard their voice in response to my own. From hunger, fatigue, heat of the sun, and excitement, I returned home about 2 P.M., with severe headache and fever. The next day I was worse, and continued ill for several days. The reader has here my first initiation into the African fever, and I might add that not a few may trace their first attack to similar imprudence. In such a climate a stranger should never leave his home before breakfast, nor undertake very vigorous exercise before he has passed the ordeal of acclimature.

CHAPTER III

Journey To Abbeokuta

The Crowthers — River Ogun — Ogboi Creek — Nymphaea
— Rhizophora Mangle — Villages in the Swamp — Steam
Navigation on the Ogun — Fish-Snares — Current —
Rocky Bed — Crossing on Calabashes — "Agayen" —
Subterranean Streams — Aro — Orange Cottage.

I remained at Lagos nearly six weeks, and my colleague,
Dr. Delany, not having arrived, I determined on at
once setting out for Abbeokuta. I left on the 29th of
August, accompanied by Messrs. Samuel and Josiah
Crowther, sons of the worthy native missionary, the Rev.
Samuel Crowther.

The journey from Lagos to Abbeokuta is usually
made by canoes, up the river Ogun, the waters of which
empty into the bay of Lagos. Somewhat west of its em-
bouchure is the Ogboi creek or cut, communicating with
the Ogun about ten or twelve miles from the bay. Canoe-
men always prefer reaching the river by means of this cut,
as the distance direct up the river is greater. There was
abundance of the beautiful water-plant "Nymphaea,"
now in flower, in places where the current was gentle.
The land on both sides the cut is low, swampy and thickly covered with mangrove, *(Rhizophora Mangle.)* Notwithstanding this, there are two villages in the midst of
the swamps, the inhabitants of which enjoy good health,
affording an example of a fact often noticed in the West—
Indies and tropical America, that people might live with

impunity in the midst of regions from which is constantly distilled the most dangerous miasma.*

The Ogun is navigable for steam-vessels of not over
five feet draft during seven or eight months of the year,
namely, from about a fortnight after the first rainy season in May, to December, about a month after the cessation of the last rains. After this time the quantity of
water diminishes rapidly, so that in February and March
an infant could easily ford it at places where it was not
long before as deep and wide as the Schuylkill at Philadelphia.

Vessels of the same draft can during the other four
or five months always ascend as far as Gaun, about one
third the distance. There being plenty of water at the
time I ascended, the journey to Abbeokuta took five
days. When the river is very high, or, as in the last of the
dry season, has but little water, the journey takes from
ten to fifteen days. In the former case it is necessary to
proceed very slowly and cautiously along the margin of
the water, where frequent obstructions are encountered,
and in the latter, the water being in many places only a
few inches deep, the canoes must often be unloaded and
sometimes carried over places where they could not
possibly float. At any time, however, except in the height
of the rainy season when the roads are much flooded, the
journey can be performed by land in two or three days.
The water is of a whitish tinge, from holding in suspension argilaceous matter and minute fragments of the
constituents of granite, particularly feldspar. There is
abundance of fish, to catch which the natives attach snares
to strong ropes made from the stems of a species of creeping palm, *(Calamus,)* passed across the river and fastened
on both sides to trees. These ropes offer some impediments
to navigation, frequently upsetting canoes, and causing
the loss of their freight. The current, to within ten or

* See similar example in Backie's Narrative, p. 195.

fifteen miles of Lagos, is very strong, due doubtless to the regular but very marked elevation of the interior country. There is generally an annual overflow of its banks. Although far more water falls in the former rainy season in May, June and July, than during the latter in September, October and November, yet the river never overflows till in the latter season, since the former rains are eagerly absorbed by the soil, which with everything else is then exceedingly dry from the prevalence of the harmattan winds immediately previous. Many large trees are then washed away and drifted into the channel, which is very troublesome to travellers on the river. There are extensive forests on the banks, from which fuel could be obtained in abundance, and which would furnish considerable freight in the form of timber to both Abbeokuta and Lagos. It offers also fine facilities in some places for water-power.

Above Abbeokuta, on account of the very rocky character of its bed, the Ogun is not navigable even for canoes. At places, however, where it intersects the roads, canoes could in the rainy season be used with advantage to convey goods and passengers across, but the natives use instead large calabashes, on which the passenger sits, the ferryman swimming and pushing his freight before him. They not only prefer the use of calabashes, but will have nothing whatever to do with canoes, and affect to despise those who use them. Not unfrequently I heard the term "aguyen" reproachfully applied by the people of the interior towns to my interpreter and other persons from places on or near the sea-coast. The word simply means canoe-men.

I crossed the Ogun in three places above Abbeokuta; the first time between Oyo and Isehin, next between Biocu and Beracudu, and finally between the last place and Abbeokuta, distant respectively five days, two days, and two hours' journey from Abbeokuta, the day's journey being from twenty-five to thirty miles. At these places

I found the bed of the river covered to such an extent with masses of granite rock, that it could be easily crossed dryshod by stepping from stone to stone, although fully twenty-five yards wide. I found also the water wider and deeper than it is from Abbeokuta to ten miles below. The reason of this perhaps is that the irregular rocky surface of its bed above Abbeokuta retards the progress of the water, and for the same reason it is not absorbed as it is below Abbeokuta, where the bed is sandy. We found all through the country brooks and rivulets apparently dry in some places, while at other points lower down the course, the water was gushing out clear and sweet. It is possible too to procure water by making slight excavations in the apparently dry sandy beds of what had been in the rainy season impassable rivers.

On the 4th September we arrived at Aro, where we found horses awaiting us, for the Crowthers had sent before to order them. Aro is the landing-place for the city of Abbeokuta in the rainy season; Agbamiya, a point lower down the river, being used in the dry season. It, the former is four miles below Ake, the business centre of the city, and about a mile and a half from the city gate. Above Aro the river is too rocky to permit canoes to ascend into the city. This place is doubtless destined to become of considerable importance; already all the merchants have depots there, and hereafter will also find it of advantage to make it their residence, when it is likely to be included in the city limits. In little more than an hour after we left Aro, we were comfortably domiciled at "Orange Cottage," the beautiful little dwelling of my kind companions, the Crowthers.

CHAPTER IV

Abbeokuta

Introduction to the "Alake" — Royal attire — Wives, over
one hundred — Ogboni Elders — Native Game, *Wari* —
Visit to the Chiefs.

Acting-Consul Lieut. Lodder had furnished me with a
letter of introduction to his Majesty Okukenu, Alake of
Abbeokuta, which I was anxious to present. The Reverend Henry Townsend of the Church Missionary Society
kindly accompanied me. My reception by the King was
very cordial. I explained to him the object of my visit to
the country, which he was pleased to hear. He observed
that for people coming with such purposes, and for missionaries, he had great "sympathy," and would afford
every encouragement; but that some of the people (emigrants from the Brazils, Cuba, and Sierra Leone) who
were now coming into his dominion, especially traders,
gave him much trouble. His body above the loins was
nude; otherwise his attire consisted of a handsome velvet
cap trimmed with gold, a costly necklace of coral, and
a double strand of the same ornament about his loins,
with a velvet cloth thrown gracefully about the rest of
his person, under which he wore his shocoto, a sort of
loose trowsers reaching only to the knees. One of his
wives (he has more than a hundred) was seated on the
same mat fanning him. He fondled on his knees an infant, and eight or ten of his other little children, all
about the same age, were gamboling around him. On his
right were seated several very old men dressed in white
cloths, elders of the Ogboni council, with one or other of

whom his majesty usually plays at the native game of *wari,* a description of which is given in another place. He offered me the only chair in his establishment. The Reverend Mr. Townsend, being an intimate acquaintance, sat on an end of his mat. A few slaves, by the by, his chief administrative officers, also sat near him. He presented me on my departure a head of cowries, worth nearly fifty cents. During the next few days I visited the principal chiefs, to explain the object of my visit and to make to each a small present. Though humble, these presents were well received and in every instance a return present of cola nuts, *(cola sterculia acuminata,)* or of cowries was given. The natives generally at first regarded me as a white man, until I informed them of my connection with the Negro. This announcement always gained me a warmer reception.

The reader here will permit me to digress to explain a matter respecting which there has hitherto been some misconception. It has been asserted that the native African does not manifest under any circumstance the same deference for colored men, as he does for white men; and so fully is this believed, particularly in the United States, that both my colleague Dr. Delany and myself were frequently cautioned respecting the danger to which we should be exposed in consequence of our complexion. It is indeed true that more respect has been accorded to white men, on account of their superior learning and intelligence, than to the generality of semi-civilized black men from the Brazils and other places, who now live in the Aku country; but it is a great mistake to think that the same is withheld from colored men similarly endowed with their white brethren. Let any disinterested person visiting Abbeokuta, place himself in a position to notice the manner in which such a person, for instance, as the Reverend Samuel Crowther, or even his son of the same name, each a pure Negro, is treated, and he would soon perceive the profound respect

with which Africans treat those of their own race worthy
of it. The white man who supposes himself respected in
Africa, merely because he is white, is grievously mistaken.
I have had opportunities to know, that if he should, presuming on his complexion, disregard propriety in his
bearing towards the authorities, he would receive as
severe rebuke as a similar offense would bring him in
England. One of the chiefs of Abbeokuta, Atambala, was
with us one day when a young missionary entered, and
passed him with only a casual nod of the head. As soon
as he was seated the haughty old chief arose and said, in
his own tongue: "Young man, whenever any of my
people, even the aged, approaches me, he prostrates himself with his face to the ground. I do not expect the same
from you, or from civilized men, *(oyibo,)* nevertheless
remember always that I shall demand all the respect due
to a chief of Abbeokuta." A sufficient apology was given,
and the matter ended, not without, it is hoped, teaching
a salutary lesson.

The king of Abbeokuta, whose person is considered
too sacred for the popular gaze, is never permitted to
leave the palace except on special occasions, and then
he only goes into the open space without the palace-gates,
one of his wives being in attendance to screen his face
with a large fan. So with the king of Oyo, who once or
twice only in the year exhibits himself to the public, deco-
rated in his best robes and wearing a crown of coral. At
these times any one can stare at his majesty with impunity. In Ilorin the king may not be seen, except as a mark
of special favor, even by those to whom he affords the
privilege of an audience.

If the reader will permit the expression, Abbeokuta
might be said to be in form an irregular circle. The circumference of its outer wall, for in some parts of the city
there are three walls, is about twenty-three miles. It was
originally formed of over one hundred townships, each
independent and governed by its own chief. The people

are of the Egba tribe of the Akus, sometimes incorrectly called Yorubas. About fifty years ago, wars with the surrounding tribes, particularly with the Yorubas, had disorganized their nation, the greatest number of their people being enslaved, and sent to the Brazils, Cuba, and other places; many of them were also recaptured by British cruisers and taken to Sierra Leone. A few flying before their relentless enemy, and wandering from place to place, at length found refuge beneath a shelf of rock now called "Olumo;" this hiding-place is said to have been before the den of a band of robbers. Advantage was taken of the security thus afforded, by others of the Egba tribe, and their number continued to increase until they felt strong enough to form a town and build a wall. In a short time that town, as before stated, contained the remnants of over one hundred townships, and became too powerful to be successfully assaulted by their enemies. The walls now include a number of huge hills of superior building granite, the quarrying of which will doubtless yield large profit to its inhabitants at no remote day.

They called the town very appropriately, "Abbeokuta," which means under a rock. It is now estimated to contain more than one hundred thousand inhabitants, and its population is fast increasing by accessions, not only from the surrounding tribes, who find in it greater security for life and property, but also from many of those, and their descendants, who were sold away as slaves.

Although the people have increased, one is at a loss to divine what has become of the chiefs of so many townships. One after another they have fallen off, and their successors have either never been appointed or are too insignificant to command attention. The treaty we concluded with the authorities of the place was signed by only seven chiefs, the king's signature not included. To them we were sent specially by the king, an act which seemed to indicate, either that they alone were of sufficient consequence to take part in such a matter, or that they, by common consent were deemed the representatives of the rest.

The language of the Egbas is the same as that of the Yorubas, Ijebus and other neighboring tribes, concerning which the author of "Polyglotta Africana" makes the following just remarks: "For the last few years they have very erroneously made use of the name Yoruba, in reference to the whole nation, supposing that the Yoruba is the most powerful Aku tribe, but the appellation is liable to far greater objection than that of Aku, and ought to be forthwith abandoned; for it is, in the first place, unhistorical, having never been used of the whole Aku nation by any body, except for the last few years conventionally by the missionaries; secondly, it involves a twofold use of the word 'Yoruba,' which leads to a confusion of notions; for in one instance the same word has to be understood of a whole, in another only of a part; and thirdly, the name being thus incorrect, can never be received by the different tribes as a name for the whole nation."

Viewed as to its power of enforcing order, and affording security for life and property, the government of Abbeokuta is as efficient as a civilized government can be, and it accomplishes these ends with the greatest ease and simplicity. Punishment is always summary and certain; notwithstanding, nobody complains of injustice. The penalty for theft is extreme, being either decapitation or foreign slavery. Before the advent of missionaries and civilized people adultery was sometimes also a capital offense; now it is modified to heavy fines, the amount of which is always proportioned to the position and wealth of the offender. Cases of adultery often occur, and must be expected until they are taught to abandon the disgusting system of polygamy.

The tenure of property is as it is among civilized people, except as to land, which is deemed common property; every individual enjoys the right of taking unoccupied land, *as much as he can use,* wherever and whenever he pleases. It is deemed his property as long as he keeps it in use; after that, it is again common property. This custom is observed by all the Akus.

The surviving relatives of one buried on any lot of ground, have a right to that ground which nothing can tempt them to relinquish, and from respect to the sentiment, no one would invade, on any pretext, particularly when the deceased was a mother or father. Mr. S. Crowther, Jr., has long desired to possess a strip of land contiguous to his place of business, but no offer of money can induce the owner to part with it, although he is very poor; because his father lies buried there.

CHAPTER V

Native Authorities

Peculiarity of Government — "Ibashorun" or Prime Minister
— Shukenu — "His Highness Ogubonna," Friend of
Civilization — "You are of my own kindred" — Atambala
— Agé — Mr. Crowther and the Doctors — Order of
Succession — Departments of Government — Shodeke.

The government of Abbeokuta is peculiar, combining
the monarchical, the patriarchal, and no small share of
the republican. Almost every free man, woman and child
is a member of the Ogboni Lodge, of which there is one
in every township or chiefdom. These lodges are presided
over by elders of their own election, and the elders at the
decease of the chief choose his successor from his relatives,
generally his brother, seldom or never from among his
own sons, as hereafter explained. The successor of the
king is also choosen by the chiefs and elders combined,
their act being subsequently ratified by the people, assembled *en masse*. It is in this that the republican element
of the government of Abbeokuta is recognized. There is,
as already observed, a king, the Alake, or chief of Ake,
which place ranks first among the numerous townships.
He is a good-natured fat old gentleman, giving himself
only so much concern about public affairs as to secure the
good will of his rather turbulent chiefs, to whom perhaps a ruler of more active temperament would be less
welcome; there are times, however, when he has been
roused to great energy and decision of character. Next
in order of authority is the Ibashorun or Prime Minister,
who is also in times of war commander in chief. He too is

a man of rather cumbersome proportions, powerful on
account of his wealth and the number of soldiers his
household furnishes in time of war, still, not personally
celebrated for military prowess. The chief next in order
is Shukenu, perhaps more corpulent than the Ibashorun.
Wealthy, powerful, haughty and courageous, he is nevertheless not free from the charge of cruelty. Scarcely a
chief in Africa afforded us a more hearty welcome. Ogubonna, or as the English, to whom he is well known, style
him, "His Highness Ogubonna," comes next. He calls
himself, not inappropriately, the Friend of Civilization;
he is a man of large stature, fine proportion, and in all
as fine-looking a Negro as I ever saw. No one could mistake him for any other than a chief, so commanding and
dignified is his bearing. On the occasion of my first visit
to his Highness, as usual he was informed of my African
origin. "From what part of Africa," asked he, "did your
grandmother come?" As this was a point on which I
possessed no information, I could not give him a satis-
factory answer. He remained silent for a short time, and
at last said: "How can I tell but that you are of my own
kindred, for many of my ancestors were taken and sold
away." From that day he called me relative, and of course
as every other African had as good a claim to kindred-
ship, I soon found myself generally greeted as such.

Adjoining the American Baptist Mission Station, at
which we sojourned while at Abbeokuta, is the compound of the chief Atambala. Less powerful and wealthy
than his colleagues, he is still a very important personage in the councils of the nation, chiefly on account of
his cunning. Every important mission requiring the exercise of such characteristic, is intrusted to him, and it is
seldom that he fails: he is also a great orator. In personal
appearance he is tall, but not as stout as the other chiefs
spoken of above, and although fully eighty years old, he
maintains much youthful vigor and comeliness. I am
indebted to him for many kind offices. There are the

names of three other chiefs attached to our treaty, but my acquaintance with them arose from only a single interview, and I am therefore unable to speak of them. I might, however, be permitted to mention that at our interview with Agé, whose name is found mentioned last in our treaty, as usual it was necessary to mention my origin, for the Africans are not as keen in the recognition of their descendants, as are the Americans of the same class of persons. On learning this, he took hold of my hand and shook it heartily; and drawing me toward him, he threw his arms about my neck, and pressed me with warmth. He has since died: for many months he was a cripple. No one has been more conspicuous in the affairs of his country, or was more respected by his people, than this good old man.

There are many doctors—physicians, I might have said—throughout the Aku country; and they are as jealous of their profession, and as opposed to innovation in practice, as the most orthodox disciple of AEsculapius amongst us can be. Shortly after the return of Mr. S. Crowther, Jr., from London, where he received the training of a surgeon, several of these doctors, hearing that he was prescribing for many who were before their patients, assembled *en masse* in the market-place, and after due deliberation issued an "injunction" that he should forthwith abandon his practice. Some of the foremost of them were deputed to communicate the decree of the faculty. They were cordially received, and heard with patience. After some conversation, Mr. C. informed them that he was willing to obey, but only after a trial on both sides should prove him to be the less skilled in the mysteries of the profession. To this they consented. Time was given for preparation on both sides. In the afternoon the regulars appeared, clothed in their most costly garments, and well provided with orishas or charms attached to all parts of their persons and dress. In the mean time Mr. Crowther had also prepared to receive them. A table was placed in the middle of the room, and on it a dish in which were a few drops of sulphuric acid, so placed that a slight motion of the table would cause it to flow into a mixture of chlorate of potassa and white sugar. A clock was also in the room, from which a small bird issued every hour, and announced the time by cooing. This was arranged so as to coo while they were present. Mr. Crowther then made a brief harangue, and requested them to say who should lead off in the contest. This privilege they accorded to him. The door was closed, the curtains drawn down. All waited in breathless expectation. Presently the bird came out, and to their astonishment cooed twelve times, and suddenly from the midst of the dish burst forth flame and a terrible explosion. The scene that followed was indescribable: one fellow rushed through the window and scampered; another in his consternation, overturning chairs, tables and every thing in his way, took refuge in the bed-room, under the bed, from which he was with difficulty afterwards removed. It need not be added that they gave no more trouble, and the practice they sought to break up was only the more increased for their pains.

Although the person made king must be of the royal family, yet a son seldom succeeds, but usually a brother by the same mother, or a son of a sister, also of the same mother. Such a person is certainly a relative, while from circumstances growing out of the system of polygamy, the son of from fifty to two hundred wives might not be the child of the husband. Property also descends in the same manner.

The appointment of the king devolves on the chiefs and elders of the Ogboni, the latter of course all old men. Some of them are men of great influence themselves, and as their power would be limited by an efficient monarch, they are not likely to choose such.

The King, or Alake, as he is called, is not, as in civilized countries, the executive: his office seems to be more to preside at all important councils. He exercises other functions not well understood by strangers. The government is divided into several departments. The Elders constitute the judiciary. The officers of the Ogboni,* a secret order, exercise legislative functions. The executive department devolves on Oro, an imaginary deity, of which mention shall be made hereafter.

The present Alake succeeded Shodeke, a man so venerated as to be ranked among the demigods. Every one who knew him has something to recount of the virtue of Shodeke.

The support of the king and chiefs is derived from the offerings of their slaves, and of those who bring controversies to them for settlement.

* This order is accessible to persons of any age or sex, but not to slaves.

CHAPTER VI

Miscellaneous

African Cities — Forms of "Compounds" — Native Food — Clothing — Industry — Percolator — Blacksmiths — Iron-smelting — Weaving — Farming Implements — Indigo — Palm-oil Factories — "Taffi" — Personal Habits — Cola-nuts — Native Affability — Onoshoko, "Father of the King" — Polygamy — Slavery — African Honor — Symmetry of Form — Calisthenics — Archery — Native Games of Skill — Stray Fact — Wild Bees — An Adventure — Funeral — Processions — Discovery of Abbeokuta.

In African native cities there are no streets such as would be called so in a civilized country. The houses or compounds are scattered according to the discretion or taste of their owners; lanes, always crooked, and frequently very narrow, being left between them. These dwellings are sometimes very large, including in many instances accommodation for from twenty to two hundred inmates, especially in those of some of the wealthier chiefs, which are sometimes tenanted by over three hundred people.

The usual form of a compound is square, and is bounded by a wall against which the rooms are commonly built. The walls are of mud, but are sometimes very straight and smooth. In some of the mission-houses, which are likewise of mud, but plastered, a stranger would not suspect the material.

In the area within the inclosure are gathered their sheep, goats and so forth, at nights. In almost every one of these dwellings there is a large dove-cot, in which are bred hundreds of common domestic pigeons. They are very fond of raising chickens, ducks and other poultry.

The food of the Egbas, as well as of all the tribes between Lagos and Ilorin, is very simple, consisting chiefly of a preparation called *eko:* corn is macerated in water until fermentation ensues. It is then crushed between stones, and the chaff separated by washing. The milky liquor is then boiled in large pots until it assumes a consistency somewhat stiffer than cream, which as it cools becomes as firm as jelly. The taste is rather unpleasant at first, but one seldom fails to like it after persisting in its use. A portion of it nearly as large as a penny-roll, wrapped in leaves, is sold for five cowries, or about a mill. An adult native consumes from four to eight at a meal, taking with it as a relish a few spoonsful of *obé,* or "palaver-sauce," as the Sierra Leone folks call it. Palaver-sauce is made by cooking together palm-oil, pepper, ocros,* locust-seed, ogiri and several esculent herbs. Leaving out the ogiri, which stinks dreadfully, *obé* is certainly very fine, but the natives greatly prefer it with ogiri, just as certain Epicureans do tainted venison. Ground beans and pepper, fried in oil, called *acras;* cooked yams, beaten with water in a wooden mortar, *fufu;* with certain other preparations of corn, rice, etc., also form part of their diet. Native beer or *oti* is plentiful, cheap and sometimes good. It is made either from maize or Guinea corn. As with the brewing of beer in civilized countries, the grain is suffered to germinate in order to develop saccharine matter. They have, however, no means of arresting fermentation, and hence the beer can not keep. Another very fine drink is made from the sap which flows from incisions made in the palm-tree.

The people are not nude, as many suppose Africans to be generally. Of course we except children, and even they are not always so. The apparel of a man consists of a shocoto, cloth and cap. The shocoto is a sort of loose trowsers, fastened with a string directly above the hips.

* Abelmoschus (Ilibiscus) Esculentus.

He dispenses with the cloth when at labor. Instead of this cloth the wealthy wear a tobe, a loose large garment, worn over the shoulders, and falling below the knees: they are generally handsomely embroidered. Sometimes, however, a cloth of velvet, silk or some other expensive material is substituted. Instead of the shocoto, men and boys are sometimes seen with garments made exactly like the kilts of the Scotch Highlanders; the cloth too is worn in much the same way as the Highlander's plaid. The attire of the women is even more simple, consisting of one or two cloths passed round the body. They wear besides a sort of turban, and in a few instances, another cloth over the breast and shoulders. The costume of some Africans costs as much as that of many of the most extravagant dandies of civilized countries.

We met several of those individuals who though entirely of Negro parentage, are white, from the absence of pigmentum or coloring matter from the skin, hair and eyes; both in features and texture of hair, however, they still resemble the Negro. But little is known of this phenomenon, notwithstanding the fact that it is common to all races of men, and even to inferior animals, white horses, birds, mice, etc., being often seen. A fact which we observed, is perhaps not yet known, namely, that between the albino proper, and those in whom there is a normal development of pigmentum, there are individuals possessing more or less color, so that if a series were formed embracing both extremes, the difference between any consecutive two would be hardly perceptible. The first digressions are characterized by a reddish tinge of hair, and complexion in harmony, but difficult to describe. These characteristics are observed still more prominent in other individuals, and thus on, till some are found with complexions as light as mulattoes, although not otherwise like them. From these the deviation still continues, till at length the perfect albino is found. Albinos, whether of the Indian, Negro or white race, are not uncommon in America, but they seldom attract attention, as without particular observation they seem like ordinary white men. For instance, one of the most prominent editors of a daily newspaper in New York, is an albino. The term was first applied by the Portuguese towards these people. They can not well endure exposure to bright daylight, their eyes lacking the protection which is afforded to others by the color in the iris, etc.

Not long since, and even now, there are not a few who regard the African to be like the snake or alligator, a lazy creature, whose life is spent basking in the sunshine, and subsisting on roots and herbs or whatever else of food within reach of his arm. A Negro friend of mine mentioned to no less a personage than a professor in a medical school in America, that he had read in the work of Denham and Clapperton, that women are commonly seen in Africa spinning by the road-side, and selling boiled potatoes, roast-meats, etc. "Nonsense," said he, "that is all English romance: can you believe such folly?" Nevertheless I assert, and appeal to every one who has visited this section of Africa to verify my assertion, that there is not a more industrious people on the face of the earth. Rise as early as you please and enter a native compound, and you will there find the women engaged at their varied occupations. Go at night as late as you please, and there by the feeble light of her lamp she is seen in the act of labor, spinning, weaving or preparing food for the ensuing day. There is not a child among the Akus— I say nothing of other African tribes—who is not instructed in some means of realizing a living. The men are builders, blacksmiths, iron-smelters, tanners and leather-workers, tailors, carpenters, calabash-carvers, weavers, basket, hat and mat-makers, farmers: the women weave, spin, dye, cook, brew, make pots, oils, soap and I know not what else.

Not many years since, much attention was excited among practical chemists by the invention of the Percolator, an apparatus for extracting in a very short time the virtues of medicinal herbs, etc. Essentially the same contrivance is used, and has been used from time immemorial by the native Africans, in making lye from ashes for the manufacture of soap, and for dyeing. A small aperture is made in the bottom of a large earthen vessel, which is covered with straw and then filled with ashes. This is placed over a similar vessel, so as slightly to enter it. Water is then suffered to percolate slowly through the first vessel into the second, which as it does so extracts all the soluble matter from the ashes.

Although the native blacksmiths frequently execute very fine productions of their art, yet their apparatus is very rude. They work sitting on the ground. Their bellows is hewn out of a block of wood about three feet long, and six or seven inches deep, in the form of two cups connected by a tube, to the middle of which another tube of clay is attached, through which the current of air is propelled. The two cavities are each covered with a sack of untanned hide, and a stick of wood about three feet long is fastened to each sack. A little boy having hold of the ends of these sticks, lifts and depresses them alternately, and thus secures the action. Although different in appearance, these bellows operate on the same principle as those of civilized construction. For fuel they use charcoal made from the hard shell surrounding the kernel of the palm-nut.

I passed through two iron-smelting villages on the road between Oyo and Isehin in Yoruba, but they were not in operation, as the war, of which mention shall be made hereafter, had driven the inhabitants into the larger towns for protection. The furnaces, or the portion of them above the surface of the earth, are made of clay. They are in the form of cylinders, about thirty inches high; the diameter of the bases about six feet. A hole is made in the upper base, communicating both with six or seven similar holes around the convex surface, and, by a small orifice, with a large cavity underground and beneath the cylinder. In this, immediately under the orifice, I found a mass of slag. They use charcoal for fuel, which they produce in abundance in the forests in the midst of which these villages are usually located.

The apparatus of the weavers is very simple. There are two kinds, one used by the men, producing cloth of only a few inches in width, and another by the women, producing cloth as wide as of English manufacture. The men can make cloth of an indefinite length: the apparatus used by the women limits the length of the cloth to about two and a half yards. I forbear a description of either of these contrivances, as such as I could make would hardly be intelligible.

The implements of the farmers are only two, a billhook and hoe. The hoe is not bad in itself, but very badly mounted for use by a civilized farmer. The handles are short, rendering it necessary for the operator to stoop in using them. The soil is prepared by heaping the surface-earth in hills, close together and regularly in parallel lines. Cotton, yams, corn, cassava, beans, grow close together in the same field.

The beautiful blue, almost purple dye of their cloths is not from the common indigo-plant of the East and West-Indies, but from a large climbing plant. The leaves and shoots are gathered while young and tender. They are then crushed in wooden mortars, and the pulp made up in balls and dried. For dyeing, a few of these balls are placed in a strong lye made from ashes, and suffered to remain until the water becomes offensive from the decomposition of vegetable matter. The cloths are then put in, and moved about until sufficiently colored. There are dyeing establishments in all the towns from Lagos to Ilorin.

Palm-oil factories, as one would suppose from the quantity of the oil exported from Lagos and other parts of the West African coast, are very numerous. The process of extracting the oil is simple. The nuts are gathered by men. From one to four or five women separate them from the integuments. They are then passed on to other women, who boil them in large earthen pots. Another set crush off the fibre in mortars. This done, they are placed in large clay vats filled with water, and two or three women tread out the semi-liquid oil, which comes to the surface as disengaged from the fiber, where it is collected and again boiled to get rid of the water which mechanically adheres to it. The inner surface of these clay vats, having at first absorbed a small quantity of oil, is not afterwards affected either by the water or oil. It is said that palm-oil loses its color by being kept for some time at the boiling temperature.

No part of the palm-nut is wasted. The oil being extracted, the fibre, which still retains some oil, is dried and used for kindling. The kernel is used for making another oil, *adi,* excellent for burning in lamps and making native soap. The hard shell or pericarp is burnt for charcoal and used by the native blacksmiths. They prepare several other kinds of oil, such as agusi, beni, and ori, or shea butter. The last, which possesses medicinal virtues, is now exported from Abbeokuta.

Palm-oil, considering the profit which it brings the manufacturer, the abundant growth of the plant which yields it, and the great and increasing demand for it, is destined to become of great commercial importance.

The native women all through the country prepare from the juice of the sugar-cane, by boiling, a sort of "taffi." The cane is cut in short bits, crushed in a large wooden mortar, and the juice wrung out, filtered and boiled to the consistence of candy. While at Ilorin and without sugar, we often used this preparation to sweeten our coffee. The reader who knows anything of the process of sugar-making will perceive from this that all the knowledge necessary to make these people sugar-makers, is that a small quantity of lime must be added to the juice in order to correct the acidity which begins to generate as soon as it is expressed. In this way many of the peasantry of the West-Indies prepare their own sugar, and often also for sale.

The Akus are great traders. Such a thing as over-reaching them in a bargain is unknown. In no instance do they ever charge for an article what they expect to get for it. "How much for this?" says the purchaser. "One head," replies the vender. "Won't you take forty strings?" "Bring on your cowries," is the reply. "Won't you take thirty strings?" "Bring on your money:" and thus on until the minimum is attained, when he replies: "Not a cowrie less." If the price suits the purchaser, well; if not, he passes on to another trader, when much the same dialogue ensues.

Several of the personal habits of the natives are remarkable. The men universally shave, not only the beard, but the eye-brows, within the nostrils, (the native razors are adapted to this,) and frequently the entire head. Many leave a strip of hair from the forehead, over the crown of the head, down to the back of the neck. The Mohammedans leave also a little tuft of hair on the chin. We met two or three men at Ilorin with whiskers. The margin of the eye-lids is blackened with pulverized sulphuret of antimony, which every native carries about with him for the purpose. The women dye the palm of the hands, finger-nails and feet with ground camwood. Sometimes when about to participate in religious observances, their entire person is colored in this way. They pay great attention to the teeth, using the chewed ends of certain roots for the purpose of brushes, as do the people of the West-Indies, where the custom was doubtless introduced by Africans. Except some little children, we met nobody who did not use tobacco. It is used in the form of snuff, not taken into the nostrils, but on the tongue. A small quantity of benin-seed and of *lubi,* a native impure carbonate of soda, is ground with the snuff. They use the

Brazilian roll-tobacco, about twenty per cent of the weight of which is treacle. There are a few who smoke, principally emigrants from Sierra Leone, Cuba and the Brazils.

As might be expected, the use of ardent spirits is very common; yet the natives are seldom seen drunk, the regulations of their Ogboni lodges forbidding it.

Cola-nuts, *(cola acuminata,)* a bitter and slightly astringent vegetable, are used by all, although in some places expensive. It probably counteracts the effects of the laxative character of their food. Whenever any one wishes to show particular mark of respect to his guest, he presents him, with great formality, a few cola-nuts. A little boy or girl brings a covered vessel, the best in the house, and prostrating, presents it. Abundant thanks and salutations follow. They have a proverb which says: "Anger draws arrows from the quiver: good words draw cola-nuts from the bag."*

There is not a more affable people found any where than are the Akus. Not even Frenchmen are more scrupulous in their attention to politeness than they. Two persons, even utter strangers, hardly ever pass each other without exchanging salutations, and the greatest attention is paid to the relative social position of each in their salutations. Equals meeting will simply say, *acu;* but one addressing a superior affixes some word to *acu,* thus, *acabo, (acu abo,†) acuni,* etc. The superior usually salutes first, and when the disparity of position is great, the inferior prostrates. The young always prostrate to the aged. Women kneel, but never prostrate. Sons, without reference to age or rank, prostrate to their mothers or senior female relatives. They never suffer any thing to interfere with the observance of these courtesies. There is an appropriate salutation for every occasion for instance: *acuaro,* good morning; *acuale,* good evening; *acushe,* for

* See Crowther's Vocabulary of the Yoruba language.
† One vowel dropped for euphony.

being industrious; *acabo,* or *acuabo,* (*ua* as diphthong,) for returning from a journey; *acatijo,* for long absence; *acujoco,* for sitting or resting; *acudaro,* for standing or walking; *acuraju,* expressive of sympathy, in distress or sickness; *acueru,* for bearing a burthen; *acualejo,* for entertaining a stranger. So rich is the language in salutations, that the above list could have been increased indefinitely.

At Oyo, the capital of the Yoruba nation, there is an old man, apparently in a very humble position, for no one is more condescending and courteous than he. He is, nevertheless, no less a personage than the Onoshoko, or "Father of the King," an officer of state so called. In the event of the king's demise, the privilege of choosing a successor devolves on him; hence his position is really very exalted: besides, he is the party with whom the king is bound to advise on all important affairs. It is customary for men in high positions, the king's relatives, chief Balaguns, and so forth, to construct in front of their houses certain turret-like contrivances, called by them *akabi.* The king offered Onoshoko to construct akabis in front of his house, as his position and rank demanded them. "No," said the old man, "Onoshoko is well enough without akabis. Let not any one be able to say, from my example, that he too must have akabis: honor belongs to the king only." He is the only man in the kingdom who is privileged to approach the king without prostrating, nevertheless he insists on doing so, explaining his conduct always by the remark that he, in his respect to the king, would ever be an example for others to copy. The king himself, determining not to be outdone, whenever Onoshoko enters the palace-yard, prostrates to the old man; and it is common for those about the palace to see one of them stealthily approaching the other, in order first to assume this position of respect.

Except with the few Africans who have been brought under the influence of Christianity, polygamy is universal. A man's position in society is estimated either by his bravery in war, or his wealth; and he can only manifest the latter by the number of his wives, children and slaves. From this circumstance men are frequently reported wealthy, and yet in emergencies can not raise ten bags of cowries, (about $40.) Wives are commonly engaged at an early age, frequently before six or seven years old. This is done by paying to the parents a stipulated sum, and occasionally making presents both to them and the betrothed. When the engagement is concluded, a bracelet is placed about the wrist to signify the new relation she sustains. She remains with the parents until of proper age to be taken home to her husband. If she comes with honor, two or three days after, adorned with costly cloths and jewels, and with music, she marches with a large company of maidens through the city, to receive the congratulations and presents of her friends, which are generally on such an occasion very liberally bestowed. Otherwise, the parents are made to refund the whole amount advanced in engaging her, and the guilty partner to her infidelity, if known, is prosecuted for adultery. If the intended husband is a youth, never before married, his mother, or less frequently his father, makes the engagement for him; and the parties are respectively kept in ignorance of each other until they are both of suitable age to live together.

A less troublesome way of procuring a wife, with many, is to resort to the slave-marts of Ilorin at once, money in hand, and make their choice. The latter, of course, are slaves, as well as their children, between whom, however, and other slaves, there is some distinction. Wives procured according to the first of these methods, although not regarded as slaves, are practically as much so as the others, for like them, at the death of their lord they become nominally, and often really, the wives of his eldest son, except, of course, his own mother. They have, however, the privilege of choosing the next elder son, or of observing ever after a state of celibacy, which but few women would choose, as it is regarded reproachfully.

According to their means of procuring them, men possess from a single wife to two or three hundred. Except the chiefs there are few, however, who have more than about twenty. The Yoruba king of Oyo, Adelu, who is reputed the wealthiest man of the Akus, maintains about three hundred wives.* They are never suffered to leave the palace-yard, except on certain days, when they march in procession through the town in charge of eunuchs, of whom the king has a large number. Men are not suffered to approach them in these excursions. The King of Ilorin and other great personages of his court also keep their wives always confined. In this case, however, they are supported. In Abbeokuta, where even the wives of the king must support themselves, they are permitted to go abroad, and are generally among the most industrious traders of the place.

Inquiry is sometimes made as to whether wives agree among themselves. I answer, they do, as well as a number of women living in the same house can under other circumstances: at any rate, their disputes do not arise from the fact that they are all the wives of the same husband. There is always one, only one, who is intrusted with the domestic affairs of her lord, and to her all the others pay the greatest deference, and they expect the recently married to receive more favor than others: making this philosophic calculation, they are saved much of what, under a different and purer system of morals, would be highly irritating and disgusting.

After polygamy it may be appropriate to make a few remarks respecting its sister evil, slavery, which exists all through this section of Africa. Although the term "slav-

---

* Including the surviving wives of his father, who as already mentioned, are all nominally his, he is said to have about one thousand.

ery" is the only word by which the institution can be properly designated, it is certainly not of the same character as the American institution, there being but little disparity between the condition of the master and that of his slave, since the one possesses almost every advantage accessible to the other. Slaves are often found filling the most exalted positions: thus at Abbeokuta all the king's chief officers are his slaves, and they are among his most confidential advisers. On certain state occasions, one or other of these slaves is often permitted to assume in public the position of the king, and command and receive in his own person the homage and respect due to his master. So in Ilorin, Dungari, the prime minister of the king, daily sits in the market-place to receive the homage of the populace intended for the king, and yet Dungari, really the most important personage of the kingdom, and in rank even above the king's own sons, is a slave. Instances of this kind might be afforded almost indefinitely.

Slaves are procured chiefly by conquest, sometimes in warfare as justifiable and even more so than the wars waged among civilized nations; at other times predatory, and undertaken solely for their capture. Not a few incur slavery as a penalty for crime. Some are sold to defray either their own debts, or it may be the debts of others for which they have become liable; and frequently children are kidnapped and sold away into distant parts.

Although but a few years since every heathen town in this region abounded with slave-markets, there is now, doubtless through the influence of Christian civilization, nothing of the kind seen; and although it would be unsafe to say that slaves are not sometimes sold, yet if so, it is done secretly. The first and only marts we met for "this description of property," were at Ilorin, a Mohammedan kingdom. There was there, besides several small numbers exposed in different places throughout the town, a large market, the Gambari, almost exclusively devoted to their sale, and in which there were certainly not less than from five to six hundred. Christian America and Mohammedan Ilorin do with complacency what the heathens of Yoruba and Egba feel it a disgrace to practise.

At Ilorin we sojourned with Nasamo, the king's sheriff, in whose company only we were permitted to walk about the city. On arriving at the Gambari market in one of our excursions, he pointed to the slaves and jocularly asked whether I wished to purchase. I embraced the opportunity to show him the wrong of making slaves of our fellows, and the great injury which it inflicted not only upon those who suffer, but also on those who practise it. Nasamo fills a high position in the state, and is the master of a large number of slaves; nevertheless he is himself a slave, and doubtless thought of his youthful home and dear parents from whom he was stolen. He admitted all I said, and observed that he wished there was no such thing; but while it existed it was better that they be exposed in the markets than that they should be sold privately, "for then bad men would seize the defenseless and our children, and we would not know where to find them."

The Mohammedans do not sell their co-religionists into slavery: they sometimes hold them as slaves, but only when they were bought as heathens and converted after coming into their possession; but these are never after sold. Here is a vast difference from that class of Christians, so called, who buy and sell the members of their own church, the partakers of the same communion with themselves. How much better are such than the heathens, or even these benighted Mussulmans?

Although, as I have before shown, slavery in Africa is not like slavery in America, or even as it is in Cuba, yet it is still a fact which must not be disregarded, that, more or less, it is slavery—such, it is true, as the teachings and example of good men might quietly but certainly in time overthrow, but which might also by an obverse course assume most of the abhorrent phases of the

American institution. My own opposition to slavery does not arise simply from the suffering and ill-treatment which the bondman endures, for in that case I would have to acquit perhaps the majority of American masters. I oppose it because a human being is by it reduced to the condition of a thing, a mere chattel, to be bought or sold at the option of his fellow-man, whose only right to do so is the accidental circumstance of superior power—a power which the good should use to protect rather than oppress the weak. I oppose it because I feel the common instinct that man has an inalienable right to "life, liberty and the pursuit of happiness." Hence I do not regard a slave-owner, even when he makes his slave as comfortable and happy as a slave can be—in all other respects, it may be, as well off as himself—I do not, I say, regard such a person as therefore less guilty: indeed, if there is one class of them whom I detest more heartily than another, it is that class whose course is to render the slave, if possible, contented with his condition.

From this view, therefore, I place my opposition to African slavery on the same ground as to American slavery, and God helping me, shall labor as earnestly for the overthrow of one as for the other.*

Rev. Mr. Townsend has a small fund at his disposal for assisting slaves to redeem themselves. He has helped by this means several to obtain liberty. The money is usually paid for them without any other condition than a promise to repay it when able to do so. I was told of one instance where a party so helped had not been heard of

---

* The following distinctions or grades of servitude prevail: one absolutely free through all generations is termed, *"Omo olu wabi."* The issue of the child of slave parents, marrying an *"Omo olu wabi,"* is deemed *"eru idili,"* or a slave connected with the family. An absolute slave is called *"eru."* One in pawn, placed in that condition by another, is termed *"wafa:"* one voluntarily placing himself in pawn is *"Faru so fa."* A favorite slave, *"eru,"* at the death of his master is seldom if ever considered any longer an *eru,* but becomes *"eru idili,"* and generally marries in the family, in which case his children, if by free mothers, become absolutely free.

for two or three years: when he was almost forgotten, he one day appeared and refunded gratefully the whole amount, pleading bad health for not doing so before.

One of the most marked characteristics of the Africans, not only in this section, but all along the Western coast, is the grace and symmetry of their forms, so well yet so unostentatiously displayed by their ordinary costume. Nor can there be any wonder on this account, considering their freedom from all those habits of civilized life so contrary to nature, and which tend so much to the physical deformity that so often offends good taste.

One never passes a group of boys at play without witnessing some of the most dexterous performances of tumbling, wrestling and other exercises tending to the development of the muscular powers of the system. In their dances too they exhibit evolutions, throwing at once every muscle into action, which would almost be regarded as impossible except witnessed.

In the towns further interior than Abbeokuta, in which the use of fire-arms has not yet become general, one frequently sees groups of boys contesting in feats of archery, with great skill. In Oyo bets are only permitted in these exercises. There are several fine games of skill practised by the Akus. A favorite one is the "wari." The apparatus consists of twelve cups arranged in two rows, hewn out of a single block of wood. Four bean-like seeds are placed in each cup, and the game is begun by each party alternately taking the contents of one cup of the row next himself and distributing them, one by one, beginning at the cup next to that from which he took them. When one party can throw the last three or four of his beans into the cups of his antagonist, containing not more than one or two beans each, he seizes the contents as his prize, and thus they continue until the beans are all taken, when each counts what he possesses, the victory being of course accorded to him who has most. There is perhaps not a house in which one or more of these apparatus is not kept, for the entertainment of the inmates. They are found too, at all the "beer-shops," if the reader will permit the application of that term to the places at which the native *oti*, or corn-beer, is sold. I never made a more acceptable present to any one, than of four dozen pretty glass balls, or glass marbles, if you please, to the Alake of Abbeokuta, to use in his game of wari. Another game, in which they are frequently seen engaging with much interest, is the *dili*, a kind of tee-ta-too, more complicated, however, and certainly more interesting than that memorable game of our school days. A large square, divided into thirty-six smaller squares, is traced on the ground, on the opposite sides of which the contestants sit. Each is prepared with twelve "men" differently colored. The parties put down one piece alternately, until all are disposed of, when the game is continued by each moving his men from place to place, until he can arrange three of his own on successive squares on a line, which feat entitles him to one of his adversary's men. The effort of each then is, first to procure this arrangement of his own, and next to prevent his adversary from doing likewise. Of course the party capturing most men wins the game.

I insert here a stray fact, lest it should be forgotten. In Abbeokuta and throughout the Aku country, old women are seen *nursing* infants, *not their own,* as in many instances they were far beyond the period of life when such a thing is at all possible.

Wild bees are very common in Africa. One day a large swarm alighted near our house. I essayed to take them in a box, and after two or three unsuccessful attempts, abandoned the undertaking, as it seemed utterly impossible to induce them to take up with a civilized abode. Next morning passing near the box, which was thrown carelessly under a tree, I was surprised to find, that they had quite changed mind, and were busily laboring in their new domicile. They continued several weeks, when ceasing to hear their busy hum, I examined, and found that they had again departed. They carried off, of course, all the honey, but left plenty of wax, which I prepared and brought with me as a sample of African beeswax. The natives thought me a charmed man, because, forsooth, I was not stung to death in the undertaking.

This section of Africa is sometimes the theatre of terrible thunder-storms. In one of these, my colleague, Dr. Delany, accompanied by Reverend Mr. Reed, missionary at Oyo, was caught one night returning from a visit to a friend, some distance from our dwelling. The doctor rode a young horse, unaccustomed to the road; Mr. Reed's could find its way back on any road it had travelled. The rain fell in torrents, and it was dismally, totally, absolutely dark; being out myself that night, I could not see my hands, and sometimes, waiting for the flashes of lightning to show the path, my servant would stumble over me, unable to discover any object before him. Every one knows the impossibility of keeping, blindfolded, in a given direction, so we continually deviated from the narrow path, and were in imminent danger of falling into one or other of the numerous excavations from which the natives procure clay to construct their walls. A large rock intercepted the path my friends took returning home, over which Mr. Reed's horse, after some urging, passed, but the Doctor's obstinately refused to follow, and Mr. Reed's as obstinately refused to return. At last they concluded to pass round a little to the right of where they stood to rejoin each other, in trying to effect which both lost their way. Mr. Reed got home with but little trouble, but the Doctor spent half the night wandering over the least inhabited portions of the city, wet to the skin, the rain all the time pouring. He had been but a few days at Abbeokuta, and of course knew nothing of the language. Coming to a native compound, he essayed to attract attention by the use of the two or

three words, the pronunciation (not the meaning) of
which he knew indifferently. With a loud voice, (the
Doctor is a second Stentor,) he cried *acushe!* (a term of
salutation to the industrious.) The natives were aston-
ished, and instantly extinguishing their lights, they fled
to the recesses of their dwelling, and, although the Doctor
exhausted his whole vocabulary in the effort, he could
not induce them to stir. After one or two more fruitless
attempts at other houses, he at last brought to his aid a
few resolute men, who perceiving that he had lost his
way, conducted him safe to the dwelling of Mr. Samuel
Crowther, Jr., whither I arrived at the same time after
a long search to find him.

A funeral in this section of Africa is not unworthy
of notice. A brother of the chief Atambala having died
during my sojourn at Abbeokuta, I went over to his
house to condole with him on his loss. I found the old
chief in no condition to receive the sort of condolence I
was prepared to offer, as both himself and almost every
other person present was intoxicated. His compound*
was crowded, a large number of his friends being there
to participate in the ceremonies. Drums were beating, the
women singing, and as many as had sufficient command
of their legs were dancing. They permitted me to see the
corpse, and to my astonishment I found it wrapped with
cloths, in exactly the same manner as are Egyptian mum-
mies. The cloth is usually the best the friends of the deceased can purchase. On this occasion they used one
which I had presented the chief a few days before. It was
laid in an open piazza, the walls around which were
draped with velvet and other costly cloths. All this time
there was moving through the city a procession, made up
of drummers, men bearing a board covered with cloths
to represent the corpse, women singing alternately songs
of lamentation and of praises to the dead, with other men

* Walled inclosures in Africa, comprising several dwellings,
are called by the civilized people "compounds."

firing guns, and all dancing and otherwise enacting the most extravagant gestures.

The deceased is always buried in the house in which he lived. Sometimes a stone is placed on the spot, on which offerings to his manes are occasionally deposited. In some cases, where the party was greatly respected, on account of his position on earth, he becomes after death the subject of religious adoration.

The Africans are not behind either the English or Americans in their love of pageantry. The writer does not remember a day spent at Abbeokuta without having witnessed something of this sort. The most frequent were processions of societies for mutual saving. They are formed chiefly of women. Once a week each member deposits a certain amount, the aggregate of which is drawn by one member, who of course continues her deposits, and does not draw again, until all in turn have done likewise. There is no disadvantage in drawing last, as those who do so, receive a consideration for the use of their weekly deposits by the other members.

Before 1839 little if any thing was known of Abbeokuta. The Yorubas and Egbas recaptured and taken to Sierra Leone were sold away before any such place existed, and no travellers had before been in the neighborhood, but at this time, vague rumors began to spread along the coast that the different tribes of the Egbas had united themselves, and had built a new city, powerful from its natural defenses not less than for the brave hearts and strong arms of its people. These were joyful tidings indeed to the Egbas at Sierra Leone, in the bosom of most of whom was immediately kindled the strongest desire, again to be united to their long-lost relatives and friends. Conquering a thousand difficulties, they eventually carried out the object of their desire, and in the short time between 1839 and 1842 we are told by Miss

To My Motherland

Tucker* in her admirable little book that no less than 500 of them left Sierra Leone for their country.

Simultaneously with these occurrences, the people of the Brazils and of Cuba, Egbas, Yorubas, and other Aku tribes who had obtained freedom, began to return. From all sources there are now scattered throughout the country, but chiefly at Lagos and Abbeokuta, over five thousand of these people, semi-civilized generally, but in some instances highly cultivated, being engaged as teachers, catechists, clergymen, and merchants. Industrious, enterprising, and carrying with them, one here and another there, a knowledge of some of the useful arts, they have doubtless been the means of inaugurating a mighty work, which, now that it has accomplished its utmost, must be continued in a higher form by the more civilized of the same race, who for a thousand reasons, are best adapted to its successful prosecution.

The hand of God is in the work, and although many discouragements and impediments might intercept the path of you who would labor for such an end, there is nothing to fear. Persevere, persevere, and the Power, which has already been a safeguard through so many dangers will aid your efforts to the end.

* "Abbeokuta, or Sunrise within the Tropics." Although Miss Tucker has never been to Africa herself, yet her statements are perfectly reliable, as they come from the best sources.

CHAPTER VII

Religion

Shango exorcised — Existence of Spirits — Ifa — Agugu —
Oro — Aspect of a City on Oro-day — Gymnastic Sports
— Pugilistic Encounters — Missions.

There are many Mussulmans among the Akus, but chiefly
the people are heathens. They acknowledge one supreme
being, of whose attributes they have as clear a conception
as civilized people generally, but they do not worship
him directly, but through subordinate deities representing those attributes. Thus in Shango, the god of thunder, lightning and fire, and the most revered of their deities, the Omnipotence of God is worshipped. Oro represents the retributive power, and Ifa the Omniscience of
God. They profess to be sometimes possessed by these
deities. The Reverend Mr. Stone, of the American Southern Baptist Mission at Ijaye, once exorcised Shango in a
very summary manner from a mischievous boy living in
the neighborhood of his dwelling, who, in retaliation for
some affront of his parents, had procured a fagot with
which he attempted to fire their dwelling. Had he succeeded, a great conflagration might have ensued, from
the combustible nature of the materials of the houses.
The inmates of the jeopardized dwelling made no other
attempt to arrest him in his projects, than pitifully imploring the deity to leave him. Mr. Stone, however, hearing of the affair, procured a rod, and seizing the young
scamp soon dispossessed Shango, and so well too, that the
god is never likely to possess him again.

They believe in the spirit after death, and it its

power of being present among the living for good or evil purposes, hence they frequently resort to the graves of the deceased with offerings, consulting them in affairs of importance, and imploring their protection from the dangers of life.

Ifa, one of their inferior deities, is much resorted to as an oracle. He has a numerous corps of priests, who realize great profit from the offerings made the god, to induce favorable responses. He is consulted by means of a sort of checkerboard, covered with wood-dust, on which the priest traces small squares. The party consulting the god hands him sixteen consecrated palm-nuts, which all the votaries of Ifa carry constantly. He throws them into a small urn, from which taking a few, the number being left to accident, he disposes them at random on the board, and from the order they assume, determines first whether the offerings shall be a goat, a sheep, or otherwise; next he ascertains whether the god is satisfied with the offering; if not, he manipulates further to ascertain whether a pair of pigeons or fowls should not be added. The preliminaries being thus arranged, he enters into his business, all the time holding a free and easy conversation with the applicant, through which he is sure to ascertain the kind of responses most welcome.

The *Agugu,* a fantastically attired individual, is frequently seen at Abbeokuta and other places interior. He represents the spirits of the departed, who are frequently consulted through him. No one is permitted to say he is a man, nor to touch him, under penalty of death. If he touches any one, the party touched must die—a dangerous power, it seems, to place in the hands of ignorant men, nevertheless, one never hears of its abuse. He is so dressed as to leave no part of his body exposed, and speaks in a guttural voice, assumed as a disguise.

Next to Shango, *Oro,* as wielding the executive functions of the government, is certainly the most terrible of their subordinate deities. Whenever a malefactor is to be punished, he is given to Oro, and after that no one knows his fate until his head is seen nailed to a tree in an open place before the king's palace. Every night, after the women are within doors, what is called the voice of Oro is heard around the city. It is on this account that the women of Abbeokuta are not permitted to be abroad after dark. The penalty is death to any woman for saying that she knows how the voice is produced, although it is certain that all know. Any man would also be slain for revealing it. This voice is a peculiar whirling noise, produced by a simple mechanism which the reader must conceive for himself, as a description might involve the writer in trouble on his return to Africa. The town is sometimes given to Oro, generally when any important matter is to be considered. This occurred twice during my sojourn there. The day preceding, announcement is made by the town-crier, who goes around ringing, or rather striking a substitute for a bell. On the first occasion I went out early in the morning, determined not to lose, if possible, any part of the ceremonies of the day. The city, usually from the earliest dawn as busy as a hive, was apparently deserted. It was like a body from which animation had fled; and this, all this because woman was not there, her voice was unheard, and her cheerful smile beaming from her countenance on the stranger, even as she toils beneath her heavy yoke, was not seen. A few men and boys were occasionally met, all looking as if discovered in the perpetration of some guilty action, because, forsooth, they were compelled to perform some office regarded, according to their customs, as proper only for women. All the gates of the compounds were carefully closed and watched. I sought and procured admission to two or three of them, and found the women engaged as usual in their varied occupations, except of course, in those which the circumstance compelled men to perform. I continued my perambulations without meeting any thing remarkable until about ten o'clock A.M., when a large number of persons gathered on the open ground in front of the king's palace, singing very prettily and keeping time by striking together two small pieces of very hard wood, which each carried. In a few minutes the king's messenger or lieutenant, with his suite, came out, representing the king. He thanked the company for their praises to the king which formed the burthen of their songs, and having for a few minutes joined with them in a dance, he presented them some cowries and retired. Later in the day I repaired to another part of the city, where I learned several of the elders and chiefs were to meet. Much of the ground was already occupied by young men and boys in active competition for the applause of the crowd which was always liberally accorded to those who performed satisfactorily with their Oro apparatus. Here and there also were other groups, engaged in tumbling, and other active gymnastic sports, which they accomplished excellently. A procession was formed by the elders of the Ogboni lodges and the king's people, and with drums, etc., beginning with the king they went from chief to chief. Of course they remained without the gate. The chief comes out and all together enjoy a vigorous dance. They then sit down, all but one, who praises the chief to his face. A few strings of cowries are then distributed and the procession moves on. Returning homewards late in the afternoon I met some terrible fights. In one instance particularly, a young fellow was most unmercifully whipped. His offense seems to have been of the sort in which one of the other sex was participant. Punishment for these offenses is often reserved for such days when, as on election-days with us, there is greater freedom to engage in pugilistic encounters with impunity.

The next Oro day was only a week before my final departure from Abbeokuta. It was on the occasion of holding a council to consider the duty of the Egbas in relation to a war between the people of Ijaye, their friends and allies, on the one side, and Oyo, and Ibadan on the other. Early in the morning the chiefs and great men of the town, in great state and with many followers, began to assemble in front of the king's palace, at which the king, surrounded by the male members of his household, was seated. There was present the largest concourse of persons I ever witnessed. The young men and boys were engaged as on the other occasion. When all who were to participate in the council had arrived, the king and chiefs repaired to an Ogboni Lodge near, where their business was transacted in secret. This concluded, they returned to the square, to inform the people on what they had determined, and to procure their concurrence, which at Abbeokuta is very essential, particularly as the rulers have no power to execute their designs without the popular arm.

There are five missionary stations, with a school attached to each, at Abbeokuta, and about the same number at Lagos. The congregations of these churches consist principally of people from Sierra Leone. There are many native pupils who also attend the services at the churches, but the number of adult converts is small, except as above remarked, from among the people from Sierra Leone.

All the people from Sierra Leone, as well as many of the natives speak English, and some also read and write correctly. I have seen at Abbeokuta several boys, who have never been out of that town, having a pretty correct knowledge of most of the branches of a common English education, English grammar, arithmetic, geography, etc., besides a good acquaintance with Scripture history. They make apt scholars.

Journey To Yoruba

Our Caravan — Atadi — Extortion of Carriers — Ilugun —
Peter Elba — Open Air Accommodation — Articles left
by the roadside for sale — Ijaye — Kumi — Telegraphic
drums — Interview with Chief — "Palaver with the water"
— Great Market — The Drivers — Carriers —Value of a
Shirt — Departure for Oyo — Fever again — Visit to King
Adelu — Exchange of Presents — Tax collecting — Snake-
Charmer — Adeneji — Small Pox — Ogbomishaw — Dr.
Delany, Fever still again — Scarcity of Water.

Having completed our business at Abbeokuta, we began
to prepare for a journey through the entire extent of the
Aku country, terminating at Ilorin, but were unable to
carry out our intention for several weeks, owing to the
illness of myself first, and my colleague next. At last we
both found ourselves well, and after two or three days
spent in purchasing horses, employing servants, carriers,
and effecting other provisions, we finally left Abbeokuta
at mid-day on the 16th January, 1860, for Ijaye. Our little
caravan consisted of twelve persons, namely, of ourselves,
two boys, one to the care of each horse, an interpreter, a
cook, six carriers, besides several natives met on the road,
who kept with us, as they were journeying in the same
direction. The same evening we sojourned at Atadi, a
small Egba town, where we were kindly accommodated
by the "visitor" of the Church Missionary Society, a
worthy, pious man, whose example and teachings are
effecting much for those among whom he labors. He possesses a neat little house, which is very comfortable
though built of mud and in the native style.

By daylight the next morning we expected to resume our journey, but were unable to obtain a relay of carriers for several hours; not that there were not several to be had, but finding that we were compelled to employ them, or be greatly incommoded, they seized the opportunity to exact more than three times the sum usually paid. Besides, they soon discovered that our interpreter, into whose hands all these things were committed, was a native of the coast, and therefore unacquainted with the manner of proceeding. There was no alternative but to submit to their extortion. No where are people quicker to perceive an advantage, and more ready to use it. We left Atadi about ten A.M. The road was exceedingly busy, as there were thousands of persons bearing palm-oil and other commodities to the coast for sale.

The next town at which we encamped for the night was Ilugun. When we were within five or six miles of it, one of our boys, Peter Elba, an intelligent sharp boy, who speaks English and reads and writes well, began to break down, his feet becoming sore and swollen, as he had never walked so much before. Tired of riding, I dismounted and placed the poor fellow on the horse the rest of the way. This was intended as much for my own accommodation as for his relief; nevertheless I never heard the last of it, as the poor fellow, deeply grateful for the act, told it to everybody he met, either the interpreter or cook being generally near, to confirm or exaggerate his statements.

The headman of the little town having treated some missionaries unkindly, whether designedly or not I am unable to say, we were advised not to sojourn with him, but to pass through the town and put up at the house of an old man, living a short distance beyond the wall. We did so, as it is sometimes wise to take the advice of the missionaries. As soon as the headman learned that strangers had arrived, he sent a messenger desiring us to come to see him, which I did, accompanied by our interpreter, and was very kindly received. He could not present us a lamb or kid, because, said he, the young persons are not at home to catch them. This was equivalent to asking for a present, which I granted in the form of a tin box of matches, and a small looking-glass. He complained that both ourselves and other civilized persons passing through his town, had treated him ill, by not stopping at his house. I frankly explained the reason, namely, his unkind treatment of missionaries who had sojourned with him before. He protested that he had never designed any ill himself, and would not suffer to inflict any if he knew it. After all, I believe the whole matter was the result of misunderstanding, as he did not seem like one who would willingly harm any body, much less civilized people. Although the party with whom we sojourned had a large house, he really had no accommodation within it for travellers, so that we were compelled, as we have repeatedly done before and after, to sleep on a mat in the open air, where, however, being tired, we enjoyed a good repose, without any serious consequences. So much for the "pestilential night air of that baneful clime."

The next morning when we were ready to leave, poor Peter could not walk; so leaving some cowries for his expenses, we were obliged to leave him to come on with the mail-man, who was expected to pass in a few days. He reached Ijaye before we departed for the next town, Oyo, but was unable to accompany us further. We never saw him again, as on our return from the interior we were unable to enter the city which was surrounded by hostile forces. His abode with the missionaries is, however, a guarantee of his personal safety.

On the road to Ilugun we met in several places fruits and other articles exposed for sale, without any person near to watch them. There were several little heaps of cowries left by those who had purchased. A few cowries were also deposited near each article to indicate its price. It is incorrect to suppose, however, that these articles were entirely unprotected. Suspended from a rod there is a small bundle of dried grass—Shango's torch—hanging always over the articles for sale, which is an appeal to the god that he should set fire to the house of any one wicked enough to steal them. This is even a greater protection than the presence of a person could be, for there are those expert enough to elude human vigilance, who would never expect to do likewise to Shango.

Crossing what was then, in the dry season, a gentle brook, but which at other times is a river of considerable magnitude, we entered the gate of the city of Ijaye, and were conducted to the station of the American Baptists by a boy whom we met at the gate, dressed in a shirt of civilized manufacture, a sure indication that he was belonging to the "mission family." The occupants of the station, Messrs. Phillips and Stone, and the wife of the latter, were out at the time, but soon arrived, and invited us into the house. In a few minutes we were provided with as fine a supper as we ever enjoyed in Africa.

Ijaye is one of the largest of the Yoruba towns, containing not less than eighty thousand inhabitants. It is ruled by Kumi, entitled Arey, a man, intelligent, active, haughty, cruel, ambitious, stubborn and despotic, yet an excellent ruler, if we judge from the decorum of his people and the respect which they show him. By the people of the surrounding towns he is much hated, and will not be permitted to maintain his position longer than they can help. The town is a part of the Yoruba kingdom, but Kumi has for several years disputed the legitimacy and defied the authority of the king at Oyo, and has actually set up himself as his rival.

Accompanied by the missionaries mentioned before, we made his excellency a visit, a day or two after our arrival. He was not at home when we reached his palace, but his officials received us kindly, and promised to call him immediately, which one of them did by making a loud peculiar noise with a drum, which, with its drummer, is kept for this and similar purposes. These drummers can, we learned, communicate, nay, converse with each other at any distance within the sound of the instrument. After we were seated a few minutes the chief entered, attended by a large retinue, at the head of whom he walked with much grace and dignity. He seated himself in a piazza, the old men and officers of his court betook themselves to the left, the right side was reserved for us and our party, and the general crowd seated themselves promiscuously in front of us in the yard. Our interview was very cordial. We mentioned the object of our visit to the country, and obtained his consent, joyfully accorded, that our people should come to live in peace in his town, and he promised that they should have all the land they required. About to depart, I presented my hand to shake, which, forgetting himself, he was about to do, when the surprise of the missionaries and some other individuals of the crowd arrested him, and he drew back his hand. From superstitious motives, he never shakes hands with "Oyibos," but would have shaken ours, had it not been for the sensation exhibited at the time.

Several of the people of Ijaye lost their lives in the river, while fishing, which induced the Arey to make a law that no one should ever fish in that river again. He said that the river was angry because its children were killed, and therefore revenged itself by killing his children, as he calls his people. Liking the sport, but unwilling to break the law, the Rev. Mr. Phillips sent to request his permission to fish in the brook. He replied, that as long as neither he nor his people make any palaver with the water, the water could make no palaver with them, white man could do as he liked, but when the palaver came, he must keep it to himself.

The most noticeable feature of Ijaye is its market, covering an area of over twenty acres, and attended three times per week by from fifteen to twenty thousand persons. In it are found, besides native produce, commodities from almost every section of the globe: swords, sandals, silk-yarn, otto of rose, paper, beads, etc., from Egypt and other Mediterranean States of Africa; and cloths, cutlery, tin and earthen wares, guns, gunpowder, rum and tobacco, from England, the United States, France, Germany and the Brazils. Among the principal articles of native produce were sheep, goats, fowls, butter, Indian-corn or maize, rice, yams, *(Dioscorea Bulbifera,)* casava, *(Jatropha Janipha,)* sweet-potatoes, *(Convolvulus Batatas,)* Guinea-corn, *(Sorghum vulgare,)* beans, several varieties; cotton, raw and manufactured; clothing; mechanical and agricultural implements of iron (native smelting;) brass, pewter and glass rings, and other trinkets, etc. As large and populous as is the market, it is conducted with the greatest order. There is a particular place appropriated for the sale of each class of goods: thus in one place may be seen spinners offering their yarn to those who weave; in another, weavers offering their cloths; then those who sell iron-ware, sitting in their own quarters, and next to them the dealers in beads and other ornaments: here is the meat-market, and there the wood-market, and the clothing-market, and the place for the sale of live-stock, etc. etc. One man manages the entire affair with the greatest of ease. The same characteristics exist in all the other markets we visited from Lagos to Ilorin, but no where else were they so extensive.

We continued at Ijaye for a fortnight, spending the time in visiting the objects of interest in the neighborhood, taking photographic views, and otherwise making ourselves as comfortable as possible. On account of threatened hostilities between Ijaye and Oyo, the next town, we were unable to procure carriers when ready to resume our journey, and our interpreter, participating in the fears of the natives, would do little to help us in procuring them. We were finally obliged to go to seek them ourselves, in which we succeeded by lending each carrier a shirt, for so great is the respect entertained for the civilized, that even the assumption of the garb affords protection and the liberty of passing unmolested through a hostile country.

We were favored while at Ijaye with some fine opportunities for observing the peculiarities of the notorious *drivers*. These creatures are neither more nor less than ants, resembling nearly the black ants of this country, and identical with those of the West-Indies, where, however, they are less numerous. They are usually seen in countless myriads, marching in line with great order and apparent discipline. They never attack dwellings, except vermin or the like are suffered to accumulate; then they come, and usually again retire in a few hours, entirely ridding the place of the objects of their attack. Of course before these visitors the occupants of a room must retire: the only inconvenience is, that one is sometimes obliged to do this at midnight. The bite of a single ant is not very painful, but of course the same can not be said of twenty or thirty simultaneous nips on different parts of the person. The inducement to dance is then irresistible. They never leave their line of march to attack an object not molesting them. I have myself stooped over a large train for an hour, watching their progress. The instant you touch them, however, fifty or sixty of the largest and most formidable dart off towards you, when a retreat is prudent. Immediately they return to the line again. It is curious to observe their tactics in attacking larger animals, a rat for instance. A single ant attaches itself to it: the poor creature naturally stops to rid itself of the paltry aggressor, but this delay enables others to join in the attack: for a few minutes a desperate combat is waged, and many an ant, persistently retaining its grasp on the flanks of the victim, is parted asunder by the effort to detach it. Overcome chiefly by fatigue from its own vigorous exertions, the rat at length passively resigns itself to the voracity of its assailants, making now and then only a convulsive effort indicative of the extreme torture to which it is subjected. An effectual way of ridding an apartment of them is to fill the mouth with salt, and when it is moistened with saliva, to blow it over them. They then hasten away with great precipitation. It is not the salt, but the saliva, I think, which is offensive to them, for once at Ijaye, unable to procure salt, I took water into my mouth, and after it was well mixed with the secretion I blew it out at them with the same effect as if salt was used.

It is obvious that while these curious creatures are occasionally the cause of some inconvenience, they are also the instrument of much good, in destroying vermin, which in such a climate might otherwise become intolerable. I never saw or heard of a bed-bug in Africa, their absence being doubtless due to the aggressions of the *drivers.*

On the 4th February we left Ijaye for Oyo, from five to seven hours' journey, in a north-eastern direction. For the two or three days preceding I was troubled with an attack of bilious fever, from which I fancied myself free, but in less than two hours after leaving, it returned with great violence; nevertheless I continued the journey, but was exceedingly ill when I reached Oyo, so as to have given our kind friend the Rev. Mr. Reid, of the American Baptist Mission, whose house was our home, a great deal of trouble. The next day I was better, and by a timely administration of remedies continued well all the rest of our sojourn in Africa. Here we met Mr. Meeking, of the Church Mission Society, a very worthy young man, whom we must here heartily thank for his many kind offices. Accompanied by these gentlemen and interpreters, we made a visit to Adelu, the king of the Yoruba nation, who welcomed us very cordially to his town. There is not another chief or king in the whole Aku country who is surrounded by more of the circumstances befitting his rank, than this man. His compound, or if you please, his palace, is the largest in the country, accommodating over fifteen hundred persons—wives, children, slaves, etc. The number of his wives is said to be fully one thousand. Many of these, however, are only nominally so, for according to a custom among them, the wives of a father at his death become the wives of his son, and frequently we find very old women calling themselves, on account of the position in society it gives them, the wives of one or other of the kings or chiefs, who in reality were only the wives of the grandfathers of such.

It was necessary to send a messenger the day before, to announce to Fufu, the king's lieutenant, our intended visit to his majesty, as, because we were strangers he would only receive us in state, and required due notice to effect the necessary preparations. He was seated under an *acabi*, one of the turret-like arrangements already mentioned, surrounded by his wives, his head reclining on one, his feet resting on another; one fanned him, another wiped the perspiration from his face; one held an umbrella of many colors over his head, and another a small vessel carefully covered up, in which his majesty occasionally deposited his salivary secretions,* which accumulated fast in consequence of the quantity of snuff he takes in the mouth, in common with all the native adults, and often even the children of this region. His dress consisted of a costly tobe and shocoto of the same pattern, both nicely embroidered, a cap of red silk-velvet, and Mohammedan sandals. On his wrists he wore massive silver rings, and a strand of large corals about his neck.

In front of the acabi, on both sides of a passage left by which to approach his majesty, were several of his slaves, the principal officers of his household, several men with long trumpets, on which they blew loud blasts, applauding those points of the conversation deemed wise or witty, and several eunuchs.

* They have a superstition that their enemies can hurt them by procuring their spittle and subjecting it to certain manipulations.

As usual, we explained the object of our visit to Africa, with which he was as much pleased as any of the other native authorities with whom we had before treated. We made him a small present, and received according to custom a return present of a fine sheep and three heads of cowries. Our interview was an exceedingly pleasant one, and every day we continued at Oyo after that, a messenger was sent to inquire after the health of the king's relatives, as he ever after called us.

A tax was being collected for the expense of the war which the king was preparing against Ijaye, the manner of collecting which we had an opportunity of observing. It was very simple. At each of the gates, which are only wide enough to suffer a horse to pass easily, there stood two men, one on each side, elevated on blocks of wood, who as the people passed through returning from their farms, abstracted from the baskets a few yams, ears of corn, or of whatever else their loads consisted.

One day in going through the market we saw a man sitting by the way-side, to whom many people as they passed gave a few cowries. As we approached nearer we found that he was one of the celebrated snake-charmers, and had at the time one of these reptiles about his neck and body as large as a man's arm: of the length we could not well judge, as much of it was coiled under his garment.

My other boy, Adeneji, here took the small-pox, and of course could not accompany us further. We left Oyo on the 8th February, and two days after arrived at Ogbomishaw, at which we sojourned only one day. We visited the chief, informed him of the object of our visit, exchanged presents, took an excursion over the town, and left early the next morning. Except a fine park, we found no object of interest peculiar to this town. Although a large place, of fully fifty thousand inhabitants, there were no missionaries. The American Baptists have a fine station there, but no missionary has occupied it for more than a year. There is no impediment whatever, and it seems a pity that it should be left thus uncared for.

Early in the morning of the 10th February, we left Ogbomishaw for Ilorin, the terminus of our journey. On account of the difficulty of procuring carriers, we were compelled to wait at the gate until nearly four in the afternoon. In the mean time Dr. Delany began to experience symptoms of returning fever; nevertheless, as it was necessary to hasten our journey, he persisted in going. We had not left two hours when the symptoms became so aggravated that he was obliged to dismount and lie by the road-side. Leaving our cook with him, I rode on as fast as possible, to find a place at which we could sojourn for the night, and fortunately found a small farm village about four miles further on. I then rode back, and met him about two miles from where he was left.

It was, fortunately for us, the dry season, when it is really more comfortable to sleep in the open air, which notwithstanding the Doctor's health we were obliged to do, as there were no accommodations for us under shelter. We left early the next morning to reach Ilorin, one long day's journey from this village. It was perhaps the most uncomfortable day's journey we ever had, as we could not procure a draught of clean water, the brooks and springs being almost all dry, except here and there a little pool so stagnant, dirty and nauseous that only severe thirst induced us to touch it. This was, however, a trouble that could easily have been provided against, by each party taking a small bottle of this necessary liquid for his own use.

Within three or four miles of Ilorin we rested at a farm-village to change carriers, etc., and take each of us, horses and all, a long draught of water, under such circumstances an invaluable luxury.

CHAPTER IX

Ilorin

Magnificent Conflagration — Grassy Plains and Forests —
Freedom of the Country from Beasts and Reptiles; why —
Extravagant Welcome — Nasamo the Executioner, and
his Dwelling — Wifeless — Royal Present of Food —
Prisoners — Interview with the King — Schools — Ara-
bians — Mulatto — Musical Instruments — Banjo —
Beggars — Looms — Gambari Market — Escort.

There was just light enough to enable us to see the dim
outline of the walls as we approached Ilorin, and by the
time we were within the gates it was dark, but the atmosphere was illumined by a brilliant light from the
burning of grass in the plain to the right of the city—a
magnificent spectacle. Except between Abbeokuta and
Ijaye, where there is a dense forest through which it requires fully five hours to pass, forming the division between the territory of the Egbas and Yorubas, the country is clear, with only low scrubby trees much scattered,
with an undergrowth of rank tall grass. In some places,
from what cause it is difficult to say, there can be found
no other kinds of vegetation than this grass, particularly
in the neighborhood of large cities. Every year, after the
harmattan winds, the natives set fire to it, causing an immense conflagration, sweeping over the country like a
tornado.

From the mission-house at Ijaye, southward over an
elevated country without the gate, we have seen a line
of fire fully a mile long, driven by the wind so furiously
as to entirely clear a space of ten or fifteen square miles in

less than two hours, and still progressing out of sight, making a terrible noise. As it burns, thousands of birds and other small animals are driven out, and are immediately seized by hawks, which during the dry season are very abundant. It is from these fires, doubtless, that there is so little forest land and so few wild beasts, serpents, etc., in this country. During the whole time we were in Africa we saw only three living serpents, one about the neck of the man near the market at Oyo, one at Abbeokuta, and a small, but they say a very venomous one, on the road towards Isehin, where I also saw a few fine deer, which are always expert enough to get out of the way of these fires. We also saw a fawn bounding at full speed over the plain near Ilorin. The fire which so beautifully illumined the darkness as we entered the city was of the kind above referred to.

We met at the gate quite a concourse of persons, chiefly women, who gave us an extravagant welcome, and brought food and water. We partook of the latter only, and hastened to the house of Nasamo, the sheriff o public executioner, to which we were directed by th advice of the Rev. Mr. Reid, who had not long befo visited Ilorin. His dwelling, at no time adapted to t purposes of hospitality, was still worse now that a rec fire in his neighborhood had compelled him, as well a his neighbors, to remove the thatch from his roof. entire building and grounds were comprised in an of not over thirty feet square, and his space acco dated, with ourselves, more than eighteen person sides our horses. Nasamo, though evidently not le seventy or eighty years old, is yet vigorous both i and physical constitution. He was the first im personage we met without a single wife: he had made him the father of three or four daughters, her death he has lived a widower. One of his dau tends to his domestic affairs.

Early the following day we sent our int

salute the king, and inform him of our visit to his capital, asking to be permitted as soon as possible to pay our respects to him in person. The interpreter was conducted to Dungari, the king's prime-minister, who received, and conveyed the message to his master. Shortly after we received a return salutation from his majesty, together with a large vessel of well-prepared native food, sufficient to feed both ourselves, and attendants for the day, also a similar present from Dungari. These presents were continued for the whole time we remained in the town, but after three or four days our servants and the other inmates of the compound retained, and consumed it among themselves, without even informing us of its arrival, a liberty we cheerfully granted for several reasons.

Every day we were requested to prepare to visit the king, but were continually put off with some slight excuse till the fourth day, when we were led into his presence. This unnecessary delay occasioned us considerable inconvenience, for we were in the mean time virtually prisoners, not being permitted to go out of our uncomfortable quarters until we had first seen his majesty, and obtained his gracious consent to see the town; and even after this consent was obtained, we were only permitted to go out accompanied by Nasamo. The excuse for this was, that he would protect us from harm by the people, a poor excuse, as we had not the least cause of fear, every one being remarkably civil and respectful towards us.

Our interview with his majesty, King Shita, was very interesting. Quite unexpectedly he permitted us at this first interview to see his face, a privilege he never accorded publicly to any who had before visited the place, at the same time informing us, that it was because he regarded us as his own people, descendants of native Africans. Besides the direct subject of our mission, we conversed on the forms of civilized government, his majesty asking many questions respecting Queen Victoria, and

the ruler of the country from which we came, of whom the American missionaries had before informed him. As a "ruse," he invited us to accompany him to his mosque, to which he said he was just going. We accepted his invitation, but when we prepared to go, he laughed and again seated himself, saying that he was glad we seemed to have no prejudices against his religion; he was seated on a mat in a long piazza, usually entirely screened, but on this occasion the screens were drawn up just where he sat, so as to expose him to view, but still keeping out of sight many of his wives. He is an old man, and like the king of Abbeokuta has had the misfortune to lose an eye. He is not a pure Negro, but like many of the Fulanees in his town, one of his parents, most likely his father, must have been an Arabian; his physiognomy therefore is not purely Negro. He is a man of small stature, but well proportioned, and was neatly attired in a white tobe, turban, and red cap. He was surrounded by a number of well-dressed men, priests, officers of his court, eunuchs, etc., all of whom sat in a clean sheltered space before his piazza, but on the ground. We were placed about four yards in front of him, to the right of the company, except Dungari, who with our interpreter was on the right of us. Although the king understands Aku well, and therefore could converse directly with our interpreter, yet the customs of his court require, that all that is said be communicated to him in Fulanee by Dungari, who as before remarked, (see page 193) is, except the king, the most important personage of Ilorin. He is by birth a Fulanee, but of the blackest type of Negroes, as are indeed ninety-five per cent of them; those who are lighter in complexion, or differ in physiognomic conformation, being more or less of Arabian intermixture. In common with many of the people he reads and writes Arabic, to teach which, there are quite a number of schools in the town. We saw there, in the market-places chiefly, several Arabians, some of whom had travelled immense distances across the continent, for purposes of trade, in which they all engage. Other travellers speak of "white people" in Ilorin, but although we spent as long a time there as perhaps any traveller had done, we were unable to find a single individual even as light as myself, though of twenty-five per cent negro blood.

One girl about twelve years old was met, who was evidently the child of some slave-trader of the coast, as she was certainly a mulatto whose father was a white man and not an Arabian, than whom she was much lighter in complexion. Every person of Ilorin is said to speak both the Aku and Fulanee languages, and we found no exception among those who were not foreigners.

The musical instruments of the people of Ilorin more nearly resemble those used in civilized countries, than those seen in other sections of Africa nearer the coast. In a large band which performed before the palace, there were several wind instruments, two or three of which were like our clarionets, and others resembled an English postman's trumpet. An old man came to play and sing for us very often. The instrument he used was the exact counterpart of the Banjo, only smaller, but played in the same way and producing similar music. Accompanied by our *soi-disant* jailer, we made several excursions through the town. Except the existence of numerous mosques and markets, there is no material difference in the appearance of it from others.

There were plenty of blind beggars, a sight quite unusual in other African towns, where we seldom ever saw a beggar. They are attracted to the place doubtless from the custom among the Mohammedans, (a religious custom,) of often ostentatiously distributing money among them.

As an example of the extent to which cotton fabrics are manufactured, we encountered one day in a ride of less than an hour more than one hundred and fifty weavers, busily employed at their looms. These weavers are seen also in the other towns, where they were formerly as abundant, but the influx of better and cheaper fabrics from England has very nearly superseded the necessity of them.

To the Gambari market, allusion has already been made as the greatest depot for the sale of slaves, besides which, there were exposed for sale fine horses, donkeys, mules, horse-trappings, swords, leather work, silk clothing, tobes, antimony, salt, cola nuts, stationery, etc., etc.

Tobacco is much cultivated by the people of Ilorin. They do not cure it like the Americans.

The day before we departed we received a special invitation to exhibit our curiosities—my watch, fowling-piece, etc.—to the king, which gave him much pleasure, and induced the remark from Dungari: "Verily, if I had not a strong mind, I would embrace the customs and religion of such a people."

The next day we took leave of the king, who made us a second fine present of two mats, two pairs of beautifully wrought sandals, and three heads of cowries "to pay our expenses down." At our first interview, after receiving ours, he had made us a present of equal value. A horseman and two foot-soldiers were sent with us, as an escort, and quite a multitude followed us out of the town, wishing us a safe journey and blessings of every kind. The people of Ilorin are not all Mussulmans, there being also a large, almost equal proportion of Yorubas, heathens; these, headed by a powerful Balagun, occasion King Shita considerable trouble, and might one day remove him and his party from power, an object openly avowed. We saw a large number of convicts about the streets, their legs chained so as to permit them a very limited and peculiar locomotion. Such prisoners are not found in other towns, being either sold into foreign slavery or decapitated as the penalty for their offense—the former, a kind of punishment the teachings of their religion forbid the Mohammedans inflicting on their own people.

CHAPTER X

Return

"Two horsemen," and their adventure — Exchange horses —
What about Vaughn — Progress arrested — New route —
Voices in the bush — Village in Ashes — Isehin — A
Hunting Party — Dead man by the Roadside — Ibadan
Soldiers, another adventure — "Enough, Enough, white
man, go on!" — A city on a hill — Berecadu, and its de-
fenses — Night travel in Africa — Abbeokuta again —
"The Dahomians are coming" — Deputation — The Doc-
tor is come, and how he did it — Final Departure for the
Coast — The Carrier Nuisance once more — Troubles —
Heroic Woman — Safe at Lagos — Departure — Krumen
— A Slaver.

On the morning of the third day after our departure from
Ilorin we reached Ogbomishaw, where we intended to
remain only that day, to rest, and proceed early the next,
as we were anxious to reach the coast to obtain our letters; but we were disappointed, as no carriers would stir
out of the town on account of the hostilities raging
amongst the people of Oyo, Ibadan, and Ijaye.

Having spent the day in fruitless search for carriers,
we had just returned to the house, which, through the
kindness of the American Baptist Missionaries, we were
permitted to occupy, when two horsemen rode up to the
door, and dismounting, entered, weary, starved and almost in rags.

These were the Rev. Mr. Stone, and a colored American carpenter in the employ of the missionaries. The surprise of seeing them so unexpectedly, and under such distressing circumstances, being somewhat allayed, Mr.
Stone briefly related to us his adventures as follows:

A colored man named Vaughn, an American, had selected for his abode a locality about three hours' journey from the city of Ijaye, on the road towards Ibadan. The Arey ascertaining that the Ibadans were moving against him, sent information to the missionaries, that they should go and bring their friend within the city, otherwise he could not answer for his safety. Mr. Stone, accompanied by Russel, almost immediately set out on horseback to apprise Vaughn of his danger, and persuade him to come with them. The horse on which Mr. Stone rode, was purchased some months before from the Arey, and was well known all through the country as his favorite war-horse; he was one of the largest, and except that the infirmities of age were becoming manifest, one of the handsomest among the Yoruba horses; besides, only a few weeks before, two large, warlike, Mexican saddles were received from America, which the horses wore at the time of the adventure. They progressed on their journey unmolested until they reached the house of Vaughn, and unfortunately found it already entirely deserted, with much of his property destroyed, and scattered over the ground. There was every indication that the enemy was there and that something serious had befallen their friend. Nevertheless they concluded to proceed to the next village, about one hour's ride, to ascertain, if possible, his fate. They had progressed a few miles when they encountered a body of Ibadans who commanded them to halt and remain with them until the Balagun of the party arrived. Our friends, presuming on the respect always shown to civilized men, and the virtue of the horses, thought fit to disregard the injunction, and giving reins and spurs to their steeds would certainly have soon left the Ibadans far in the rear, had not suddenly before them, and on every side, a large number of soldiers, like spectres made their unwelcome appearance, and actually pointed their long guns at the fugitives, and would have fired, had they not immediately abandoned their design of so unceremoniously forsaking their company. Some, indignant at their attempt to escape, would have done them bodily injury but for the interference of their superiors. After all, they were pretty roughly used, their clothes torn, their hats stolen. There was no alternative, so they passively submitted.

In a few minutes the Balagun arrived, and sent the captives in charge of a few armed men to Ibadan. Arriving there, they were immediately taken before Ogumola, the chief of the city, who after much questioning, suffered them to depart. The timely interference of the Rev. Mr. Hinderer of the Church Mission, stationed at Ibadan, conducted much to their being dismissed with so little trouble. The circumstance of Mr. Stone's riding Arey's war-horse, looking, as well as the other horse, so martial in his caparison, induced the soldiers to regard him and his companion as spies, and hence the cause of their capture; and it was only after good evidence was afforded, that the horse was purchased from the Arey, and also that their mission without the walls of Ijaye was a peaceable one, that they were dismissed.

Not wishing to return by the same road, they attempted to pass through Iwo and Oyo, to Ijaye, but arriving at Iwo, they learned that the road to Oyo was in possession of soldiers who would not suffer any one to pass; on this account they were obliged to proceed to Ogbomishaw. They arrived as before narrated, hungry, tired, and pitifully distressed in mind, particularly Mr. Stone, on account of his wife, who must have suffered extreme agony from the apprehension that harm had overtaken her husband.

Not wishing again to be annoyed on account of the horse, Mr. Stone offered to exchange him for mine, a fine young animal, but not worth in money-value more than half his, to which I consented, as, being well known to the King of Oyo, I could take the horse into his capital without suspicion of connection with the rebel chief.

To My Motherland

The next day we heard that some Egba traders were expected at the farm-village near Ogbomishaw, and that their carriers, who would have to return thence to Oyo, would be glad of the job of taking our parcels thither. I immediately went off to the village, and had the good fortune to engage them. I then hurried back to Ogbomishaw, and having completed our preparations, the next morning we were on the way to Oyo. Mr. Stone, in order I suppose to get as far as possible from association with the animal, rode ahead of us, so as to reach that place a day before us.

We never met a single living soul on the road to Oyo, several thriving villages being now quite deserted, the inhabitants taking refuge in the larger towns.

We arrived at Oyo early on Sunday morning, and proceeded to the compound of the Rev. Mr. Reid, of the American Baptist Mission, whom we did not find, as both he and Mr. Meeking, of the Church Missionary Society, accompanied by a messenger from the king, had gone to Ibadan, to seek Mr. Stone, who had arrived on Saturday evening, and, expecting us, had kindly ordered breakfast, of which, with a keen appetite, we were just about to partake, when Mr. Reid also rode up to the door. He did not go all the journey to Ibadan, having been informed at Iwo that the object of his search was safe and had gone to Ogbomishaw, thence to reach Oyo. Mr. Stone immediately after breakfast set out for Ijaye, to relieve as soon as possible the distress which his wife and friends endured on his account.

As for Vaughn, the party whom Mr. Stone had gone to seek, a few days before he had procured from Ibadan a number of men to assist him to remove his things into that town: unfortunately he got into a quarrel with some of these, one of whom struck him a blow on the head with his weapon, wounding him severely: he returned the blow, and leaving the man apparently dead, fled to Ibadan. Except his money, and a few other articles of value which he had before secured, he lost all his property by this adventure.

We continued at Oyo more than a week, not being able to procure carriers for our parcels. We could have gone on ourselves without any fear of harm, but it was impossible to leave all our things: it was at the same time essential to reach the coast within a month, as our funds were insufficient for a longer stay. After some consultation, it was determined that I should make an effort to get to Abbeokuta down the valley of the Ogun through Isehin.

Accordingly, leaving all the parcels in the care of the Doctor, taking with me only the means of living on the journey, and accompanied by our cook and interpreter, the latter to return for the Doctor if carriers could be found, we left Oyo on the morning of the 6th of March, and arrived at Isehin about eight o'clock the same evening. The road, at best but little frequented, was now completely deserted, and in many places almost impossible on horseback. Two or three hours from Oyo, we came to the iron-smelting village already referred to.

It was apparently entirely unoccupied, and I dismounted and examined the construction of their furnaces: remounting and again attempting to go forward, my attendants hesitated, declaring they heard voices in the bush ahead.

I affected to despise their fears, and moved forwards, bidding them follow, which they did at a very respectful distance. True, we had not advanced a hundred yards when we perceived several groups of armed men on both sides of the road a little way ahead: as we approached, they directed their weapons towards us in rather a threatening manner, yet they did not seem hostile; so urging my horse to a brisk trot, I rode amongst them, laughing and cheerfully saluting them as I approached. They could not help laughing too, but when I presented my hand successively to the first three or four, neither would touch it:

passing the others, I presented it somewhat insistingly to one who seemed the leader: he shook it, several others following his example. They merely inquired whence we came, and suffered us to pass.

About two hours after, we crossed the Ogun and suddenly encountered one of the saddest spectacles in Africa, a village only a few days before full of life and activity, now entirely depopulated, its inhabitants captured as slaves, itself in ruins and ashes. The people belonged to Oyo, and were collected there on account of the employment of ferrying passengers over the Ogun during the rainy season. The King of Oyo having a short time before captured a few of the people of Ijaye, Arey in retaliation sent an expedition against the place, and suddenly pouncing upon the unsuspecting inhabitants at midnight, took every individual and burnt the place.

During this day's journey we saw the largest number of wild animals, deer, monkeys, etc., especially near the river; and as we passed through the village we perceived a flock of Guinea-hens covering an area of over an acre. As before mentioned, we arrived at Isehin about eight in the evening. Mr. Elba, the native reader of the Church Mission, and father of the boy already mentioned, kindly afforded us accommodation. We tarried long enough the next day to pay our respects to the king. We found his majesty attired in his hunting costume, horses, attendants, dogs and arms, all ready to depart, consequently he could not afford a lengthy audience, but was very courteous, and presented me a small smoked animal not unlike the armadillo, a present, I was told, significant of much respect, but which I could not sufficiently appreciate, particularly as it partook of the qualities of venison when most acceptable to certain palates. We also called on the chief Balagun, who gave us a hearty welcome and a few dried fishes. The number of inhabitants does not exceed twenty thousand, and the town is one of the only two in this section, Iwo being the other, which have existed before the troubles which led to the formation of Ijaye, Abbeokua, etc. We left Isehin about eleven A.M., and reached Awaye, the next town, the same evening. The road was quiet and deserted, the people every where fearing to leave home on account of the unsettled condition of affairs. There was the body of a man near the road, a mile from the town, where it had lain for more than a week. A few of a straggling party of Ijaye soldiers lurking in the neighborhood, having unsuccessfully pursued some farmers, were returning to their companions, who fired on them, mistaking them for the fugitives, and unfortunately killed one. The chief ordered that his body, which of course his companions had no time either to take away or bury, should remain, as a lesson to similar marauding parties.

Not more than half an hour after our arrival, the chief waited on me in person to salute me and welcome me to his town. He is the youngest chief in the Aku country, but certainly one of the most intelligent, to judge by his conversation. He sent me a large bowl of milk for supper, and the next morning a fine pig, although he knew I was not in a position to make him a return present. He was very anxious that some civilized person should come to live in his town. It is strange that while, including teachers and catechists, a place like Abbeokuta should have ten or twelve missionaries, besides an indefinite number of native readers or visitors, there should be only an ignorant visitor, whose sole qualification is his ability to read, allowed to a town of from sixteen to twenty thousand people.

My horse and men being tired, we rested all the next day at Awaye.

A woman with her son and daughter besought me to permit them to go under our protection to Abbeokuta. I told her she was welcome to all the protection I could afford, and we left together the next morning early. At about eleven o'clock, when halfway on our journey to Bi-olorun-pellu, we suddenly met about two hundred Ibadan soldiers. My servants, who were before me, attempted to pass by the foremost of them, but were very roughly arrested. Myself and the rest of the party soon came up and were all immediately surrounded. They kept us, while discussing the fate of my people, for nearly two hours. At length they demanded a present as the condition on which they would allow us to proceed. I had nothing to give, having left Oyo with only two suits of clothes, one on my back, the other in a small bundle. My other things consisted only of a gutta-percha sheet and some cooking utensils. I told the man who carried them to open the things and allow them to take whatever they desired: seeing we had nothing, they informed my interpreter, after a little consideration among themselves, that we could depart peaceably, but they must keep as their captives the woman and her two children. It was too distressing to see three human beings about to be deprived of their liberty. The old woman wept bitterly, but her tears were apparently unheeded. I told them that it was impossible for me to leave these people; they had placed themselves under my protection, therefore I could not permit them to be taken away, except with myself also; that they could take my horse, my watch, my money, all I had, in short; but I would not permit them to take these people. They hesitated, I saw they were moved, and I kept up my entreaties. At length the balagun or captain, to whom I addressed myself, and who remained silent all the time I spoke, with almost a tear in his eye, exclaimed, *"Oto, oto, oyibo, molo!"* "Enough, enough, white man, go on." When one of his party attempted to take away a tin cup my interpreter carried, he drew his sword, declaring that it was at the peril of any one to touch us. Some of his people seemed much disappointed. We hurried away, and four hours after were climbing an immense rock, rising like an island from the surrounding plain, on the summit of which is situated "Bi-olorun-pellu," "*If the Lord wills.*"

The party we had so fortunately escaped from, belonged to the same who had arrested the Rev. Mr. Stone, for they knew the horse, and two or three of them contended that he was the same, while others more skilled in logic showed that it was impossible, for the reasons that he was sent to Ibadan, that he was not ridden by the same oyibo, and that he had not on the same saddle. The argument was conclusive, so they contended no longer; but there seemed to be still a few who, by an occasional shake of the head as they viewed the animal, continued to indicate a lingering skepticism. The horse, in his turn, seemed to recognize his old acquaintances, and looked all the time as suspicious as possible.

The people of this town, like those of Abbeokuta, flying from place to place before a relentless enemy, had at last betaken themselves to this naturally impregnable position, and in view of its safety called it, "Bi-olorun-pellu," for, said they, only by the Lord's will, and not by the power of man, can we be removed hence. I never perhaps endured greater labor than in the effort to get my horse up the almost inaccessible cliffs, although assisted by our party, even the women; and when at last we succeeded, the poor beast was much bruised. There are only two passes into the town, one by which it is entered from Isehin, and the other from Berecadu. Three men at each of these could successfully defend the place against any number. It could also hold out against a long siege, for not only is there always a supply of provisions stored away to last for at least two years, but the interstices of the rocks and other places unattainable except by the inhabitants, are susceptible of cultivation, although the amount of produce thus obtained would hardly be equivalent to their ordinary consumption. The same evening we arrived I called to pay my respects to the chief, from whom I received the usual kind treatment: he presented me, as did the chief of Awaye, with a fine pig. The Balagun also gave me a large "rooster." I left the next morning with a thousand blessings from the people, for the woman who with her children I had aided in saving from slavery, had told the matter to all her friends, as she did also at Berecadu and at Abbeokuta, and they, with all the warm gratitude of the African's nature, were exceedingly lavish in their acknowledgments of the deed.

We arrived at Berecadu on the evening of the same day, without any incidents on the journey worth recording. At one of the crossings of the Ogun, we met a large company of Ibadan soldiers, again lurking like wild beasts to seize any unsuspecting native who in such times should venture out to their farms. They had taken possession of a few huts on the banks of the river, used in the wet season by those who make a business of crossing passengers on large calabashes as already described.

First one, evidently the balagun, came out and saluted us very kindly, then another, and still another, until there were more than thirty standing around us. I strove to appear myself, quite at ease, and shook hands and joked with them, but the woman and her son and daughter gave them a "wide berth," while the interpreter and cook, the latter of whom I shall better call Johnson, could ill repress their fears, although they behaved well.

Berecadu is a town of about thirty or thirty-five thousand inhabitants, judging from the extent and character of its only market. The people are partly Yorubas and partly Egbas, paying tribute to both nations, but obliged to guard against both also, as each seems determined to compel the paying of tribute to itself alone. Its defenses are so well contrived that it would almost be as difficult a place to take as Bi-olorun-pellu, except by surprise, and this is not likely, as a large number of armed men, "keepers of the city," are stationed every night at the gates.

There are two walls encompassing the whole city,

leaving a space of about two hundred yards between them, and this space contains a dense forest, with an interlacing undergrowth, utterly impassible to an enemy except by the use of means incompatible with the dispatch of warfare.

We sojourned with the Visitor, who lives in the compound of the chief, to whom I as usual paid my respects and explained the object of my visit. He is almost the most miserable person of the town, old, blind, neglected and in dirt and rags, yet cheerful and apparently much concerned for his people. There is a second chief or regent, who is charged with the municipal administration.

Leaving Berecadu shortly after midnight, we arrived at Abbeokuta in time for breakfast. Except in the warmest part of the day, it is always pleasant to travel in Africa, but it is particularly so at night or near day-break: the country then seen by the mellow light of the moon, or by the gray twilight, seems twice as wild and magnificent, and the flowers distill their perfume in greater abundance: now and then, it is true, one hears the dismal screech of some nightbird, or the yell or howl of some small animal disturbed in his repose by intruding footsteps, but these serve only to break the monotony; and besides, there are the gentle cooing of doves, and the cheerful voices and merry laughter of your native attendants, sufficient to cheer any heart.

Whenever it was practicable, we always preferred travelling at such times; and although much is said in disparagement of night air in Africa, certainly in our case, if injurious at all, it was not as much so as the effects of the sun.

We found Abbeokuta in considerable commotion. Only a few days before, the Dahomians were known to be advancing against the city, but informed doubtless by their spies of the reception that was prepared for them, they suddenly wheeled about and retraced their steps, not without committing much depredation among the people through whose territory they passed.

Every one was also speculating on the war in the interior, and its probable consequences and duration. Being the only person who had returned thence for a fortnight, every one wanted to hear news from me: the king and chiefs desired an interview particularly, respecting the Ibadans we met on the road, who were suspected to be loitering there to join the Dahomians in their contemplated attack.

The morning after my arrival I was waited upon at the house of my kind friend Mr. Samuel Crowther, Jr., by a large deputation of the relatives of the woman who came with me from Awaye. She was not with them herself, being ill from the effect of her fright and the fatigue of such hurried travelling; but there were the son and daughter and her other children, brothers, sisters, aunts, uncles, cousins, and their husbands, wives, children, etc. They brought with them presents of chickens, eggs, fruits, cola-nuts and many other suitable gifts.

The interpreter had accompanied me with the object of returning to inform the Doctor whether carriers could be obtained on the route, and if so, to come with him and our luggage after me to Abbeokuta; but the condition of the road, as the reader already knows, rendered it impossible even for the interpreter to return alone.

My next plan was to return myself, taking with me the letter-bags of the missionaries, which they were very anxious to receive; but both the interpreter and Johnson, who belonged to Lagos, wanted to go home, the former because his mother was at the point of death, the latter because he was longing to see his wife, but he promised to return in a week, and to indicate his sincerity refused to take his wages until then. True to his word, he came at the appointed time, and we were about to set out the next morning, my horse waiting, when our native boy Adeneje, who was left at Oyo with small-pox, came in with a note from my colleague informing me that he had just arrived at our usual place of abode at the Baptist Mission House. After making several fruitless efforts to procure carriers, he was at length favored by the king with the protection of a detachment of soldiers going to join the Ibadans against Kumi, Arey of Ijaye, a few of them being also detailed to the duty of carriers, an office they seemed to regard as derogatory to the dignity of soldiers, judging from the trouble they gave him. The king also sent with him a special messenger to indicate that he was the king's friend, and as such should receive proper consideration. He made the journey through Iwo and Ibadan. When he arrived at the latter place he could only procure carriers for a portion of our things, the Rev. Mr. Hinderer, with whom the Doctor sojourned at Ibadan, kindly consenting to take care of the rest for us. The reader will remember that we had already left a large portion of our property at Ijaye, which though safe, we could not procure, as we were unable to enter the city. From both these circumstances we lost most of our collections, and also some fine photographs.

By the first of April we had completed our arrangements, and were to leave on the morning of the third for Lagos. Carriers were engaged for the journey, as we intended to travel by land, it being the dry season; but when the time arrived we were as usual put off and annoyed by their unconquerable love of gain, and desire to make if possible a fortune out of us. They would come, examine the parcels, and charge three or four times more than the labor was worth. One refuses to pay, and they walk off. After great trouble you procure another set; they serve you in the same way; then the first return and abate somewhat, but the charge is still too great, and you refuse to pay it; they walk off again, expecting that as you are in a hurry, you will call them back, which of course you do not, having acquired some wisdom by your past experience in the country. They go out of sight for twenty minutes, and at last return again, asking an honest price, and the bargain is completed. Surviving all the annoyance, which I assure the reader is much worse than I can depict, we at length left Abbeokuta about nine o'clock in the evening on the fifth of April, intending to sleep that night at Aro, and depart early the next morning; but having attained that point, our relentless carriers placed down their loads, and declared that as they were heavy they would not carry them any further without more pay. This they did because the next day being Oro-day, it would be impossible to get others, and we could not delay a day longer without the risk of losing our passage to England. I was at a loss what to do, but of all things I would not submit to their extortion. At last Mr. Pedro, an intelligent young native, kindly volunteered to procure a canoe to take down the things, thus enabling us to dispense with the carriers entirely. After some effort he succeeded. It was then concluded that the Doctor, accompanied by Johnson, should proceed by land, while I should go with the canoe to look after the safety of our things. The Doctor left about ten o'clock A.M., the things were placed on board, my horse sent back to Abbeokuta, and stepping into the canoe it was pushed off. We proceeded with much labor for about two miles, when it was found impossible to go further: there was not enough water to float it. We were then left in a worse dilemma than at first, for a little more pay would have secured the services of the carriers. Leaving the canoe, I returned to Aro, to procure if possible the aid of a man to push it on, and fortunately met Messrs. Josiah Crowther and Faulkner, the latter a respectable young man from Sierra Leone, who seeing and pitying my unlucky position, sent a few of their laborers to take the luggage down to Agbamiya, a point further down the river, from which place there is always enough water to float a loaded canoe. These laborers instead of returning with the things to Aro, and proceeding thence by the direct road, attempted a short cut and went three or four miles out of the way, so that we never arrived at Agbamiya until about six in the afternoon. Arriving there, by a little more trouble and the offer of good pay on condition of leaving that night, I procured another canoe, and away we went at last.

There is always trouble travelling in Africa with luggage, but it is far less in the interior than among the semi-civilized, neither Christian nor heathen, natives of the coast, who acquiring all the vices of the white man, know little and practise still less of his virtues.

I never experienced real hardship until in this little journey between Abbeokuta and the coast. No sooner had we fairly started than it began to rain heavily, and it continued raining more or less until we reached Lagos, so that, sleeping and waking, I was wet the whole time, forty-eight hours; but I warded off the effects by helping the canoe-man with a paddle the entire way, by which means we also arrived at Lagos earlier. One more unpleasant incident, and I shall relieve the reader. It seemed that the canoe in which we travelled was purchased from an Ijebu, and not paid for. When two thirds down the river, the canoe-man stopped at a small market-village, not expecting to meet there his creditor, but did unfortunately. Some altercation ensued, when the Ijebu began to take the things out of the boat, in order to repossess himself of his property. I remained quiet until he attempted to remove my things, when I interposed. He turned from me, and began to talk very angrily with the canoe-man. Both became more and more excited. At this time another canoe with several men and women came up, and all these took part in the row, which grew more fierce every instant. I saw some of the crowd running away, who in a few moments returned, and with them about thirty men, all armed with knives, their chief at their head. They rushed at the poor man, and the chief seizing the resistless creature was about to slay him, when a woman heroically threw herself in the way of the weapon, and saved him. The row continued fully an hour longer, and terminated at last only from the sheer exhaustion of all concerned. Without an interpreter, and my own knowledge of the language being very limited, I was unable except by conjecture and an expression understood here and there, to learn the details of the dispute.

We arrived at Lagos on the evening of the 7th of April. Dr. Delany accomplished his overland journey in the same time, so that we met crossing the bay, and landed together. The next day, Sunday—Easter Sunday—we attended divine service, and heard a sermon from our venerable friend the Rev. Samuel Crowther, who was now spending a short time with his family, and expecting to return to his labors up the Niger in a few days. Let me here, as well for my colleague as myself, record my acknowledgments and thanks to him, his family, and to the many kind friends we met with in our travels, not omitting our friend Capt. Davis, who kindly furnished us a passage in his boat to the steamer, free of expense.

On the morning of the 10th of April we bade adieu to Lagos, and after an unusually fine passage across the bar, embarked on board the Royal Mail S.S. "Athenian," Capt. Laurie, for Liverpool. The steamer, as in the outward voyage, stopped at the intermediate places on the coast, and at Teneriffe and Madeira. She had on board a large number of Kru men, returning from different points of the coast, where they had been serving either on board men-of-war or trading vessels. These men are of incalculable advantage, as without them it would be impossible to work the ships, European sailors being unfit to labor in such warm latitudes, and not understanding so well the management of boats in heavy surfs. No where, I believe, can people be found so at home in the water. At Cape Palmas and other places on the Liberian coast, the steamer stops to allow them to land, which they do in very small canoes, brought off from the beach by their countrymen, in which no other human beings would venture. They make a fearful noise as they are departing and preparing to do so, and if not hurried off by the officers, would detain the vessel much longer than necessary. Sometimes the steamer starts before they have all left, and then without the slightest hesitation they throw into the water such of their property as will float, taking the rest in their hands, and jumping overboard swim with the greatest ease to their canoes. Such a scene occurred in our ship. Those who were still on board when the steamer started, had a number of swords, iron pots, pistols, kegs of powder, etc., the wages of their labor, which they prefer rather in goods than in money. I saw several jump into the water with swords in both hands, but there was one who had five swords and two iron pots, certainly not weighing less than thirty-five or forty pounds. Their canoes often upset, but this they consider quite a matter of course; a dexterous jerk from one side rights them again, and in another instance they are in their place bailing out the water.

At Freetown, Sierra Leone, we saw a large slaver, brought in a few days before by H.M.S.S. "Triton." Her officers and crew, consisting of over thirty persons, were there set at liberty, to be disposed of by the Spanish Consul as distressed seamen. They were as such forwarded in the same ship with us to Teneriffe. No wonder that the slave-trade should be so difficult to suppress, when no punishment awaits such wretches as these. What scamp would fear to embark in such an enterprise, if only assured that there was no personal risk—that he has only to destroy the ship's flag and papers on the approach of a cruiser, not only to shield himself and his crew from the consequence of his crime, but to receive the consideration rightly accorded distressed honest men. These villains, of course return to Havana or the United States, procure a new ship, and again pursue the wicked purpose which their previous experience enables them to accomplish with all the more impunity.

The incidents of a voyage to England under every variety of circumstance, have been so often described, that I shall both save myself the trouble of writing, and you, dear reader, the tedium of perusing them.

CHAPTER XI

Conclusion

Willingness of Natives to receive Settlers — Comparative Healthiness of Coast and Interior — Expense of Voyage — Protection — How to procure Land — Commercial and Agricultural Prospects — Time of arriving at Lagos — The Bar — Extent of Self-Government — Climate — African Fever and Treatment — Cotton Trade — Domestic Animals — Agricultural Products — Minerals — Timber — Water — African Industry — Expense of Labor — Our Treaty — *Finis.*

The native authorities, every where from Lagos to Ilorin, are willing to receive civilized people among them as settlers. It is hardly fair to say merely that they are willing; they hail the event with joy. They know and appreciate the blessings which must accrue to them by such accessions. They would, however, be opposed to independent colonies, the establishment of which among them, not only on this account, would be highly inexpedient.

The sea-coast, from the prevalence of mangrove-swamps, is unhealthy, but it is a fact that many persons, even Europeans and Americans, enjoy good health there, and many of the deaths are more to be attributed to alcoholic indulgence than to the character of the location. Abbeokuta, and all other interior towns we visited, are healthy, but even in these an occasional attack of bilious fever must be expected for a year or two, or until the process of acclimature is completed. Emigrants should remember that in new countries it is always necessary to exercise great watchfulness and discretion.

The expense of a voyage to Lagos directly from America, should not exceed $100 for first-class, and $60 for second-class: via Liverpool, besides the expense of the voyage thither, it would cost $200 for first-class, and $150 for second-class: $25 should include all expense of landing at Lagos, and of the journey to Abbeokuta.

The best protection on which a settler should rely in Africa, is that which all men are disposed to afford a good and honest man. The proper kind of emigrants want no protection among the natives of the Egba and Yoruba countries. We have had, however, from Lord Malmesbury, late Foreign Secretary in the British Cabinet, a letter to the Consul at Lagos, by which the protection of that functionary, as far as he can afford it, is secured for settlers.

Although land for agricultural purposes may be obtained, as much as can be used, "without money and without price," yet town lots will cost from $2 to $50 and even $100. Some fine fellows may get a very suitable lot for a trifle, or even for nothing; much depends upon the person.

The commercial and agricultural prospects are excellent, but there is much room for enterprise and energy. There is a decided demand for intelligent colored Americans, but it must be observed that one who is only prepared to roll barrels would have to compete with the natives under great disadvantages. Agriculturists, mechanics, and capitalists, with suitable religious and secular teachers, are most required.

Emigrants should never leave the States so as to arrive at Lagos in the months of June, July or August: the bar is then bad, and there is great risk to person and property in landing at such season. For safety I might include the last of May and first of September. During all the rest of the year there is no danger. The difficulties of the bar are not, however, insuperable; small vessels can always easily sail over it into the fine bay within, where they can load or unload with little trouble and without risk. It is not so easy to go out again, however, for then it would be necessary to "beat" against the wind, but a small steamboat could at once take them out in tow with perfect safety. I was informed that slavers used always to enter the bay: they could, of course, afford to wait for a favorable wind with which to get out.

Emigrants going to Abbeokuta, according to the second article of our treaty, will be permitted the privilege of self-government, but this can only be municipal, and affecting too only themselves. There is no doubt, however, that in time it will assume all the functions of a national government, for the people are fast progressing in civilization, and the existing laws, which from their nature apply only to heathens, would be found inadequate for them. Even now, as soon as any one of the people assumes the garb or other characteristics of civilization, they cease to exercise jurisdiction over him. He is thenceforward deemed an "oyibo," or white man.* The rulers, of course, will not be unaffected by those influences which can bring about such changes in their people, and thus they too will find it expedient to modify the laws to meet the emergency. But emigrants must ever remember that the existing rulers must be respected, for they only are the *bona fide* rulers of the place. The effort should be to lift them up to the proper standard, and not to supersede or crush them. If such a disposition is manifested, then harmony and peace will prevail; I am afraid not, otherwise.

Of course the succession of seasons in northern and southern latitudes below the 24th parallel, does not exist. There are two wet and two dry seasons. The first wet begins about the last of April, and continues until the close of June. The second begins in the last of September,

---

* This term, which literally signifies stripped off, was applied to white men, from the belief that their skin was stripped off. It is now applied indiscriminately to civilized men. To distinguish, however, between black civilized and white civilized men, the terms *dudu* for the former, and *fufu* for the latter, are respectively affixed.

and ceases with the end of October. The period between June and September is not entirely without rain. Both the wet seasons are inaugurated by sharp thunder and lightning, and an occasional shower. The harmattan winds prevail about Christmas time. They are very dry and cold: I have seen at 8 A.M., the thermometer at 54° Fahr., during the prevalence of these winds. The mornings and evenings, however warm the noon might be, are always comfortable. The general range of the temperature is between 74° and 90° Fahr. I have experienced warmer days in New York and Philadelphia.

With due prudence there is nothing to fear from the African fever, which is simply the bilious fever, arising from marsh miasmata common to other tropical countries, as well as to the southern sections of the United States. I have, myself, experienced the disease, not only in Africa, but in the West-Indies and Central America, and know that in all these places it is identical. Emigrants to the Western States of America suffer severely from typhoid fever, which often renders them powerless for months together; but with the African fever, which is periodical, there is always an intermission of from one to three days between the paroxysms, when the patient is comparatively well. Persons of intemperate habits, however, are generally very seriously affected. I suffered five attacks during my sojourn in Africa. The first, at Lagos, continuing about eight days, was induced by severe physical exertion in the sun. The four other attacks were in the interior. By a prompt application of suitable remedies, neither of them lasted longer than four or five days, and were not severe. The treatment I found most efficacious was, immediately on the appearance of the symptoms, to take two or three anti-bilious pills, composed each of two and a half grains comp. ext. Colocynth, and one fourth grain Podophyllin, (ext. Mayapple root.) For the present of a box of these pills I am indebted to Messrs. Bullock & Crenshaw, druggists, Sixth, above Arch street. This treatment always had the effect of greatly prostrating me, but the next day I was better, although weak. I then took three times daily about one grain sulphate of quinine, as much as will lie on a five-cent piece. This quantity in my own case was always sufficient, but it must be observed that the same dose will not answer for every constitution. It should be taken in a little acidulated water, or wine and water. Mr. Edward S. Morris, 916 Arch street, has a preparation which from experience I found better than the pure quinine. The practice of physicking while in health to keep well is very unwise: try to keep off disease by living carefully, and when in spite of this it comes, then physic, but carefully. Many suffer more from medicines than from disease. Quinine should not be taken during the recurrence of the fever. Hard labor or unnecessary walking in the sun must be avoided, but with an umbrella one might go out for an hour or two with impunity in the warmest weather.

Cotton from Abbeokuta has been an article of export to the British market for about eight years. In the first year only 235 pounds could be procured, but from that time, through the efforts of Thomas Clegg, Esq., of Manchester, and several gentlemen connected with the Church Missionary Society, London, the export has more than doubled every year, until, in 1859 the quantity reached about 6000 bales or 720,000 pounds. The plant abounds throughout the entire country, the natives cultivating it for the manufacture of cloths for their own consumption. Its exportation is, therefore, capable of indefinite extension. In the seed it is purchased from the natives at something less than two cents per pound. It is then ginned and pressed by the traders, and shipped to Liverpool, where it realizes better prices than New Orleans cotton. The gins now in use by the natives affect injuriously the fibre, so as to depreciate it at least two cents per pound. Properly cleaned, it would bring far more than New Orleans cotton, and even as it is, the value is about four cents more than the East-Indies product. The plant in Africa being perennial, the expense and trouble of replanting every year, as in this country, is avoided. There are flowers and ripe cotton on the plants at all seasons of the year, although there is a time when the yield is greatest. Free laborers for its cultivation can be employed each for about one half the interest of the cost of a slave at the South per annum, and land at present can be procured for nothing. These are advantages not to be despised.

The domestic animals comprise horses, which are plentiful and cheap; mules and asses at Ilorin; fine cattle, furnishing excellent milk, which can be purchased at about two cents per quart; sheep, not the woolly variety; goats, pigs, dogs, cats, turkeys, ducks, chickens, Guinea-hens, (also wild ones in abundance,) pigeons, etc. Of agricultural products there are cotton, palm-oil, and other oils; Indian-corn, which is now being exported; sweet potatoes, yams, cassava, rice; Guinea-corn, a good substitute for wheat; beans, several varieties; arrow-root, ginger, sugar-cane, ground-nuts; onions, as good as can be obtained any where; luscious pine-apples, delectable papaws, unrivalled oranges and bananas, not to mention the locust and other fine varieties of fruit.

Of minerals there is an abundance of the best building granite. I have seen no limestone, but Lagos furnishes, as already observed, an unlimited supply from oyster-shells. Plenty of rich iron-ore, from which the natives extract their own iron.

Of timber there is plenty of the African oak or teak— *roko,* as the natives call it—which is the material commonly used for building. Of course there are other fine varieties of timber. Water is easily procured every where. In the dry season some find it convenient to procure it from wells only a few feet deep, say from three to twelve feet. The Ogun furnishes good water-power; there are also fine brooks which could be so used, but not all the year. The sugar-cane I have seen every where.

There is certainly no more industrious people any where, and I challenge all the world besides to produce a people more so, or capable of as much endurance. Those who believe, among other foolish things, that the Negro is accustomed lazily to spend his time basking in the sunshine, like black-snakes or alligators, should go and see the people they malign. There are, doubtless, among them, as among every other race, not excepting the Anglo-American, indolent people, but this says nothing more against the one than the other. Labor is cheap, but is rising in value from the increased demand for it.

———

The following is a copy of the treaty we concluded with the native authorities of Abbeokuta:

TREATY

THIS Treaty made between his Majesty Okukenu, Alake; Somoye, Ibashorun; Sokenu, Ogubonna, and Atambala, on the first part; and Martin Robison Delany and Robert Campbell, of the Niger Valley Exploring Party, Commissioners from the African race of the United States and the Canadas in America, on the second part, covenants:

ARTICLE FIRST

That the King and Chiefs on their part agree to grant and assign unto the said Commissioners, on behalf of the African race in America, the right and privilege of settling in common with the Egba people, on any part of the territory belonging to Abbeokuta not otherwise occupied.

ARTICLE SECOND

That all matters requiring legal investigation among the settlers be left to themselves to be disposed of according to their own customs.

To My Motherland

ARTICLE THIRD

That the Commissioners on their part also agree that the settlers shall bring with them, as an equivalent for the privileges above accorded, intelligence, education, a knowledge of the arts and sciences, agriculture, and other mechanical and industrial occupations, which they shall put into immediate operation by improving the lands and in other useful vocations.

ARTICLE FOURTH

That the laws of the Egba people shall be strictly respected by the settlers; and in all matters in which both parties are concerned, an equal number of commissioners, mutually agreed upon, shall be appointed, who shall have power to settle such matters.

As a pledge of our faith and the sincerity of our hearts, we, each of us, hereunto affix our hands and seals, this twenty-seventh day of December, Anno Domini one thousand eight hundred and fifty-nine.

OKUKENU	his × mark	ALAKE
SOMOYE	his × mark	IBASHORUN
SOKENU	his × mark	BALAGUN
OGUBONNA	his × mark	BALAGUN
ATAMBALA	his × mark	BALAGUN
OGUSEYE	his × mark	ANABA
NGTABO	his × mark	BALAGUN OSE
OGUDEMU	his × mark	AGE, OKO

M. R. DELANY
ROBERT CAMPBELL

059185

Witness:

SAMUEL CROWTHER, JR.

Attest:

SAMUEL CROWTHER, SR.

We landed at Liverpool, Dr. Delany and myself, on the 12th of May, 1860, in good health, although we had been to—Africa!

FINIS